THE WATCHLIST

The Most Chaotic Chapters of Human History Lie Ahead

REGINALD K LISEMBY

All italics added are the author's emphasis.

Cover Design: Reginald K. Lisemby.
Cover Image: Reginald K Lisemby.
Cover Photography: Reginald K Lisemby.

The 2020 edition is printed by Amazon Publishers.
The 2020 edition is owned and copyrighted by *Crumbs from the Jewish Table,* Dr. Reginald K Lisemby.

Researched, compiled, edited, rewritten, designed, composited, and all photographs by the author, Dr. Reginald K Lisemby.

Author's Comment to the Reader: *Thank you for your investment in this book, and it is my humble desire that you will consider your read of this book inspiring, thought-provoking, informative, enlightening, and even entertaining. For more information on other books I have written go to my Amazon page.* https://www.amazon.com/-/e/B07NP1SB8P

Write to me:
Reginald K Lisemby
P.O. Box 22654
Chattanooga, TN 37422
reglisemby@gmail.com

DEDICATION

This compilation is lovingly dedicated to Jacob Kent, Faith Victoria, Judah Christian, and Gideon Elijah – four loves of my life who will need to know the answers to the questions in this compilation. I hope all four of you will read, learn, teach and share this important biblical knowledge with others. The time of the end is near! If He delays and I go first, I will see each of you around His throne!

"…declaring the end from the beginning and from ancient times things which have not been done, saying My purpose will be established and I will accomplish all My good pleasure."
Isaiah 46:10

"Surely the Lord God does nothing unless He reveals His secret counsel to His servants the Prophets."
Amos 3:7

"Wrong will be right, when Aslan comes in sight,
At the sound of his roar, sorrows will be no more,
And when he shakes his mane, we shall have spring again."
C.S. Lewis, The Lion, the Witch, and the Wardrobe

"Something told the wild geese, it was time to go.
Though the fields lay golden, something whispered "snow!"
Leaves were green and stirring, berries luster-glossed,
But beneath warm feathers, something cautioned, "frost!"
All the sagging orchards, steamed with amber spice,
But each wild breast stiffened, at remembered ice.
Something told the wild geese, it was time to fly,
Summer son on their wings, winter in their cry."
Rachel Field

"Yea, the stork in the heavens knows her appointed times,
and the turtledove and the crane and the swallow observe the time
of their migration; but my people know not the judgment of YHWH."
Jeremiah 8:7

TABLE OF CONTENTS

ACKNOWLEDGMENT

Psalm 37:4 says to delight yourself in the Lord, and He will give you the desires of your heart. As a young man my desires were to be like *Yeshua*, and second, to have Crystal Faith McNeely as my wife. Crystal is my wife for 32 years at the time of this writing. I remain hopeful and anticipating for a likeness to my Lord.

PREFACE

After the crucifixion, death, burial, resurrection and ascension of *Yeshua* to heaven, and upon His return to earth, He presented Himself to His *talmidim* or disciples in Galilee. During those forty days *Yeshua* spoke to them of the things pertaining to the coming kingdom of God. The good physician, *Lukas* records His Words for us in Acts 1:1-11. One of the questions His *talmidim* asked *Yeshua*, was if He was going to restore the kingdom to Israel at that time. He had fulfilled the sacrificial system of the former old and obsolete covenant (Hebrews 8:13) by bearing upon Himself the sins of the world, and He had returned from heaven to reign! *Yeshua's* answer is recorded in verse 8, *"and He said to them, It is not for you to know the times or season which the Father has put in His own authority...."* My question to you who read this book is this. Do those words spoken by *Yeshua* to His *talmidim* then, two-thousand years ago, apply to us today? Aren't we to know the times and seasons which our Father has established? Aren't we to anticipate God's times and seasons? The sun, moon, and the stars were created for signs and seasons (Genesis 1:14; Psalm 104:19).

> *"Then God said, Let there be lights in the expanse of the heavens to divide the day from the night; and let them be for signs and seasons, and for days and years."*

> *"He appointed the moon for seasons; the sun knows its going down."*

During His three-and-one-half years ministry, *Yeshua* spoke much about the kingdom, and some of His last words to His followers were about His return. *Yeshua* is coming again! But, is *Yeshua* coming bodily to reign? Perhaps, Second Coming was on the Feast of *Shavuot* or Pentecost recorded in Acts 2, when His Spirit blew in and upon the one-hundred-twenty followers of *Yeshua* who had gathered? Isn't it possible that His kingdom is the Church, those of us who are indwelt by Him?

For those of us who anticipate *Yeshua* to return bodily, as the hybrid Son of Man and Son of God, and reign from the Holy Land over all the earth for one-thousand literal years, as spoken (six times) in Revelation 20, aren't we to know when He is coming? Aren't there signs of His Second Coming? Of course, there are! Yeshua revealed to us signs of His re-visitation so that we, His people may prepare? And, just as Yeshua said, the sun, moon, and stars will be communicating that the time is near?

What about the *Rapture*? Aren't we to anticipate two bodily returns of *Yeshua* to the earth, one for His church at the *Rapture*, and then another return [later] with His bride, the Church at His *Second Coming*? Why would *Yeshua* be coming to this world three times? His first coming at His incarnation, His second visitation in the atmosphere to *Rapture* His Church, and third, His *Second Coming* to the earth to reign as King? Is *Yeshua* going to physically sit on the Davidic throne, in Israel, and be the world Czar? Why does the Son of God need to sit on an earthly throne when He is presently seated on the throne of heaven? Aren't we to know God's messianic plan?

The *Rapture* and the *Second Coming* are separate visitations of our Lord in the last days, and there are events which precede, accompany, and follow each coming of *Yeshua*. Is *Yeshua* returning in the *Rapture* only for those who have made themselves ready, those obedient to the Holy Spirit and the Holy Scriptures? Or, is *Yeshua* coming for all believers regardless of their spiritual temperature? Will all the redeemed be *raptured*, even carnal Christians, even the disobedient? Will babies and children who have not reached *the age of accountability* be raptured, or will they be left-behind to mature so that they can make a free-will decision concerning *Yeshua*? Aren't we suppose to know the answers to these questions?

The term *Rapture* does not appear in the Holy Scriptures so why should we believe in the *Rapture*? Is the *Great Tribulation* another term for *Yaaqov's Trouble*? If so, will the Church go through the *Great*

Tribulation, since the church is not *Yaaqov* or Israel! Perhaps the Church will be raptured before the *Great Tribulation* begins? Our Lord experienced great tribulation as did His *talmidim* after Him. In fact, most died horrific deaths. Many in the first church in *Yerushalayim* were martyred. So, why shouldn't the Church experience great tribulation? Why should the last-days Church receive less suffering than the first-days Church?

Is the resurrection of the Jewish people out from the death camps and ovens of the Holocaust, back to their ancestral and biblical land called Israel, prophetic? Are the spirit-filled believers in *Yeshua*, the Church, the new *Israel of God*? What relationship does the modern Jewish nation of Israel have with *YHWH* since the majority of the 9.7 million Israelis are outside biblical and salvific faith in *Yeshua* and are unregenerate?

Does the Bible speak of a third temple to exist in Jerusalem in the last days, and should Christians be excited to hear of such a temple? What purpose does a one-thousand-year millennium serve? Isn't the present *church-age* the millennium? What will life be like during the millennium? Aren't these things for us to know?

Is the *antichrist* going to be a Jew? Might the *antichrist* be alive today, and if so, can we discern who he is and his program?

Will there be sacrifices during the millennium? Will the rule of *Yeshua* be political?

What is the relationship of the *War of Armageddon* and the *War of Gog and Magog*? Could these wars happen now? Is the *New Jerusalem* going to be a satellite city, or a literal city on planet earth.

To answer these and other important questions that pertains to biblical prophecy and *eschatology*, reading, studying, and knowing the Divine Library is paramount. The Holy Scriptures are inspired, holy, inerrant, infallible, sacred, and trustworthy. The Word is also living, and, therefore, how one interprets the inspired, holy, inerrant, infallible, sacred, and living texts is of zenith importance. One's *hermeneutic* or interpretation of the Holy Scriptures will determine how he or she obtains answers to important questions of *eschatology*. For example, there are myriad Christian faiths and denominations due to differences in style of worship, music, and other, but the majority of differences have to do with Christian interpretation of the sacred Holy Scriptures.

There are opposing interpretations of the pre-incarnate appearances of *Yeshua*, the virgin birth of *Yeshua*, the deity of *Yeshua*, the messiahship of *Yeshua*, the implications of discipleship, the mode of baptism, the security of the believer, the resurrection of the dead, the gifts of the Holy Spirit, the reality and location of heaven and hell, whether *hades* and *Gehenna* are symbolic or literal places, the sovereignty of God, the responsibility and accountability of man, gifts of the Spirit, and, the eschatological scenarios of last days events.

Disagreement on any one of these things listed above does not implicate the Holy Scriptures to be faulty or untrustworthy. The Holy Scriptures are absolute. In fact, the Holy Scriptures are the one sure thing that will remain true and last forever (1 Peter 1:25; Matthew 24:35; Luke 21:33; Isaiah 40:8 Psalm 119:89).

"But the Word of God endures forever" (1 Peter 1:25).

"Heaven and earth will pass away, but My Word will last forever" (Luke 21:33).

"Your word O YHWH will last forever" (Psalm 119:89).

This being true, it is important, then, to have a correct interpretation or *hermeneutic* of the sacred texts.

My name is Reginald Kent Lisemby, and as a believer in *Yeshua* Who is my savior and Lord, I am committed to the inspired, infallible, inerrant, and sacred texts as God gave them in the original languages. God inspired the authors upon whom He breathed, and we are recipients of those inspired texts, the Holy Bible, the divine library, the living Word of God.

To help us understand more exactly what God revealed, we need language studies, concordances, lexicons, commentaries, and good and various translations. The foremost and cardinal rule of biblical interpretation is that the Holy Scriptures be interpreted according to their historical, grammatical, and cultural contexts. If the reader of the sacred texts has the correct biblical hermeneutic or interpretation, he will more accurately discover the meaning that the inspired biblical author intended his audience to have of his texts. The biblical authors were writing to an audience. They were not scribbling in a trance to no one in particular. The biblical authors were cognizant thinkers and writers, and when they were writing their texts, they were not zombies without their mental facilities. They did not robotically receive and scribal the Word of God. They were not mechanical in their recording of the divine library.

The biblical authors lived in a historical setting and their texts are a "web of words" influenced by inspiration and also by their history, culture and language. The biblical authors chose words they knew and words they anticipated their readers would know. The authors were reader-conscious and anticipated a response from the audience to whom they were writing. The biblical authors were selective in their vocabulary or word choices, their semantics or word usage, and how they structured their writings, whether as narrative, prophecy, poetry, epistle, or apocalyptic genre.

A correct interpretation of the holy scriptures -in their historical, grammatical, and cultural context- is accomplished through a series of necessary skills. One important skill is being committed to learn and use the original languages. Hayim Nahman Bialik once said, "He who reads the Bible in a translation is like a man who kisses his bride through a veil." God intends that we gain a deep understanding of His Word, and He intends that we not be lazy in biblical reading, biblical study, language study, and acquisition of a good hermeneutic, so that we may accurate interpret His Word.

Every believer of Yeshua is a theologian, although we might be shallow in the scriptures. Every believer anchors his soul to the fact that God's Word is knowable. To gain insight and enlightenment of God's Word we must invest much time to read, meditate, and study the Word. The believer must invest money to acquire the right helps to instruct him in the biblical languages that God chose to reveal Himself. A translation regardless of the version is a translation and is never near enough to God's original disclosure! We MUST study Hebrew and Greek!

As for translations, I recommend studying the Holy Scriptures using several renditions. A parallel Bible is helpful because it has multiple versions in one compilation. I also recommend a good concordance and excellent commentaries since commentaries are explanations of the sacred texts from scholars who have learned the original languages and have studied the historical, grammatical, and cultural contexts of the Holy Scriptures as a whole.

To correctly interpret the Holy Scriptures, I highly recommend a study of Hebrew, Jewish customs and traditions, Jewish history, biblical Judaism, and messianic prophecy. The Holy Scriptures are not a collection of disjunctive and unharmonious texts. The Holy Scriptures are not emails or personal text-messages to us from God. We are not free to make personal and independent interpretations of the Holy Scriptures (2 Peter 1:20, 21).

We do not have a pen-pal in heaven. God does not communicate His Word only to us. Catholicism, Mormonism, the Jehovah's Witnesses, Charismatics, and some Christians believe and practice this fallacy. A prominent Southern Baptist female author by her own admission suggests that the biblical reader should ask, "what does this text mean to me?" Better be very careful here! The reader should want to know what the text(s) meant to the inspired author!

The Holy Scriptures are not recordings of inspired events. The Holy Scriptures themselves are inspired! Liberal Christians often consider the Bible to be another source that discloses inspired events that occurred in history. Oy Vey! The sacred texts are themselves inspired; they are the divine revelation of God! The Holy Scriptures give the reader *the privileged perspective* for they offer us the true events, the true facts of those events, and the true interpretation of what God chose to disclose.

The reader of the inspired, infallible, inerrant and authoritative Holy Scriptures must be text conscious. Kay Arthur of Precept Ministries says, "He gives every believer a resident teacher, the Holy Spirit Who guides us into His truth." The Holy Spirit Who inspired the biblical authors wants to connect us to the inspired Holy Scriptures.

Beloved, as believers in *Yeshua*, our hallmark is Him! We have the divine author and teacher of the Holy Texts living within us. God wants you to know everything He has disclosed, and God wants us to know His times and seasons. God wants us to know His prophecies. God does nothing without revealing His secrets to the Prophets who reveal the prophecies to His people. So said the prophets, *Y'shayahu* (Isaiah) and *Amos*.

"…declaring the end from the beginning and from ancient times things which have not been done, saying My purpose will be established and I will accomplish all My good pleasure" (Isaiah 46:10).

"Surely the Lord God does nothing unless He reveals His secret counsel to His servants the Prophets" (Amos 3:7).

Reginald K. Lisemby (Author)

Reginald. K. Lisemby

INTRODUCTION: THE END FROM THE BEGINNING

If we are to understand biblical *eschatology* which is the study of the end-times concerning God's messianic program, it is vital to accept the biblical origins of all that exists. Since God initiated a beginning (Genesis 1:1) we should anticipate an end. In between the two bookends is God's progression toward the culmination of His Messianic plan.

God Himself is eternal and has no beginning. The *beginning* spoken of in Genesis is the start or beginning of something other than God. God Who existed before *the beginning* given in Genesis 1:1, planned and inaugurated His colossal messianic plan. That plan was His design foreknown to Him before the beginning, and has streamed through the ages, and will one-day culminate at *the end.*

Between God's beginning and God's end, is God's messianic program. This messianic plan lies within the compilation of the Holy Scriptures, and you and I can know God's messianic plan by knowing His Word. In fact, we are participants in His great design since we are His children, foreknown, and begotten by Him before the foundation of the world (Romans 8:29).

God existed a billion millennia ago and a trillion millennia before that, although the Holy Scriptures tell us very little about God before the *reshit* or the beginning of Genesis 1:1. Yet, we know some things! We know that God the Father, *Yeshua* the Son, and the Holy *Ruach* or Spirit of God were dwelling together in eternity. God the Father and God the Son were sharing glory (John 17:5), and the Father was loving the Son (John 17:24). Before the beginning YHWH possessed wisdom and by it founded creation (Proverb 8:22), and the *Sefer Chayim* or Book of Life was being inscribed by Him (Revelation 17:8; 13:8; 21:27).

Before the beginning, the mystery of the crucifixion was being determined (1 Corinthians 2:7,8; Ephesians 3:9-11), and the Lamb of God was slain (Revelation 13:8; 1 Peter 1:19,20).

The Holy Scriptures tell us that at some time in the beginning, God created spiritual beings. *Archangels, angels, Seraphim, Cherubim, Watchers, Elders, seven spirits, the Angel with a loud voice, the Captain of the Lord's host* and other beings were made by God. The Holy Scriptures tell us that in the beginning a mutiny occurred in *haShamayim* ("the heavens") as the ruling *Cherub* named *Helel Ben-Shachar* meaning "Shine Son [of] the Dawn" became an adversary of God, defected, and led one-third of heaven's angelic coterie with him (Revelation 12:4). God had a purpose for allowing these beings to have free-will, to choose to become unrighteous, to become dark apostate spirits, and continue to exist. God had a greater purpose for allowing these beings to influence the federal head of the human race, our parents, *Adam* and *Havvah* (Adam and Eve) whom God had created then placing them in *Gan Eden*. God had a purpose for positioning His image in an arena of temptation. Man was and continues to be the trophy of angels and demons. God had a purpose in creating a place called *Sheol* (Hebrew) or *Hades* (Greek) that would one day be emptied into *Gehenna* or the lake of fire.

God was dwelling in perfection one quadrillion millennia ago. God had no need. God had no want. God dwelt in His perfection as holy, righteous, and satisfied. So, why did God appoint His Son to be slain? The Holy Scriptures reveal that *Yeshua* was crucified before the foundation of the world (Revelation 13:8; 1 Peter 1:19,20), meaning before God made man in His own image and before His image joined the satanic mutiny against Him, God knew He would one day slay His Son as the only resolution for the sin and fall of man whom He was intending to create.

God foreknew that His Son would be tortured and would die on a rugged tree before He created man. Why would God write a script like that? Why would God design a play where He, the playwright, would be murdered? -and by humans He was about to create? The

Potter's clay vessels would become villains to the Potter? Why would God humiliate Himself by creating and rescuing a motley crew?

The temptation of man, the sin of man, the fall of man, and the continuous rebellion of man was not a surprise to God. Before God made his first clay vessel in His own image, and breathed into him the breath of life, God foreknew man's depravity. *Yeshua* was slain before the foundation of the world, and He was predestined to become man, to be crucified as the sacrificial Lamb of God, in order to accommodate man's rebellion, sin, and depravity. This is a colossal mystery!

The *messianic* plan of God was not a sudden remedy for man's wreck. The *messianic* plan of God was calculated in eternity past, before the foundation of the world, and God's messiah was known before man's temptation, and before man's need for redemption. According to the Apostle *Kefa* (Peter), the *Lamb of God* was slain not two-thousand years ago, but before the foundation of the world.

"…knowing that you were not redeemed with perishable things like silver or gold from your futile way of life inherited from your forefathers, but with precious blood, as of a lamb unblemished and spotless, {the blood} of Christ…For He was foreknown before the foundation of the world, but has appeared in these last times for the sake of you" (1 Peter 1:18-20 cf. 1:9-12).

The apostolic brother, *Yochanon* (John) agreed.

"All who dwell on the earth will worship him, {everyone} whose name has not been written from the foundation of the world in the book of life of the Lamb who has been slain" (Revelation 13:8).

Man, God's image, was tempted by Satan the adversary (Satan means adversary in Hebrew), the father of sin, a murderer and a liar from the beginning. The adversary of God had sinned prior to God's creation of man, since the serpent was already in the garden when God created *Adam* and placed them there, and the serpent was already an evil dragon (Revelation 12). YHWH God knew that man would become like the devil. God knew that He Himself would need to become a descendant of man (not a clone of him) if He were to be man's champion and save humanity. God knew that in order to be man's champion, He would need to become man, face the same temptation, the same way, in the same place (meaning Israel is the Holy Land), and by the same evil power. The serpent in the garden of Gethsemane was that old dragon, the devil in the garden in Eden. YHWH needed to travel the venue of human descent, comply with human conception, and realize the world of humanity with its hurts, pains, woes, and sorrows. God was obligated to become man, a man of sorrows, if He were to rescue men from our sorrows (Isaiah 53:3). God did this!

God chose to become authentically human in order to be humanity's authoritative champion. God, however, had to remain authentically God. God is always God! God is His nature! God cannot become not God. When God became an embryo in the womb of a virgin, a newborn infant in Bethlehem, a nursing babe in journey to Egypt, a Hebrew toddler, and a Jewish young man, God remained God. It had to be so, since man cannot reconcile man to God, and, God separated from being a Son of Man cannot reconcile man to God. God MUST become a Son of Adam!

God came because man had become demonized. God desired to reclaim man and rebirth man and bring him back, not merely to be the *image* of God as he was in Eden, but higher, to be a Son of God, to be part of the sovereignty of Elohim! God would regenerate man in order to make man divine! When God was crucified, He was killed by demonized humans for whom He came! Humanity premeditated and murdered God! Humanity premeditated and murdered *Yeshua*, the Jewish Messiah. Demonized man walks in darkness rather than God's light, unless God in His sovereignty moves upon man and causes conviction of sin that leads man to desire God and call upon Him for salvation. Desire for God, comes from God! The willingness to call upon God comes from God!

From the beginning, God made promises to man that He would come! The compilation of the Holy Scriptures contains His promises, and they also contain the necessary resources for man to recognize the time of His coming, and to recognize Him when He comes! God's Holy Word is absolutely essential to correctly know God and to understand His messianic plan.

God was to be born as a hybrid human, fully man and fully God. God was to be birthed at a certain time, in a certain place, in a certain way, by a certain woman, and God would live His life in perfection as both God and man, keeping all His divine laws that govern heaven and earth, and also being subject to the ways of humans. God's prophetic messianic plan included His being rejected, crucified, and murdered by the very ones for whom He came to save. Yet, God according to His messianic design would resurrect from death, He would ascend [back] to heaven, He would send His Spirit to indwell His people who by regeneration would become divine beings. In the end, the Son of Man and Son of God, the champion of man, would restore man to become monarchs. Man would be with God and rule with God in a holy land, as Kings over a Kingdom.

This messianic plan if masterfully kept (every *jot* and *tittle* without error) would reconcile man and make man to be *Sons of Elohim*, the essence of deity. Man would regain the true pristine Holy Land, *Gan Eden*, and man would dwell as Sons of God with God. And, there would be one major addendum. No devil or dark powers to tempt man. God and man will dwell forever in perfect harmony.

This exhaustive plan of God was ordained before the ordination of the world (1 Corinthians 2:7-8; Ephesians 3:9-11).

"...but we speak God's wisdom in a mystery, the hidden {wisdom} which God predestined before the ages to our glory; {the wisdom} which none of the rulers of this age has understood; for if they had understood it they would not have crucified the Lord of glory."

God intended a *messiah* before the beginning, prior to man's need, and before man's rebellion (Romans 5:14). God intended to make His Messiah and His Messianic kingdom the hallmark of His Divine Library, the Holy Scriptures. This is the zenith theme of the Holy Scriptures! The Bible is potently *messianic*. The messiah was promised to come, and He came! The Messiah is promised to come again to complete the messianic plan of God. He is coming!

Messiah's first coming was to satisfy the Law, the demands of a holy God. He had to bring propitiation back to the altar of God in Heaven and satisfy the covenant God had made with Israel at Mount Sinai. He did that! After His resurrection He told *Miriam* (Mary) do not touch for Me for I have not yet ascended. He later returned, and told Thomas to touch and handle Him and be not faithless but believe.

Yeshua spent forty days with His *talmidim* in the Galilee and shortly after that, *Yeshua* inaugurated the new covenant prophesied by Jeremiah, a covenant not like the one He made with Israel at Sinai (Jeremiah 31:31). *Yeshua* satisfied the former, old covenant by His perfect life and death and atonement for all mankind. That old mosaic covenant has become obsolete (Hebrew 8:13). The *Brit Chadashah* or New Covenant includes a different priesthood, a different kind of High Priest, a different law, and a different city, one not made by human hands. The priesthood is no longer a Levitical one, but a *Melchizedekian* priesthood. The law is no longer ten commandments written on stone, but Messiah's law, the New Testament law written on the human heart of those regenerate by the new birth.

Man is now the *kodesh kodeshim* or the "Holy of Holies" and a temple of a different kind than the Mosaic temple of the Mosaic covenant, which was wood, stone, and gold. The sanctuary of the New Covenant where the Holy *Ruach* of God would dwell, would be man's spirit, not a building made with human hands.

The new covenant procures all sins to be eradicated and the believer to be positionally seated in the heavens, a reality not yet experienced, but nevertheless a present reality! *Sababa*! Awesome!

According to the New Covenant promises, the Messiah is to return, first, as a bridegroom to receive and elope with His bride, that is, His *kehillah* or congregation, the church, those born into His kingdom by His Spirit. He will bring His bride to the bridal chamber in heaven. As a bridegroom, *Yeshua* is coming to steal His bride, and then, later, the Messiah will return with His bride, the Church, to the earth, to the epicenter of the globe. He is coming to the Temple Mount in Jerusalem, Israel to dwell as the ruler of the entire world for one-thousand years. His reign as monarch will be a theocracy.

The Second Coming of *Yeshua* will be in the same bodily form He had two-thousand years ago, as a son of *Adam*, a descendant of *Avraham, Yitzhak, Yaaqov, Yehudah,* and *Dovid. Yeshua* is returning as a Jew, the King of the Jews, the Lion [of the Tribe] of Judah, and He is returning to reign over the entire world as *ben David*, the Son of David.

Messiah *Yeshua* was rejected at His first coming by the nation of Israel whom God had chosen to vehicle His Messiah, but had Israel embraced *Yeshua,* He as the Messiah would still have had to die on the cursed tree for the sins of all men, He would have resurrected (which He did), ascended back to heaven to make propitiation for all sins (which He did), and later return to reinstate God's Plan A (which He will do). Plan A was given us at the beginning. God's monarchs, Adam and his bride, were to reign over the earth from the Holy Land. This will be fulfilled in the millennial kingdom, yonder in the future.

Yeshua, the Second Adam, and His bride, the Church will dwell together in the Holy Land, the Garden in Eden, and rule the world. *Yeshua* will soon accomplish this finale!

Messiah *Yeshua* was Israel's Passover Lamb. *Yeshua* was Israel's Unleavened Bread placed in the ground before dark as the feast was approaching. Messiah *Yeshua* was Israel's *Bikkurim* or "First Fruits" resurrecting on Sunday the day after the Sabbath that followed Passover. On the appointed day of *Shavuot* or *Pentecost Yeshua* literally "blew in" to the upper room and possessed 120 believers who were awaiting His coming. *Yeshua* immersed His holy ones with His Spirit, just as *Yochanon* (John) had immersed his followers in water. This was the beginning of a totally new era or age, the beginning of the New Covenant dispensation.

Messiah *Yeshua* has sworn to return bodily to dwell in the land of His conception, birth, childhood, manhood, and messiahship. That land is the land of Israel. We are awaiting this fulfillment.

In God's *gadol* ("grand") messianic script, the Holy Scriptures, His only begotten Son *Yeshua* is cast as the zenith protagonist of God's program. The Son of God is the hero of the scriptures, and He walks through every page of Holy Writ so that man might see and identify Him, know Him, and anticipate His coming. Messiah *Yeshua* is present in the Holy Scriptures in types, shadows, hints, innuendos, allegories, allusions, prophecies and direct statements. This is, in fact, the hallmark purpose of the Bible. This was the *hermeneutic* or interpretation that *Yeshua* had of the Holy Scriptures.

> *Then beginning with Moses and with all the prophets, He explained to them the things concerning Himself in all the Scriptures…Now He said to them, "These are My words which I spoke to you while I was still with you, that all things which are written about Me in the Law of Moses and the Prophets and the Psalms must be fulfilled"* (Luke 24:27,44).

We eagerly await our bridegroom *Yeshua*. *Yochanon* wrote in the *apocalyptic* book called Revelation, *"the name of the Lord is the Word of God"* (Revelation 19:13). Earlier in his gospel *Yochanon* had written, *in the beginning was the Word and the Word was with God and the Word was God* (John 1:1). God has communicated to us His plan from the beginning. *Yeshua* was in the eternal beginnings (Isaiah 9:6) and He is the zenith of God's *magnum opus*.

God's passion play extends from eternity to eternity, and includes His *sofer chayim* or "book of life" which was inscribed at the beginning. This *book of life* is a book of lists, a book of names already recorded and filed in *haShamayim* or the heavens. Dear reader, you want to make sure your name is in that book!

"And those who dwell on the earth, whose name has not been written in the book of life from the foundation of the world, will wonder when they see the beast, that he was and is not and will come" (Revelation 17:8).

"All who dwell on the earth will worship him, {everyone} whose name has not been written from the foundation of the world in the book of life of the Lamb who has been slain" (Revelation 13:8).

"…and nothing unclean, and no one who practices abomination and lying, shall ever come into it, but only those whose names are written in the Lamb's book of life" (Revelation 21:27).

God's *messianic* program was conceived before the beginning. God's *messianic* plan was first written in the stars of heaven (Genesis 1:14; 15:5; 37:9-10), and if modern man had the genius of the ancients we might read God's Word in the heavens as *Adam, Seth, Avraham, Yitzhak, Yaaqov, Yoseph, Moshe* and others could read. They knew His program by reading His *cantata* in the rotations of the stars in the heavens. *Yov* (Job) a contemporary of *Avraham* spoke of the Zodiac. The Prophets wrote concerning the stars, and the *magi* observed the shining stars in the night sky in concert with the messianic prophecies of God's incarnation declared by the Prophets.

God's messianic plan was also declared in visions and dreams to holy men. God's *messianic* plan was revealed to men who inscribed His Words on *papyrus* and later *vellum* or animal skins. Scribes took those copies and transcribed or copied them myriad times. From those manuscripts came translations, paraphrases, and eventually they were printed in *codex* or book form.

From the beginning man was to be cognizant of God's program. God wants man to know His principles, precepts, and His doctrines, and God wants man to know His plan. God wants man to know the *last days* events, things that pertain to the "end of time."

There are many *eschatological* beliefs as how the end will occur, some believing that no one view of the end-times can be absolute.

These skeptics would suggest that since there are men and women with PhDs in all of the various views of eschatology, no one view can be correct. It appears to these critics that to preach biblical eschatology with certainty would be arrogance. In truth, we can know biblical eschatology. The depravity and transgression is men who do not know God's eschatological plan, because they have not studied and do not know how to interpret scripture. Since these don't know they insist we cannot know! Are we arrogant in stating with certainty that we DO know?

Many believers recognized *Yeshua* at His first coming, and those who did were those who had studied the messianic prophecies and who knew the living Word. They recognized *Yeshua* even as an infant! *EliTzavet* recognized the mother of her Lord, and exclaimed her faith! The babe in *EliTzavet's* womb, *Yochanon the Immerser* upon hearing *Miriam's* salutation recognized his Messiah though a fetus in the womb, and he was filled with the Holy Spirit. *Yochanon* (John) leaped. This may sound sensational, but it was supposed to be the norm. During the millennial kingdom no one will need to teach another "know the Lord, know the Lord." All will know Him from birth" (Jeremiah 31:34).

Sh'meon recognized his messiah, *Yeshua* when *Yeshua* was an eight-day old suckling! *Anna* recognized Him that same day, and *Yeshua* was not wearing a halo or Star-of-David diapers. Even the dark spirits know the prophecies. Demonized Herod learned quickly of his opponent and killed all the bitty baby boys in *BeitLechem*. *Yoseph* and *Miriam* escaped *Yeshua* to Egypt, and that was also foretold (Hosea 11:1-4; Matthew 2:13-15).

Yeshua's first coming was knowable and many knew! Sadly, myriad more had not studied and did not know the prophecies and the day of His visitation. It is the same today. Often, those who challenge the "knowing ones" are the ones who do not know Him, the Word. They do not know Him, the Word because they have not taken the time to study Him, the Word so as to know Him!

The majority of Christian people are shallow in their Wordology. Some Christians are actually offended by the knowledge others have of His program. These who know have dedicated themselves to knowing the Word. The shallow ones suggest that the knowing ones should only just "preach the Gospel," and have little to do with prophecy and *eschatology* since it divides Christians and Churches. These feeble folk do not know that *eschatology* is the Gospel. The Jewish prophet Amos wrote the following.

> *"The Lord YHWH does nothing unless He reveals His secret counsel to His servants the prophets… YHWH God has spoken! Who can but prophesy?"* (Amos 3:7).

God has spoken. God is speaking! God's Word contains His oracles. What prophet cannot prophesy! What Christian cannot study to know? What Christian does not want to study and know? *Shaul* (Paul) wrote to the believers in Galatia that the Gospel was preached to *Avraham*.

> *"…and the scripture, foreseeing that God would justify the Gentiles by faith, preached the gospel beforehand unto Avraham, saying, In thee shall all the nations be blessed"* (Galatians 3:8).

Yeshua said that *Avraham* knew His day and rejoiced in it. *Avraham* knew eschatology.

> *"Your father Avraham rejoiced to see my day; and he saw it, and was glad"* (John 8:56).

Avraham knew of the last days, since the last days began with the birth of *Yeshua*.

> *"God, after He spoke along ago to the fathers in the prophets in many portions and in many ways, in these last days has spoken to us in His Son, Whom He appointed heir of all things, through Whom also He made the world"* (Hebrews 1:1-2).

Avraham may not have known everything concerning eschatology. Yet, *Avraham* knew some things. So do I. Dear friend, do you know the prophecies?

I have written this book to help you in your study and search of knowing God's messianic plan and how it will culminate in the end of days. This book includes questions that I have accumulated over my years of ministry, and I have arranged the questions in a chronology of eschatology. The first questions are about the present time in which we live, questions to do with understanding prophecy, the modern nation of Israel, the church, and the importance of biblical interpretation. Then, I answer questions about those things soon to occur: the Rapture; the Bema Seat Judgment; the Great Tribulation; the appearance of the *Antichrist*; and other questions pertaining to this era. I also chose questions concerning the Second Coming of *Yeshua*, His judgments, and His millennial reign. Finally, I conclude with questions about the eternal state, the different perspectives of eschatology, and key terms to know when studying eschatology.

I have attempted to be brief and yet thorough although every question is worthy of exhaustive research. Books have been written on each individual subject. I unashamedly confess that I am biased toward some questions and have given more attention to them mainly because of my own interest.

I hope you will enjoy both the read and the study of this work, and I would be very delighted to hear from you, whether in agreement or in opposition with my answers. I remain a student, so I am hopeful for your attention to inform me, and I am dull, so I am needful for you to help sharpen me.

Thank you! Enjoy!

Question 1

Why should we assume that we are to know the eschatological signs of the end times, when Jesus answered His disciples that it was not for them to know the signs of His coming and the end of the age?

Answer

When the Lord's *talmidim* or disciples asked *Yeshua* about the future of *Yerushalayim* and the end of the age, He answered them that it was not for them to know (Acts 1:7). His words were, of course, to His *talmidim*. The New Covenant had not yet begun, the New Testament Church did not yet exist, the New Testament scrolls were not yet written, and *Yeshua* had much more to say about the question of prophecy, which He disclosed (by signs) to *Yochanon* in the final book of the Holy Scriptures, the *Apocalypse*, known in English as The Revelation. The *Apocalypse* of *Yeshua* is *Yeshua's* revelation, not *Yochanon's*. It is *"the revelation of Yeshua HaMashiach"* (Revelation 1:1) and the *Apocalypse* contains His final words. The Revelation is also a book of last days prophecy (Revelation 1:3) written to the churches.

The Revelation of *Yeshua* is exclusively *eschatological*. It is a disclosure from *Yeshua* of end-time scenarios. What is recorded for us in the Acts of the Apostles by the good physician *Lukas* was not *Yeshua's* final Words, and certainly not His final words concerning the *acharit hayomim*, or "the last days." The *Apocalypse*, the Revelation of *Yeshua* the Messiah, is His last Words!

The Church and the New Covenant began on the Day of *Pentecost* and not with the virgin birth of *Yeshua*, the incarnation of *Yeshua*, the ministry of *Yeshua,* the history of *Yeshua* given in the four Gospels, or even *Yeshua's* death, resurrection, and His ascension back to *haShamayim* or "the heavens." The New Covenant began with the outpouring of the Holy Spirit on the Jewish Feast of Harvest (Acts 2). This is the "birthday" of both the *Brit Chadesha* or "new covenant" and the church.

Our Lord's answer to His *talmidim's* question recorded for us in Acts 1:7 was in the context of the mosaic covenant or the old testament that the Jewish nation was obligated to obey. The Old Testament did not end with *Malachi,* and the New Testament did not begin with the historicity of the four Gospels, *Mattityahu, Markos, Lukas,* and *Yochanon.* The Old Covenant did not become obsolete until God gave His New Covenant which was prophesied by *Yeremiyahu* (Jeremiah 31:31) and inaugurated on *Pentecost* (Greek) or *Shavuot* (Hebrew). Not everything *Yeshua* spoke to His *talmidim* or "disciples" and to His contemporaries two-thousand years ago, all who were living under the Mosaic Covenant, is applicable to His New Covenant Congregation or Church since Pentecost, AD33.

There is no question that the biblical records within the four Gospels are true, although not everything we read in the four Gospels is applicable to the church. We must be very careful when we read the Holy Scriptures, that we understand that they have an historical, cultural, and grammatical context. The Gospels of *Mattityahu, Markos, Lukas,* and *Yochanon* are categorized by publishers at the beginning of the New Testament portion of our Bibles, although contextually, they belong to the Old Testament dispensation.

What *Yeshua* said to the Jewish nation living under the authority of the Old Mosaic Covenant, under the jurisdiction of the *Cohen Gadol* or Aaronic High Priest, led by the priestly tribe of *Levi,* living in the holy Real Estate called Israel, subject to all 611 laws of the Mosaic code and not just ten commandments, was indeed applicable to Israel "married" to the Sinai covenant. The NT Church is married to *Yeshua* and His New Covenant Messianic Law (Romans 7:4). The Church is not *antinomian*; that is, without law. We do indeed have a *Torah* or instruction to obey. However, our *Torah* or law is not the Mosaic or Sinai Covenant.. Our covenant laws are contained in the New Testament.

The Church abides under the authority of the new Messianic Covenant that *Yeremiyahu* had prophesied to come, foremost for Israel. Israel should have been anticipating the new covenant.

"Behold, days are coming, declared YHWH, when I will make a new covenant with the house of Israel and with the house of Judah, not like the covenant which I made with their fathers in the day I took them by the hand to bring them out of the land of Egypt, My covenant which they broke, although I was a husband to them, declares YHWH. But this is the covenant which I will make with the house of Israel after those days, declare YHWH, I will put My law within them and on their heart, I will write it; and I will be their God, and they shall be my people...." Jeremiah 31:31-33.

The New Covenant Church abides under the jurisdiction of the new *Cohen Gadol, Yeshua* Who is the High Priest of the order of *Melchizedek*, a different priesthood than the Old Testament dispensation and the Aaronic priesthood. *Yeshua* from the tribe of *Yehudah* (Judah) is High Priest of the *Melchizedekian* Priesthood, and His followers are obligated only to obey the new code of the new covenant He administers. We are not obligated to obey the Laws or statures of the *Torah* of the Mosaic covenant, which includes all 611 laws, and not just ten. *Yeshua* came and first spoke to those who were obliged to obey literally every *jot and tittle* of the Mosaic covenant. However, the Church abides under a new covenant. When *Yeshua* was speaking to His *talmidim* or disciples they were not [yet] immersed into that covenant. The inauguration of the New Testament Church was upon the feast day of *Pentecost*.

The Church of the new covenant is a new priesthood and every believer is a priest, unlike the old mosaic covenant where only those of the tribe of Levi were priests. Under the new covenant every believer is a king, unlike the old Sinai covenant where only Judahites were legitimate kings. The New Covenant High Priest is *Yeshua* born of the tribe of *Judah* of which the OT or *Tanakh* spoke nothing concerning High Priestly authority (Hebrews 7:14), while the old, mosaic, Sinai covenant required High Priests to be Levites of Aaronic descent.

The old covenant of *Moshe* had a Temple, which was first, a traveling tent, a tabernacle that was designed by the artisan *Bezalel* (meaning, "in the shadow of El"). The tabernacle gave way to the permanent Solomonic Temple. It sat on Mount Moriah in Jerusalem. Our [new] High Priest *Yeshua* has a Temple! His people, the Church are His Temple. We are "living stones" together constructing God's Holy House, says *Kefa*/Peter (1 Peter 2:5). Believers are the seat of God's dwelling. God no longer dwells in a man-made building in the midst of an ethnic nation. Christians, all together, comprise the holy Tabernacle of God. The authentic Temple of God is *Yeshua*'s Temple, His Church, and no longer an edifice in Jerusalem on the Temple Mount. *Yeshua*, in fact, spoke of His new covenant to the woman at the well, saying *Yerushalayim* with its Jewish Temple, and *Shechem* with its Samaritan Temple will be replaced by another Temple where man can worship God anywhere and everywhere, no longer in religious shrines, on religious estates, in religious cities, led by religious gurus. His worship will be one of spirit and truth (John 4).

A new covenant necessitates a new High Priest, a new Temple, a new priesthood, and new laws! No longer is anyone, Jew or Gentile obligated to make pilgrimages to Jerusalem, Mecca, or Rome to pay homage to God. Believers under the New Covenant are not even obligated to make a weekly pilgrimage to a building called, "the church." We worship God in spirit and in truth everywhere and anywhere we gather, because we are the church. We are not to forsake the assembling of ourselves together for prayer, praise, encouragement, confession, teaching and hearing the Word, as the author of Hebrews says we should pay attention (10:25). Yet, that assembly can be anywhere, everywhere, few or many, at any time, and as often as we wish. There is no New Testament law governing the frequency of assembly or the place for assembly regardless of what religious leaders may say.

In the scroll of *Yekhek'el* (Ezekiel 10) is a prophetic visual of what God was about to do. Because of Israel's disobedience, God rose up as a wind and He blew eastward, out of the *kodesh kodeshim* or holy of holies, leaving the holy temple, departing the holy city *Yerushalayim*, exiting over the Mount of Olives, and He was gone! Fast-forward centuries later. As prophesied and in God's perfect timing, the Spirit of God descended upon *Yeshua* when He was immersed by *Yochanon the Immerser*. Then, when the Holy Spirit of *Yeshua* blew [back] into *Yerushalayim,* as a mighty wind, in the upper room on the day of Pentecost following His resurrection and ascension, He came to indwell His New Testament Temple. Jews had gathered in *Yerushalayim* for the Feast of *Shavuot* or harvest, and they heard the Gospel spoken in sixteen known languages of the World that *Lukas* recorded for us in His *Acts of the Apostles*. God had returned to His holy city, *Yerushalayim*, to His holy temple, and to His *kodesh kodeshim*, except His new *kodesh kodeshim* or "Holy of Holies" was/is His people, the Church, not the temple of Rabbinic Judaism. We, the Church are His New Temple!

We must be VERY careful when we interpret the sayings of *Yeshua* who was born under the [dispensation of] law, speaking to a Jewish nation under the legal covenant of the law called *Torah*, as being applicable to us, the Church, who are an entirely new entity, under a new contract, with a new administration, and given a new compilation of Holy Scriptures. The sacred texts of *Mattityahu, Markos, Lukas*, and *Yochanon* are foundational books of the beginnings of *Yeshua* and His fulfillment of the Old Covenant. The epistles and letters of *Shaul*, the book of Hebrews, the letter of *Yaaqov* (James), the two letters of *Kefa* (Peter), the three letters of *Yochanon* (1,2,3 John), *Yehuda* (Jude), and the *Apocalypse* (Revelation) are all scrolls included in the New Covenant canon, and these are the new *Torah* or law of Messiah that believers are obliged to study, know, and obey. Our *Bema* judgment (see Questions 13 & 14) in heaven will be based on obedience to this law, and not obedience to the law of Moses! The Church of *Yeshua* is not without law or instruction; that would be *antinomianism* (meaning, "anti-law") which the Apostle *Shaul* fought hard against (along with *Galatianism* or legalism, and the *Judaizers*).

Yeshua, DOES want His New Testament church or congregation to know His end time scenarios. Of course, He does. The only scroll in the entire corpus of the Holy Scriptures that bears His authorship (Revelation 1:1) and endorsement (Revelation 22:16) is His *Apocalypse* which is the bookend of Holy Writ, and is entirely prophetic (Revelation 1:3)! The Revelation of Jesus Christ is His final Word to His Church, and the entire book is *eschatological.*[1] "Revelation" is the English title for the Greek term, *Apocalypse,* and this final book of the New Testament/Covenant is the only book in the Bible that declares itself to be, *"the Revelation of Yeshua the Messiah"* (Revelation 1:1). *Yochanon* or John was only the recipient of the Word, and it cost *Yochanon* dearly to receive the disclosure via the angel, and pen it.

The scroll of *Yeshua* called *Revelation* includes a blessing for those to read, hear, and obey the words of the final prophecy (Revelation 1:3). Why would *Yeshua* conclude the compilation of the Holy Scriptures which make up His Divine Holy Library with such a difficult book to understand? Why would *Yeshua* bookend the Word of God with an apocalyptic book? Why didn't *Yeshua* conclude the Holy Scriptures with a 5th Gospel, the *Gospel According to Yeshua,* or another psalm, after all He was the son of David? Why didn't He conclude the Holy Bible with another proverb since He was the one greater that *Sh'lomo?* Why wasn't His scroll that ends the compilation of the Holy Scriptures not an epistle like those *Shaul* (Paul) was inspired to write?

God wants His Church to know the end times since His concluding scroll in His Holy Scriptures is the *Apocalypse,* the *Revelation* of *Yeshua* concerning the end times. This final book of the divine library, the one *Yeshua* disclosed to *Yochanon* on the isle of Patmos, is a scroll of prophecy (Revelation 1:3), and the Words of *Yeshua* in some translations are in red, just like the Words of *Yeshua* in the Gospels. It was *Yeshua* Who told *Yochanon* NOT to seal the book, for the time is

---

[1] The amillennial view of eschatology is discussed later in the book.

imminent (Revelation 22:10). No wonder the Catholic pope, priests, bishops, and cardinals, taught and continue to teach the *Preterite interpretation* of the book of Revelation (see Question 43), that all biblical prophecy was fulfilled in the history of the church and the destruction of Jerusalem in AD 70 by the Romans.

Yeshua wants you and I to know the things that have happened, the things that are happening [today], and things that are going to happen at the end of the age. This, in fact, is the three-fold division of *Yeshua*'s *Apocalypse*.

"Write the things which thou hast seen (Revelation 1:4-20), *and the things which are* (Revelation 2-3) *and the things which shall be hereafter"* (Revelation 4-22).

It is true that *Yeshua* did not give His apocalyptic disclosure to His *talmidim* or disciples under the old administration. However, *Yeshua* gave His *Apocalypse* to *Yochanon* who was one of His *talmidim* or disciples under the old covenant, yet now no longer called a "disciple." In fact, the word "disciple" does not appear in the New Testament after the book of Acts. Believers in *Yeshua* are not disciples; disciples can fall away and be lost (e.g. Judas). New Testament believers are "Sons of God," the "Temple of the Holy Spirit," God's "building," the "body of Messiah," the "bride" of Messiah, and His "epistle" or book. *Disciple* or *talmid* was an OT term for followers of a rabbi, endorsing the rabbis interpretation(s) of the *Mishna* and *Gemara* (which came to be compiled forming the *Talmud*). Believers in *Yeshua* (Christians) are not followers of a rabbi; we are indwelt by *Yeshua*, we are His body, immersed by Him under His holy *Ruach* or spirit, and we are Sons of God.

The *Apocalypse* or Revelation of *Yeshua* was to be distributed to the seven churches that existed in *Yochanon's* day, and those seven churches represent seven kinds of churches that existed then and that will continue to exist until the Church is raptured. *Yeshua* wants us, His Church to know eschatology, since the prophetic book of *Yeshua* received by *Yochanon* was to be given to *Yeshua*'s Church (Revelation 1:3).

Yeshua's apocalypse was placed in the canon of the New Testament chronologically at the end, because it pertains to the end. The *Apocalypse* is immensely important to His New Testament Church. In fact, the scroll of Revelation is the only scroll in the canon of Scripture that states the revelation is from *Yeshua* (Revelation 1:1). *Yeshua*'s last words were not on the cross, nor were they at His ascension at Bethany, nor were His last words to His *talmidim* during the forty-day bible study in Galilee. The last words of *Yeshua* were not at His final *shalom* to His disciples as He ascended. His final words are within the book that *Yeshua* imparted to *Yochanon*, the *Apocalypse*. His last words are here in the *apocalyptic eschatological* unveiling, the disclosure, the Revelation of *Yeshua*, which has to do entirely with the end times.

> *"The Revelation of Jesus Christ, which God gave Him to show to His bond-servants, the things which must soon take place; and He sent and communicated {it} by His angel to His bond-servant John"* (Revelation 1:1).

The apocalypse of *Yeshua* is *prophecy* having to do with the end times, and it is also the only book in the Bible that is said to be endorsed by *Yeshua*.

> *"I, Jesus, have sent My angel to testify to you these things for the churches. I am the root and the descendant of David, the bright morning star. The Spirit and the bride say, "Come." And let the one who hears say, "Come." And let the one who is thirsty come; let the one who wishes take the water of life without cost. I testify to everyone who hears the words of the prophecy of this book: if anyone adds to them, God will add to him the plagues which are written in this book"* (Revelation 22:16-18).

The Bible, every book, every chapter, every verse, every Hebraic, Aramaic, and Greek *jot* and *tittle* is inspired. Yet, the Revelation of *Yeshua* which is the final scroll in the Bible is preeminent. The Apocalypse was from *Yeshua* (Revelation 1:1); the Apocalypse is the final prophecy of *Yeshua* (Revelation 1:3); the Apocalypse was endorsed by *Yeshua* (Revelation 22:16); and the Apocalypse is the only book in the Bible that promises a blessing to the one who reads, hears, and obeys its revelation (Revelation 1:3).

"Blessed is he who reads and those who hear the words of the prophecy, and heed the things which are written in it; for the time is near."

God wants His church to know His design, His plan, His program for the end of the world. God's final words recorded and placed in the canon of Holy Scripture is exclusively *apocalyptic, prophetic,* and *eschatological* having to do with the end of the age.

Har Megiddo (Armageddon) is the battlefield of the Bible. When the Jewish people returned to the land of Israel following the Holocaust, the *chalutzim* or "pioneers" changed this mosquito infested bog to become an agricultural miracle. The rounded top mountain to left of center is Mount Tabor. Nazareth the home of *Yeshua* is to the far left in the picture with white stone buildings. The mountain in the center of the picture is the Hill of Moreh (Judges 7:1).

OUTLINE OF THE APOCALYPSE

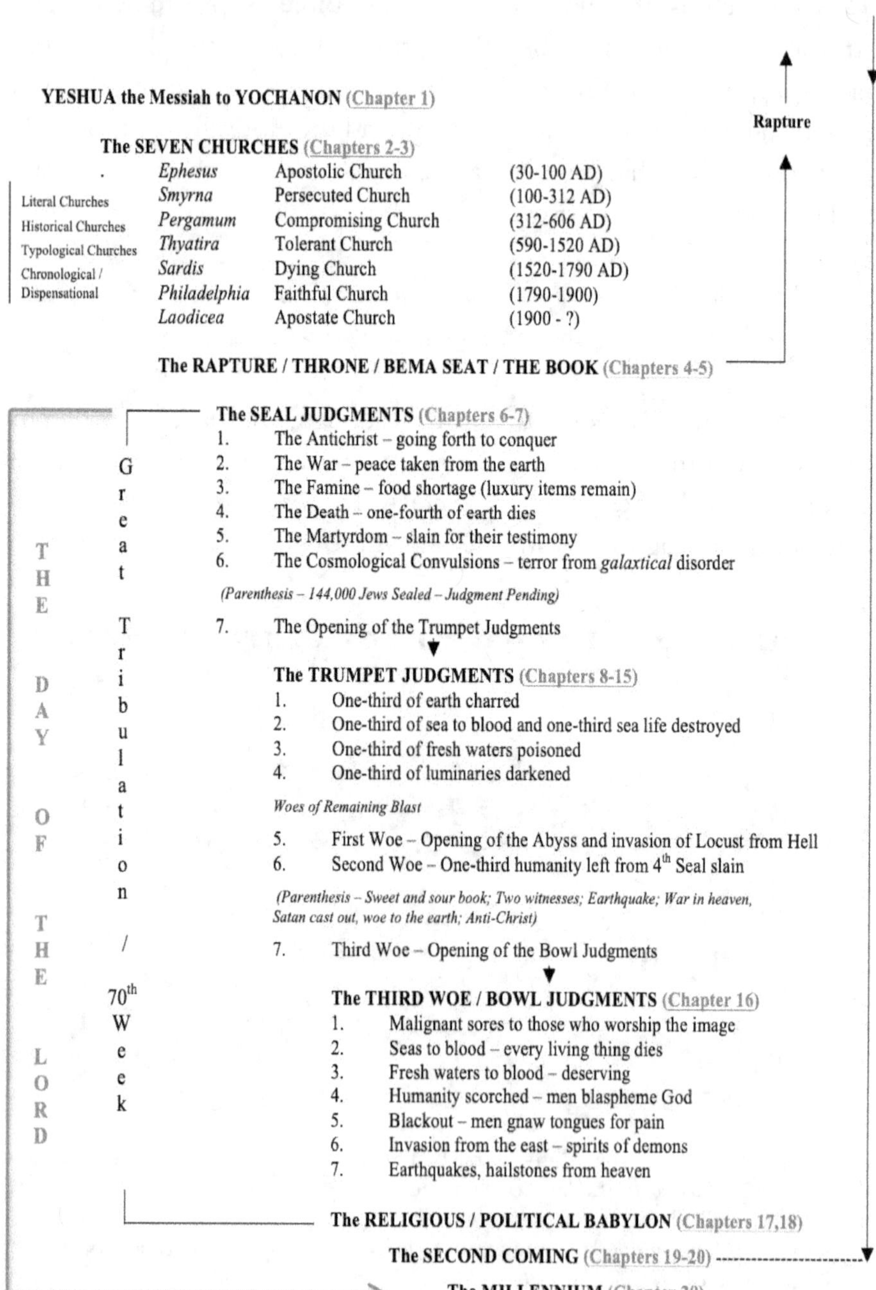

Question 2

Why is prophecy considered so important when the hallmark of the Holy Scriptures is the Gospel, the Lord's virgin birth, perfect life, sacrificial death, burial, resurrection, and ascension?

Answer

Prophecy is the forecast of God's messianic plan from *Abel*, who was a prophet (Luke 11:51) to the final biblical prophet, *Yochanon* on *Patmos* who recorded the *Apocalypses* or Revelation of *Yeshua* that in its entirety concerns the end times. God's prophets spoke to the people in their day foretelling events to come centuries even millennia in their future. The prophets foretold myriad prophecies, but one central hallmark theme, was *Messianic Prophecy*. The first coming of Messiah, the return of the Messiah for and His elopement with His bride, the Church, the Second Coming of Messiah, and His millennial kingdom and reign in Jerusalem is zenith throughout the Holy Scriptures.

When *Yeshua* came two-thousand years ago, there were an elect few who although not knowing the day or the hour of His coming they knew they were in the season of Messiah's appearance. They had been given privy of His coming by the inspired Word of God, and they recognized Him as Messiah, believed in Him, and told others, spreading the Gospel. Their enlightenment came by the messianic prophecies of the Word of God.

Yeshua came and He is coming again, and there are myriad messianic prophecies that foretell His return, first in the air to *rapture* His Church/congregation and take us to the throne room for the *Bema*

Judgment, and later His *Second Coming* to earth when He will judge the sheep and the goats, and then take His monarchal seat in *Yerushalayim* to reign for one-thousand years over the entire world.

It was of vital importance that the first century Jews and Gentiles recognize *Yeshua* when He came, and it is just as important that we are able to recognize His appearance to rapture His bride, the Church. It will also be vitally important for believers living during *the Great Tribulation* to know the time of His Second Coming. Prophecy was potently important to the first century Jewish nation, and those who knew the prophecies are the ones who recognized their savior, even when He was a babe! All of this is the Gospel! The Gospel and Biblical Prophecy are not rivals or polar. Biblical Prophecy is formidable and vitally important.

Prophecy is the spirit of Yeshua, and a witness of Yeshua.

"for the testimony of Yeshua is the spirit of prophecy" (Revelation 19:10).

The very first prophecy in the bible is Genesis 3:15 concerning the *"seed of woman."* This prophecy is called the *protoevangelium* or "first Gospel." This prophecy predicts three spiritual wars. The first war was the battle between the woman and the serpent; it has been fought. The second war is the battle between the woman's seed and the serpent's seed. This war continues until the Lord separates the wheat from the chaff. Finally, the third spiritual war is between the two champions, "He" from the woman Who was to strike the serpent's head, and "you," the serpent to whom God was talking who would strike the champion's heel. *Yeshua* is the champion from woman Who is to crush the head of the serpent. *Yeshua* crushed the dragon's head by His death, burial, and resurrection. The final blow to the dragon will be at the end of the age when the Devil is cast into *Gehenna* fire.

Genesis 3:15 is the first biblical prophecy and every other prophecy in the Bible hinges on this first one. The prophecy is about *Yeshua,* in fact, according to *Yeshua* the entirety of the Old Testament, the *Torah*, the first five books in the Bible also called the *Pentateuch*, the *Neviim* or the Prophets (both major and minor prophets, that is the large books and the smaller books), and the *Ketuvim* or the Writings which include Psalms, Proverbs, Ecclesiastes, Song of Songs, etc. are all about Him.

> *"Then beginning with Moses and with all the prophets, He explained to them the things concerning Himself in all the Scriptures…Now He said to them, "These are My words which I spoke to you while I was still with you, that all things which are written about Me in the Law of Moses and the Prophets and the Psalms must be fulfilled."* (Luke 24:27, 44).

The prophecy concerning the blessing of *Avraham* in Genesis 12 is about *Yeshua*. The prophecy concerning a priest like unto *Melchizedek* is about *Yeshua* (Psalm 110; Hebrews 7:1-22). The prophecy concerning *Yehudah* being the preeminent tribe to whom the other tribes would exonerate (Genesis 49:10) is about *Yeshua* Who is the Lion from the tribe of *Yehudah*. The prophecy concerning the *kokav* or star to descend from *Yaaqov* (Numbers 24:17) is about *Yeshua*. The prophecy concerning "the prophet like unto *Moshe*" (Deuteronomy 18:18) is about *Yeshua*. The prophecy concerning the messiah being a son of David (2 Samuel 7) is about *Yeshua*. The prophecy concerning the anointed messiah (Psalm 2; 22; 45:7,8; 110) is about *Yeshua*. The prophecy concerning the virgin born *Immanuel* (Isaiah 7:14) is about *Yeshua*. The wonderful, counselor, mighty God, everlasting Father, Prince of Peace (Isaiah 9:6) is about *Yeshua*. The suffering servant (Isaiah 53) is about *Yeshua*. The Lord reigning from His throne as priest and king over all the earth (Zechariah 6:12,13) is about *Yeshua!* The very last prophecy in the Bible is also about *Yeshua*.

> *"He who testifies to these things says, "Yes, I am coming quickly." Amen. Come, Lord Jesus"* (Revelation 22:20).

The zenith of prophecy is the Lord God, the Messiah. He is the hallmark of prophecy. *Yeshua* is walking through the pages of Holy Writ. Every story, narrative, prophecy, parable, protagonist, hint, innuendo, and every jot and tittle are pointing to *Yeshua*. He is everywhere! This is the Gospel!

Prophecy promotes intimacy with Yeshua.

"but I have called you Friends, for all things that I have heard from My Father I have made known to you" (John 15:15).

Avraham was a friend of God and God did not hide from His friend what He was about to do. In fact, *Yeshua* said that *Avraham* rejoiced to see His day, saw it, and was glad (John 8:56). The prophet *Dani'el* was highly esteemed by God and *Dani'el* heard God speak intimately (Daniel 10:10-21). According to the Prophet *Amos,* God does not move forward without revealing His paths to His servants the Prophets who were to herald His Words (Amos 3:7). God wants us to know His plan! Of course, He does!

When we read the narratives, poetry, songs, the four gospels, the epistles and the apocalyptic writings of God's Word we realize that the authors were intimate with their savior Who spoke and endeared Himself to them. We also realize that God is intimate with His people and desires to tell us of His calculations, where He is going, and what He is about to do. *Yeshua* said He was the *bread of life* and that means we should feed on Him, think of Him, remember Him, long for Him, and remember His Word which in concert with His Holy Spirit is His presence with us. His Word is spiritual food. He sustains us. His Word is a prophetic Word. Prophecy is about *Yeshua!*

Consider the following colossal events that came about by the Word of God being spoken.

- The prophetic Words of God gave *Avraham* faith whereby he was called righteous (Genesis 15:1).

- The prophetic Words of the Lord were not idle words to the hearers, but His Word is the tree of life, giving life, sustaining life, and prolonging life (Deuteronomy 32:47).

- The psalmist wrote that the [prophetic] Word was *a lamp* that enlightens (Psalm 119: 105).

- God's Word is medicinal for the depressed, hurting, lonely, accused, guilty, and dying (Proverbs 12:18, 25; 15:4; 16:30; 13:17; 18:6, 21; 19:28).

- *Shaul*/Paul encouraged believers to speak the prophetic Word of God without fear (Philippians 1:14) stating that the prophetic Word of God performs its work in those of us who believe (1 Thessalonians 2:13). This is why it is so important to get the Word in our minds.

- Food is sanctified or made *kosher* by the prophetic Word that is prayed over it, says *Shaul*/Paul to Timothy (1 Timothy 4:5).

- The prophetic Word of God reproves, rebukes, and exhorts (2 Timothy 3:16).

- *Yeshua* upholds all things by His prophetic Word (Hebrews 1:3).

- Believers are born again by the living prophetic Word of truth, wrote *Yaaqov* (James 1:18), and the prophetic Word implanted is able to save the soul (James 1:21).

- Faith, saving faith, keeping faith, living faith, overcoming faith comes by hearing the prophetic Word (Romans 10:17).

- The prophetic Word of God is living, active, sharper…. piercing to the division of soul and spirit and able to judge the thoughts and intents of the heart (Hebrews 4:12).

- The new birth, regeneration from death to life comes by the imperishable seed, the living and abiding prophetic Word of God (1 Peter 1:23). What the Word of God births cannot be unbirthed or corrupted. This is why born-again men and women are safe in God and cannot lose their salvation.

Salvation is the work of the prophetic Word of God, not of a man's behavior, or his religion, or his works.

- The prophetic Word of God is as unadulterated milk, wrote *Kefa*/Peter (1 Peter 2:2); it is nourishment for the soul of man.

- The heavens and earth were formed out of water by the prophetic Word of God (2 Peter 3:5; Hebrews 11:3).

- The present heavens and earth are being reserved for fire, kept for the day of judgment and destruction of ungodly men by the prophetic Word of God (2 Peter 3:7).

- The prophetic Word of God perfects the love of God (1 John 2:5).

- The victory of the saved during the reign of the *antichrist* and false prophet with their mark of the beast upon foreheads and hands will be by their overcoming Satan by the prophetic WORD (Revelation 12:11).

Eschatology is a study of God's prophetic Word concerning what He has predestined to do in the last days. *Eschatology* is the study of *Yeshua*'s messianic plan which entails many things believers in *Yeshua* need to know. *Yeshua* has given all things to His people, which should make us all the more intimate with our Lord God. To think that He would include us, inform us, and enlighten us is endearing!

Prophecy is an impetus that causes authentic believers in Yeshua to strive to live holy.

"And everyone who has this hope (in context, the coming of the Lord) *fixed on Him, purifies himself, just as he is pure"* (1 John 3:3).

Believers in *Yeshua* are born-again and regenerate people who trust in God's prophetic, eschatological, and messianic plan. This is our hope! While we live in this beautiful world God has created, we anticipate our Lord's coming and we prepare for His appearance. We are waiting for Him since He is returning for us.

Metaphorically, *Yeshua* is our groom and we are His bride! So, in an analogous way we are a spouse waiting for the consummation of our relationship with our bridegroom, *Yeshua*. Our relationship with *Yeshua* is authentic! We are His love, His passion, His desire. He chose us. He sealed us. He is working out our salvation, since He first loved us. He has put within us His Spirit which incites us to have a passionate desire for Him. He is love! So, we love Him. He is coming soon, and He will take us back to the place He is presently preparing for us. Isn't that romantic? We must not forget that as the bride of *Yeshua,* we belong to Him, and we are to be anticipating His soon return for us, to remove us from this secular and sinful world to His heavenly palace.

I have never forgotten when my wife, Crystal thanked me for rescuing her. I'm not sure what all she meant when she referenced our marriage, but we are on an adventure: marriage, three children, built a log home in the hills of Arkansas, experienced four years at the Moody Bible Institute in Chicago, taking the helm of *Messianic Ministry to Israel* in Chattanooga, TN, a grandson, Gideon Elijah, twenty journeys to God's backyard, Israel, and much more. Think of the treasures we have in *Yeshua*! What an adventure we have being married to *Yeshua*!

According to the Holy Scriptures we are sojourners passing through this world. We are aliens! We are not citizens of this world (Philippians 3:20; Ephesians 2:19; Colossians 1:13; 3:1)! We are citizens of the New Jerusalem that Messiah *Yeshua* is presently constructing (John 14). We are soon to *aliya* or "go up" to the New Jerusalem with Him! Thrice yearly Old Testament Israel would make *aliya* or "go up" to Jerusalem to observe the seven Feasts of YHWH. I know this feeling well, for I have made *aliya* to Israel twenty times at this writing, to see, hear, taste, touch, smell, and feel the land of Israel and the people of the new modern nation since 1948. "Going up" to heaven should be more exciting to us as we consider, plan, and prepare!

It is sad that many believers in *Yeshua* live mediocre lives and when death comes they fear death and dying. Perhaps the reason is because this world is attractive and our treasure is here; we often live so focused on things in this world, that we invest little in eternal things and heaven. There are Christians who know they are saved, yet they have not matured, they are not knowledgeable of God or His Word, and they are not ready in heart to depart this world. These are "carnal Christians" according to the Apostle *Shaul* (2 Corinthians 3:1-4). This should not be so, beloved.

Prophecy reminds us that our future is heavenward, not here. This correct focus obligates us, challenges us, and is an impetus for believers to actively pursue personal purity and obedience to our Lord, *Yeshua* Who is our bridegroom. We should be making ourselves ready for the great wedding to come, for soon we will hear these words, "*behold the bridegroom cometh; go ye out to meet Him!*" One thing is sure, you will want to be living *kosher* when He comes for you, whether in the *Rapture* or at death! The Lord spoke of the evil servant who became apathetic, slothful, and indifferent to the Master's return. The record is given by *Mattityahu, "my Master delays His coming…."* The servant did evil and *Yeshua* said his judgment was one of dread. The context of the passage pertains to the literal coming again of the Master (Matthew 24:48-51).

It wasn't by happenstance that *Zacharyah* (Zacharias) came to serve in the Temple at the most appropriate time. Both he and his wife, *EliTzevet* (Elizabeth) were righteous and blameless before God; they were *messianic* believers looking for Messiah in spite of the fact that as *Aaronic* descendants they were childless. Being childless was shameful to their religious society (Luke 1:25, 36; Genesis 30:23). Yet, they remained devoted, pure, and holy before God anticipating His advent. There was also an eighty-four-year-old widow, *Hanna* who never left the Temple, fasting day and night; she was a holy woman, and her reward was to see her redeemer up close. She held Him in her hands (Luke 2:36-38).

Biblical prophecy promotes genuine piety and devotion to *Yeshua* and our God. Prophecy challenges the authenticity of our faith. What we believe is seen by how we live and vice-versa. What we believe is displayed in our character and by our purity! Authentic believers will live holy as we prepare for the bridegroom and the mansion city, our next world. Of course, we will battle our old man, the flesh, our opponent as we live in the flesh in this world. We will fail and fail miserably, but we will continue to cry to God for help and sanctification. We want His character! Isn't that true of you, beloved?

Beloved, are you living as though your Lord will come today, or have you given in to unbelief considering the Lord's return, and grown distant to His promise of return, thinking His coming is insignificant or uncomprehensive or even irrelevant? *Kefa* (Peter) wrote that some will say, "the Lord has delayed His coming" and they will begin living for this world and its pleasures. The Holy Scriptures say that in the last days men will question the Lord's promise to return, thinking that His return is fictional, or because the Lord tarries in His return, they will mock devotion and piety of believers who are truly anticipating His return. The Lord's delay is due to love; He is not willing for anyone to perish (2 Peter 3:3).

The Church is spoken of as the Lord's bride, and we are excited to prepare ourselves for the wedding and for our groom. We know He is pure and we want to be pure like Him!

Beloved, we will soon rendezvous with *Yeshua* and have a face-to-face encounter. After our escort to heaven, there will be a consummation of our relationship with *Yeshua*. There will be full disclosure, and although sin is not in any way part of our meetup, there will be a judgment of our works. Think of it, an encounter with the living Messiah, *Yeshua, Elohim, YHWH, El Shaddai, YHWH-Yireh.* Amen, amen, and amen!

Prophecy is a venue for blessings from God.

"Blessed is he who reads and those who hear the words of the prophecy, and heed the things which are written in it; for the time is near" (Revelation 1:1-3).

The biblical book of Genesis contains the story of *Yaaqov* (Jacob) who gathered his twelve sons to himself and pronounced upon each one a prophesy that would occur upon them, *b'acharit hayamim* or "in the last days." *Yaaqov* was near death, about to be gathered to his people, and he knew it, but before his departure he desired to "bless" his sons (Genesis 49:1-33). The scriptures say that *Yaaqov* "blessed them with the blessing."

> *"All these are the twelve tribes of Israel, and this is what their father said to them when he blessed them. He blessed them, everyone with the blessing appropriate to him"* (Genesis 49:28).

Yochanon wrote something similar in the scroll of Revelation that *Yeshua* disclosed to him. He wrote that prophecy is a blessing.

> *"Blessed is he who reads and those who hear the words of the prophecy, and heed the things which are written in it; for the time is near"* (Revelation 1:1-3).

The *Apocalypse* is the most potent, prophetic, and eschatological book in the Holy Scriptures and it concerns last days events almost entirely, and to anyone who reads, hears, and obeys the *apocalyptic* book of Revelation, a blessing is promised. No other book in the Bible promises a blessing for reading the scroll. This *eschatological* scroll called Revelation contains seven blessings from *Yeshua* (Revelation 1:3; 14:13; 16:15; 19:9; 20:6; 22:7; 22:14).

Reading prophecy, hearing prophecy, believing prophecy, and acting on the understanding we have of prophecy is a blessing from God. *Miriam* (Mary) was a young teenage girl chosen by God to be the mother of our Lord. *Miriam* was not randomly chosen by God as though He rolled the dice. God had eyed *Miriam* all her life, taking note that she was setting her heart to His messianic prophesies. She had been hearing and memorizing His prophetic scriptures. The young virgin studied the *Tanakh*, what we call the Old Testament, the texts of the *Torah, Neviim,* and *Ketuvim.* In the synagogue on *Shabbat* and Feast Days *Miriam* listened when the Word of God was read or spoken, and she hid the Words of God in her heart. How do we know this? The *Magnificat*! *Miriam* was hailed by *Gabriel* to be the mother of messiah, and six times she was called "blessed" by the archangel. In return, *Miriam* blessed the Lord God, saying *"my soul exalts the Lord,"* and, then she quoted from memory twenty-three OT passages which the good physician *Lukas* recorded for us in his Gospel (Luke 1:46-55). *Miriam's* praise is called the *Magnificat.*

Miriam had memorized passages from the Torah, Job, the Psalms, Habakkuk, and other books. *Miriam* was anticipating the Lord to come! In return, *Miriam* was blessed by the Almighty because she knew His prophecies. Those who are unlearned in the scriptures might say that everything is predestined, and we cannot affect or influence God. They would argue that *Miriam* did not cause God to favor her in order to bless her. They interpret God's sovereignty as a program already written and unfolding that cannot be changed. However, the Holy Scriptures disclose a God Whose eyes roam the globe looking for one Who is devoted to Him (2 Chronicles 16:9; Zechariah 4:10). God is always looking for another *Miriam*! Are you a *Miriam*, beloved?

Prophecy reminds us of the many attributes of God, that God is omnipotent, omniscient, omnipresent, sovereign, faithful, imminent, just, and good! What a blessing, beloved! We open the gates of the prophetic word and God lifts the veil and discloses to us what He has done, what He is doing, and what He is about to do. He did this for *Yochanon* (Revelation 1:19). We "chew the cud" or meditate on His Word and God continues to give us His Word. It is disheartening that so many Christians do not behold God's prophetic Word, they do not knock on His gates, they do not seek Him or His ways, and they remain lean and barren.

Shaul (Paul) wrote in 1 Corinthians 14:1, *"pursue love, and earnestly desire the spiritual gifts, especially that you may prophesy."* The reason, of course, is that the gift of prophecy was a blessing to the NT congregation of *Yeshua* in its formation while the Holy Scriptures were being given and finalized by the Holy *Ruach*/Spirit to men. Prophetic utterance ceased with the prophet *Yochanon* and his scribing the final scroll of the Holy Scriptures, the *Apocalypse*. Any other word since AD 90 when the book of Revelation was written, that is proclaimed to be the Word of God had better be measured against the Holy Scriptures. There are no new scriptures, not the Book of Mormon, not the Koran, not those prophetic utterances given by those who supposedly speak in tongues, and there are no lost gospels.

What a blessing it is for us to behold biblical prophecies spoken millennia ago coming to fulfillment, today!

Prophecy gives us hope, encouragement, and consolation.

"…looking for the blessed hope and the appearing of the glory of our great God and Savior, Christ Jesus, who gave Himself for us…" (Titus 2:14).

"But one who prophesies speaks to men for edification and exhortation and consolation" (1 Corinthian 14:3).

Some years ago, the space shuttle Columbia exploded and was incinerated upon reentry to our atmosphere. NASA learned that a problem had occurred at liftoff. An external panel had dislocated which rendered the shuttle vulnerable to the intense heat of reentry to the earth's atmosphere. The ship was in peril from the beginning, throughout the whole journey, but who knew? We were told no one knew this horrific problem had occurred (with the possible exception of a few engineers who warned NASA that it could happen). The astronauts accomplished their mission and were coming home, about to make reentry, each astronaut thinking of his and her family and the thrill of sharing their journey, when suddenly they were no more. They died unexpectantly. How horrifically sad!

Our world is in such a state, for we too are traveling on a space ship, called earth. We, too, had a destructive fiasco in our beginning, and we too, will one day unexpectedly and suddenly be no more. What we do know for certain, is that we are not getting out of this alive!

In the beginning, man sinned and our relationship with God was severed. Man lost life with God, communication with God, and man died spiritually. Man, also died physically. God has said man might live three-score and ten years and a decade beyond that if strong. Man will not survive forever in his earth suit, and he will not survive spiritually either, unless there is reparation! The earth is dying, space the supposed final frontier is dying, all life is dying, we are dying, and you, dear reader, are dying as you read! Our present life is going to end, and our soul is going to an eternal destiny. Man is in dire need of being saved. Every man has inherited Adam's nature to sin, and we are responsible for our choices and our spiritual condition. Man is not just headed for destruction, we are born destructive, spiritually dead, and in dire need of a savior. After death, there is an accounting; we will be judged. Good news! God has given man a savior! His only son, *Yeshua* gave His life as a ransom for everyone. He is our hope!

Using another analogy, like the great ship, Titanic, man also is at peril; we are sinking. The whole human race has been irreparably damaged because the captain of the human race, *Adam* made a horrendous choice that continues to affect everyone and everything on board this planet. Just as *Adam* and *Havvah* rebelled against a holy and righteous God, we, too continue the rebellion. Our journey through life may be an enjoyable, beautiful, and an exciting adventure, and we may think this journey of life is paradise as we sip tea on the deck while the orchestra continues to play music to soothe our nerves. Yet, every man is in colossal trouble. Each one of us have sinned, we are sinking, we are [already] dying, and after death everyone will stand before a righteous judge and give an accounting. All have sinned and "the wages for sin is death" (Romans 3:23). At death each one of us will go out into eternity, alone. After death, there is judgment. *"It is appointed to man once to die and after this the judgment"* (Hebrews 9:27).

The Christian, however, has a privileged perspective and a privileged position. While living this short life ("life is like a vapor," James 4:14), the Christian is enlightened of sin, himself as a sinner, and yet God's great love for man causing Him to pay man's debt to heal his condition. *Yeshua*'s death was to redeem and save man, and the Christian knows and is sure that God will accomplish what He has promised. *Yeshua*, God's Son is our atonement, our covering, and *Yeshua* is our security since He is our salvation. The life of Christ is credited to us, and our sinful self, cursed by sin and death is credited to Him. He gets us and we get Him. His righteousness is imputed to me, and my transgressions are imputed to Him. Wonderful trade!

No man's faith is so sturdy that he or she does not need to strengthen it, and the study of God's prophetic program helps to edify and encourage the church.

"But one who prophesies speaks to men for edification and exhortation and consolation" (1 Corinthian 14:3).

Sadly, the church or congregation of *Yeshua* does not have enough of the teaching of prophecy in its diet. Perhaps it is because many churches are disoriented to its importance. Yet, according to the Bible the teaching of prophecy is the antidote for despair, because the teaching of prophecy gives hope. The teaching of prophecy gives encouragement.

The old Jewish man *Shmeon* in the Gospel of *Lukas* had studied the prophecies and was looking for the *consolation* of Israel which refers to a time according to *Yesh'yahu* or Isaiah when Israel's time of suffering would end (Luke 2:25). Like *Shmeon* we have a confident expectation that God will do what He has said; this is our hope, and to obtain and secure this hope one must study to know what God has said! We happily know that a nuclear holocaust is not going to be the end of civilization. Alien beings from outer space are not going to invade earth and destroy our planet.[2] God has said how the world will end. God has spoken His plan in biblical prophecy, and we want to know God's design.

---

[2] The Holy Scriptures do prescribe a coming invasion of spirit beings in the last days (see Question 11).

Beloved, let me encourage you to be reading, thinking, studying, and looking for the consolation of the church, and the end-times scenarios. Our Lord's coming is soon and His coming is your glory, your treasure, your reward, your life, and your hope! Your hope is not in health, because at some point your health is for certain going to fail you. It's just a matter of when. Your hope is not in a parent, child, or spouse, for they will inevitably disappoint, hurt, or abandon you. It happens daily. Your spouse, child, parent, or sibling may have to plant your body in the soil very soon. Their hope and yours cannot be in a person, institution, or a moment. Our hope cannot be in man, money, fanfare, fame, adventure, another tomorrow, or this life. Your only hope is *Yeshua*! He is your hope, encouragement, and consolation. And, He is coming!

The inspired prophetic Holy Scriptures are profitable for righteousness.

"All Scripture is inspired by God and is profitable for teaching...for training in righteousness, that the man of God may be equipped" (2 Timothy 3:16).

The *magi* or "wise men" from the east were students of prophecy. They had studied the seventy *shavuot* or "sevens" of the prophet, *Dani'el* who gave the exact time of the Lord's coming to *Yerushalayim*. Like *Yov, Avraham, Yaaqov,* and others before them, the *magoi* had studied the stars in the heavens, and reading the stars like notes of music the wise-ones knew some of God's symphony. The *magi* were students of prophecy and they left their world to make the arduous journey across rugged mountains, barren wasteland, and inhospitable plains to *Yerushalayim*, and then on to *Beit Lechem* (Bethlehem) because they believed in the inspired prophetic Holy Scriptures. Because they studied, believed, and obeyed the prophetic scriptures, they saw Baby God.

In the same spirit the young disciple *Andreas* (Andrew) after meeting the Messiah ran to alert his brother *Kefa* (Peter) saying, *"we have found Him of whom the Scriptures foretold." Kefa* followed *Andreas* to *Yeshua.* We know that *Andreas* and *Kefa* were not tobacco smoking, bear guzzling, potty-mouth fishermen. They were students of the prophetic word!

When we speak of *eschatology* we are speaking of prophecy, and prophecy declares that there is a sovereign God whose has a sovereign plan. God is not "playing it by ear" as some musicians play without a script. One of the honors I had before leaving our family ministry, The Lisembys, to attend Moody Bible Institute and offer my life to Jewish evangelism, was to play guitar for Johnny Cash and June Carter Cash. It was sensational and a high honor for Dad, Mom, we four sons and our wives to be on stage with Johnny and June as their band for a concert in Kingsland, Arkansas, the birth place of Johnny Cash and our Dad, James Travis Lisemby. Dad and Johnny were cousins (their grandmothers were sisters) and we were enchanted when Johnny turned to us after the first song, nodded his head, smiled big, and continued singing in his deep baritone voice. We knew he approved of our playing and we had his confidence.

That day I played my twelve-string Ovation Legend guitar. I had been playing guitar for more than twenty years, although I played "by ear," a musician's term meaning "the ability of performing a piece of music one has never heard, and without having seen it notated in any form of sheet music." This is a desirable skill although it has limitations. In my studies at Moody Bible Institute I took Music Theory as an elective because I love music. Within a few weeks I knew I was in trouble. I talked to my prof, I moved to the front of the class, I stayed after class and got help, and I learned to read music. I finished the class with an excellent grade (A). For the purpose of illustration, God does not play by ear! God is not making it up as He goes, but He has written His *magnum-opus*, and has deposited His messianic plan in His prophetic Word. God has a messianic plan and God has invited man to come alongside Him and know Him and know His plan. What an honor. However, to know His plan, there is a cost!

God spoke to *Dani'el* that he was to "seal up" the vision or revelation, for it pertained to the end of time (Daniel 8:26; 12:4). However, God declared to *Yochanon* that he was not to seal up the vision given to him for the time was near.

"Do not seal up the words of the prophecy of this book for the time is near" (Revelation 22:10).

What God spoke to *Dani'el*, He did not say to *Yochanon*. What *Yeshua* spoke to His *talmidim* or disciples He did not necessarily say to us, the Church. It is inexplicably important to study the Word and to know how to interpret and apply the Word. *Yeshua* told the disciples when they asked Him an *eschatological* question, *"it is not for you to know."* But, that does not mean that you and I, the Church of *Yeshua* are not to know! We have the new covenant scriptures that the disciples did not have. We have the apocalyptic book called Revelation that the *talmidim* did not have, and *eschatology* is woven throughout this prophetic book. We also have the Holy Spirit indwelling us which the *talmidim* did not have while *Yeshua* was with them, because they were under the OT dispensation. The baptism of the Holy Spirit by *Yeshua* the baptizer did not begin until the New Covenant began. It wasn't until Pentecost as we have already said, that the *talmidim* and all others who were saved became eternally indwelt with the Holy Spirit. We also have the new covenant messianic law that the disciples did not have even while *Yeshua* was with them, for they were abiding under the old mosaic code.

Eschatology is especially highlighted by the Holy Spirit in the New Testament. When you read the Gospel accounts you discover that those saints who had read and studied prophecy were the very ones who recognized *Yeshua* at His first coming. Think of the intelligentsia of Israel who were supposed to have known the prophetic Holy Scriptures and should have known the appearance of Messiah. The students of prophecy knew *Yeshua* when He was eight days of age and in diapers, while the leaders of Israel did not recognize their Messiah when He was full grown, loving sinners, performing miracles, casting out devils, and dying on the cursed tree. Those unbelieving souls are paying eternally for their ignorance! That is frightening!

The leaders of the nation of Israel thought they were kingdom heirs because they were Jews, children of *Avraham, Yitzhak,* and *Yaaqov,* yet they were *children of the devil* according to *Yeshua* (John 8:44). They knew the scriptures intellectually, but they did not possess the Spirit of the Word! They believed in a coming Messiah, but they did not possess the Spirit of Messiah. Beloved, study the scriptures. It is the Word that created the world and everything in it. The Word sustains the world. The Word births unregenerate man and makes him righteous. The Word sanctifies a man, secures man, keeps, guards, and protects man, and the Word gets him home safe although he walks through the dark.

The Prophetic Word is a Menorah Shining in Darkness.

"And so we have the prophetic word made more sure, to which you do well to pay attention as to a lamp shining in a dark place, until the day dawns and the morning star arises in your hearts" (2 Peter, 1:19).

Much of *Yeshua's* teaching and preaching was in the area of the Galilee, a place where myriads of people sat in darkness needing enlightenment. The *Galil* was primarily a pagan estate. Suddenly, a great light dawned upon the people of Galilee (Matthew 4:14-16). The light was the messiah *Yeshua* who came teaching the prophetic *eschatological* scriptures.

The Bible has over 31,000 verses and someone has counted over 8,300 of those verses to be direct prophecies. The OT has 23,210 verses and it is estimated that 6,641 verses are directly prophetic. The NT has 7,914 verses and 1,711 verses are prophetic (J. Barton Payne. Encyclopedia of Biblical Prophecy. New York: Harper and Row, 1973.

Page 631-682). What physician would discredit or ignore 27% of the human anatomy? What mechanic would disregard or ignore 27% of engine anatomy? What chef would discount 27% of the recipe? What student would discredit 27% of his notes for the exam?

Some books of the *Holy Scriptures* are entirely prophetic, like *Yesha'yahu* (Isaiah), *Yechek'el* (Ezekiel), *Dani'el* (Daniel), *Zechar'yah* (Zechariah), *Yoel* (Joel), and the *Apocalypse* (Revelation). To be a student of the Holy Scriptures is to be a student of prophecy! The Holy Scriptures are called "the Prophetic Word" and the Lord's beloved are told to "pay attention" to this prophetic word, for, *"it is a light to our feet as we walk through this dark world"* (2 Peter 1:19).

Yeremiyahu (Jeremiah) waded the sewer under *Yerushalayim* being placed there by the leaders of *Y'srael,* because he proclaimed prophecy. He had forewarned them that calamity was coming upon the nation. *Yeremiyahu* remembered the prophetic Word that had come to him concerning Israel and her rebellion. Babylon would be God's chastening rod, and *Yeremiyahu* was told to tell the prophecy to Israel. Few listened!

Dani'el was taken captive with his three Jewish friends into the dark world of Babylon. In the ninth chapter of *Dani'el's* scroll he mentions the prophetic writing of *Yeremiyahu* whom *Dani'el* had read (and had perhaps, memorized). *Dani'el* knew that Israel would not be in exile forever. God had given His Prophetic Word concerning Israel, that after seventy years the Jews would return home to the Holy Land. God's Prophetic Word was sure! In time God's Word became reality for Israel. The exiles returned home.

When *Yoseph* was in the pit of Egypt, in the dark dungeon, he was given light. He remembered the prophetic Word that had come to him in dreams while in the land of Israel. *Yochanon* was in darkness while in exile in the prison camp of *Patmos.* On one occasion he was boiled alive in hot oil. Yet, *Yochanon* in his darkness was given light, a nexus of the messianic plan of God from the beginning.

In dark times we light a candle or a bulb so that we can see. In the darkness our vision is limited. Our sight is dependent not only upon light, but the brightness of the light. In dark times we go to God's menorah, His prophetic Word to see what God has said through the prophets, and we had better pay attention! The prophetic Word of God is a compilation of 66 candles. One day we will have the living Word, *Yeshua.*

8. Prophecy is a convicting tool for evangelism.

A sovereign righteous God on His throne is the Judge of all the earth, and He has spoken declaring what will happen in the last days. This makes us a little uncomfortable, knowing that an account of our lives will be given. Sinners need to know that every soul has sinned, every soul will die, judgment awaits us all, and we can be pardoned ONLY by the blood of *Yeshua* and calling upon His name. Sinners given that truth by someone impowered by God to impart that truth, will run very fast to *Yeshua*! There is NEVER anything wrong with the Word we preach, teach, sing, write, and share. The wrong is always in the human vessel that is not consecrated to God, or in our aggressive and/or arrogant presentation of the Gospel. The Gospel is the power of God unto salvation for everyone (Romans 1:16).

Jonathan Edwards read his gospel message, *"Sinners in the Hands of an Angry God"* and people stampeded to the altar as they wailed begging to be saved. The Holy Scriptures tell us that God has given man *general revelation* of sin, righteousness, and judgment. No man is without the light that lighteth every man (1 John 1:9).

The teaching of prophecy is of interest to everyone, even unbelievers. Box office hits that are *apocalyptic* in genre prove this to be true. We must study to know what has been said and to carefully yet strategically, with Bible in hand, show the relevance of modern events as biblical prophecy being realized and fulfilled. We must be careful, of course, and not be sensational, yet what God has said in His holy Word is coming to pass in these last days.

Prophecy insulates us from heresy and fanaticism.

Prophecy helps us to know what God has said and also what God has not said. While some people retreat into *"eschatological agnosticism"* pleading ignorance on prophetic matters and arguing that no one can be sure about prophetic teachings, or that studying prophecy and *eschatology* leads to division, the truth is, *eschatology* actually helps us to be balanced and not fanatical. Prophecy helps insulate us from fallacy.

The study of prophecy provides us security from men who would manipulate us to buy their books. The study of prophecy gives us discernment from cultic men, women, and ministries. The Bible is the prophetic Word of God that insulates us from heresy, fanaticism, and from relativism. The mystics, new age apparitions, experiences, visions, odd sightings, feelings of ecstasy, meditations, prophetic calculations, and sensational *speaking in tongues* are here to stay, beloved. You and I had better know what God has said, so we can stand firm, and then be able to give an answer when these things occur! Satan is a grand counterfeiter.

Moshe laid down his staff and it became a serpent, and Pharaoh's men laid their Egyptian sticks down and theirs became serpents, also! Pharaoh's magicians counterfeited many of the miracles *Moshe* was performing by God's power, and their results were nearly the same except that Pharaoh's miracles were by another god. When *Moshe* stretched out his rod and miracles happened in Egypt, Pharaoh's men duplicated the miracles. The witch of *Endor* did indeed bring up *Shmuel* from the afterlife (much to her surprise). *Sh'mon* the sorcerer was duplicating the miracles of God until he was muted by the Apostle *Shaul*/Paul a disciple of the true God. Satan and powers of darkness oppose and counterfeit God. That's what they do best!

Believers had better know what God has said, and that there are dark spirits at work. The god of this world knows very well what our Lord has said, and beloved he will rage in the last days. He will grow strong in his opposition, for he knows he has a short time. These are indeed his last days.

"For this reason, rejoice, O heavens and you who dwell in them. Woe to the earth and the sea, because the devil has come down to you, having great wrath, knowing that he has {only} a short time" (Revelation 12:12).

I remember well the charismatic movement when it was strong in the 60s and 70s. Their message was that all spirit-filled believers must speak in tongues as evidence of having the Holy Ghost. I knew then as I know now that such teaching was not warranted by God's Word. Yet, many of my acquaintances were not insulated from deceptive teachings, because they did not know God's Word. They were deceived, spell-bound, and they were led into practices that were weird, sensational, mystic, and that appealed to pride and self. Many gave themselves to the powers. What happened? These former holy ghost, spirit-filled charismatics are now gone from the church; they have become apostate. One acquaintance of mine, Gary P. married a beautiful Pentecostal and Charismatic young lady, and he began practicing the heretical rituals of her church. Gary is now a practicing homosexual. The *holiness movement* deceived them both because they did not know the Word.

We need to remember that it was those who knew the prophetic Word that saw and recognized *Yeshua* at His first coming. Some recognized Him in His diapers, because they knew the Word. *Yeshua* wasn't wearing a halo, yet He was discovered. Others who were students of rabbinic Judaism though not students of the Word, did not recognize *Yeshua*, not even when He was thirty years of age and performing divine acts and miracles!

The prophetic Word of God enlightens, convicts, draws, regenerates, saves, insulates, protects, guards, guides, and keeps us! Prophecy is vitally important!

Question 3

Was the biblical gift of Prophecy only given to men? Weren't there also women Prophetesses?

Answer

Yes, you are correct. *Seer* was the first Hebrew term found [27 times] in the *Tanakh* or OT for those who could *see* the future. A *Seer* was not a "time traveler" as mystics propose, but recipients of revelatory information concerning the future ("to see") which they spoke and sometimes recorded (1 Peter 1:10-12).

The Hebrew term *Navi* meaning "prophet" is found 309 times in the Old Testament or *Tanakh* in noun form, and 600 times in verb form. The *Nevi* was both a forthteller and a foreteller. The true *Navi* and the false *Navi* have existed throughout history proclaiming and prophesying (2 Peter 1:19-2:3).

The true *Seer* and *Navi* was the Man of God and the Woman of God who knew *YHWH,* and was given a position he/she was commissioned to fulfill. The call was often voluntary, as the example of *Yeshayahu* or Isaiah. "*And I heard the voice of the Lord, saying: Whom shall I send, And who will go for us? Then I said: 'Here am I; send me.'*"

The phrase, "*the Servant of the Lord*" stresses the close relationship the prophet had with God as evidenced that they did not serve themselves, but God. An example is *Yekhez'qel* (Ezekiel) who was commanded not to marry.

The *Seer* and *Nevi* saw, received, proclaimed, prophesied, wrote, spoke, and acted; he/she was angelic in nature, and was "*the Messenger of the Lord*" (cf. Revelation 19:10; 22:8).

Tasks of the Prophet and Prophetess

1. He/She was a reformer calling God's people to His Word.
2. He/She was a statesman confronting kings, sages, priests, and common Jews.
3. He/She was a watchman commissioned to speak regardless of his/her personal security or circumstances.
4. He/She was an intercessor mediating, encouraging, and healing.

Tests of the True Prophet and Prophetess

1. His/Her resource was God, not divination or sorcery (2 Peter 1:20,21).
2. His/Her message was God's message, and not catered to the people as the "pillow prophets." Their message was not an adulterated message for personal gain or to be renown. The message was given to the people as he/she was directed by God (Micah 3:5-6,11).
3. His/Her life manifested fruit from God's Holy Spirit (Matthew 7:15-20).
4. He/She willingly laid down his/her life and often suffered for God (1Kings 22:27-28; Jeremiah 38:4-13).
5. He/She did not contradict God's Word. His/Her message was contemporary with God's other prophets and was built upon the message of former prophets.
6. His/Her message was authenticated. He/She had a one-hundred percent success rate (Deuteronomy 18:20).

Traits of the True Prophet and Prophetess

1. There were WRITING prophets: *Yeshayahu* (Isaiah); *Yeremiyahu* (Jeremiah); *Yekhez'qel* (Ezekiel); *Dani'el*/Daniel;

Havakkuk (Habakkuk); *Zephanyah* (Zephaniah); *Shaul* (Paul); *Kefa* (Peter); *Yochanon* (John).

2.   There were ORAL prophets: *Eliyah; Elisha; Yeshua; Philip's* four daughters; *Agabus.*

3.   There were ACTING prophets: *Yeshayahu*/Isaiah walked naked for three years; *Yermiyahu/* Jeremiah bore a yoke; *Yekhek'el*/Ezekiel played in a sand box, named a brick *Yerushalayim,* packed his suitcase and hiked a circle around *Yerushalayim,* slept on one side, and split hairs from his head; *Agabus* bound his own hands and feet to declare a prophetic message to *Shaul*/Paul; *Hoshayyah*/Hosea was the "Drama King" for his performance in marrying a prostitute.

<u>There were Prophetesses in both the Old Testament or *Tanakh* and the New Testament or *Brit Chadesha.*</u>

OLD TESTAMENT PROPHETESSES

Devorah (Judges 4:4)
Miriam (Exodus 15:20)
Huldah (2 Kings 22:14-17)
Isaiah's Wife (Isaiah 8:2,3)

NEW TESTAMENT PROPHETESSES

Anna (Luke 2:36)
Four Daughters of Philip (Acts 21:8,9)

OLD TESTAMENT FALSE PROPHETESSES

Group of False Prophetesses (Ezekiel 13:17-23)

NEW TESTAMENT FALSE PROPHETESSES

Jezebel (Revelation 2:20)

The Hulda Gate in Jerusalem, named after the OT Prophetess, Hulda. "When American astronaut Neil Armstrong, a devout Christian, visited Israel after his trip to the moon, he was taken on a tour of the Old City of Jerusalem by Israeli archaeologist Meir Ben-Dov. When they got to the Hulda Gate, which is at the top of the stairs leading to the Temple Mount, Armstrong asked Ben-Dov whether Jesus had stepped anywhere around there. "I told him, 'Look, Jesus was a Jew,'" recalled Ben-Dov. "These are the steps that lead to the Temple, so he must have walked here many times." Armstrong then asked if these were the original steps, and Ben-Dov confirmed that they were. "So Jesus stepped right here?" asked Armstrong. "That's right," answered Ben-Dov. "I have to tell you," Armstrong said to the Israeli archaeologist, "I am more excited stepping on these stones than I was stepping on the moon." (From Thomas Friedman's book, *From Beirut to Jerusalem*, New York: Doubleday).

Question 4

In the New Testament are two phrases, *"the Fullness of the Gentiles,"* and *"the Times of the Gentiles."* What do they mean; are they the same?

Answer

<u>FULLNESS OF THE GENTILES</u>

"For I do not want you, brethren, to be uninformed of this mystery so that you will not be wise in your own estimation that a partial hardening has happened to Israel until **the fullness of the Gentiles** *has come in"* (Romans 11:25).

In Romans 11:25 the Apostle *Shaul* (Paul) wrote of a "fullness" of Gentile believers in contrast to a hardening that has happened to Israel due to their unbelief. The unbelief of *Y'srael* was only partial since biblically there has always been a *remnant* of *Y'srael* who have believed and followed after *YHWH* their Lord. The European deicide charge, that all Jews of all times killed Christ, is a sinister and demonic untruth. All the *talmidim* or disciples of *Yeshua* were Jewish! There was not one non-Jew in His handpicked coterie. The first *synagogue* or congregation of believers that came to be called the *church* was exclusively Jewish. All the New Testament scrolls were written by Jewish authors with the exception of *Lukas*, although he was a proselyte to Judaism. There were so many Jews coming to faith that the Holy Spirit inspired the author (*Shaul, Apollos,* or *Priscilla*) to write a book to warn Jews from defecting to Judaism. The book is called *Hebrews*. There has always been a Jewish remnant of believers in both the *Tanakh* or Old

Testament, and the *Brit Chadashah* or New Testament -unto this present day (Romans 11:5). God's plan has always included the "whole house of Israel," which is the collective remnant of the true nation of Israel.

In Romans 9, *Shaul* wrote concerning the Jews who had descended from *Yaaqov* and he defined them as "children of the flesh," in similitude of Ishmael. True Israel are those Jews like their predecessor, *Yitzhak* also born of the flesh, yet also, born supernaturally and miraculously by YHWH. These are the "true" Jews and the remnant Israel. Therefore, the "whole house of Israel" of whom *Shaul* wrote, has not yet been fulfilled, since there are still Jews coming to faith in *Yeshua*, and there will be myriad Jews saved during the Great Tribulation, when the "whole house of Israel" will be realized.

Yonder, in the future "all Israel" will believe and a nation of miraculous born-again Jews will reign over all the nations of the earth. The king of that nation, Who will sit on the Davidic throne, will be *Yeshua*. With Him will be His regent prince, *David ben Yessi*, and the millennial *Knesset* will be the *talmidim* or disciples whom *Yeshua* said would reign with Him along with *Yeshua's* New Testament *kehillah* or church (Matthew 19:28). Together, *Yeshua*, David, the twelve *talmidim*, and the church will rule the entire world.

The Apostle *Shaul* wrote that before the *eschatological* era where every living Jew is regenerate, is realized, another *eschatological* event must be completed. That period of time is the *fullness* or completion, or the full number or [total] tally of born-again Gentiles. This "fullness" is the remnant of Gentile believers.

Just as there has always been until this present day a holy remnant of Jews who collectively make up true biblical Israel, there has always been a holy remnant of non-Jews who have come to faith and are regenerate (until this very day), who form the "fullness of the Gentiles." For example, in the days of *Noach* there was a *remnant* of Gentiles on the earth who were saved by God. There was a fullness or tally of souls aboard the Ark of refuge which consisted of *Noach*, his wife, their three sons, and their wives (Genesis 7:7). There was also a remnant of the clean and unclean creatures that went aboard the ark. In Lot's day there was a remnant or fullness realized even though they were vexed by the sins of Sodom. The remnant consisted of Lot and his two daughters (Genesis 19:30-37). Lot's unnamed wife initially left Sodom although she became stone dead for [re]turning her eyes to Sodom.

Avraham had asked the Lord if there be a remnant of 50 regenerate souls would God spare the city. The answer was, "yes!" Then, *Avraham* began the numerical descent in calculating the remnant, if there be forty, thirty, twenty, ten righteous would God spare the city. Each time God agreed, since there was a righteous remnant in the city living among the sodomites.

In *Yericho* there was a fullness or remnant. *Rahav* and her house would be spared (Joshua 6:17-25). In *Eliyah's* day there was a remnant, seven thousand who refused to bow their knees to *Baal* (1 Kings 19:14-18). The bible alludes to a fullness or completion or remnant of the work of the myriad saints throughout Holy Writ.

Eschatologically, "in these last days," God has been gathering His remnant since AD 33. He is gathering a bride for *Yeshua*. All whom God has given the Son, will come to *Yeshua* (John 6:37-39), and *Yeshua* promised never to leave or forsake us. How could He forsake us, for we are born of His imperishable seed, the living Word of God. God knows who we are, beloved. He knows our name and He knows our number just as certain as He knows the number of the stars which astronomers estimate to be innumerable, something akin to 10 with twenty zeros (10,000,000,000,000,000, 000,000 +) and that is just the stars in our galaxy alone (Psalm 147:4; Isaiah 40:26). He knows His remnant. He knows you, beloved!

According to Romans 11:25 when the *remnant* or fullness of Gentiles is obtained, that is, when the non-Jewish remnant has been regenerated by spiritual birth into the Church, God will transition His messianic plan to resume with His program for a regenerate ethnic state of Jewish believers called Israel (Romans 11).

The *fullness of the Gentiles* is a phrase for this present era of time that some call the "church age." For example, *Adam, Seth, Enos, Canaan, Mahalaleel, Jared, Enoch, Methuselah, Noach,* and all the patriarchs were Gentiles, although these do not belong to the, "fullness of Gentiles" spoken of in Romans 11:25. The term *fullness of the Gentiles* is a coined reference of the inclusion of Gentiles in the New Covenant and within the era of the Church age in which *Shaul* was writing. Remember, the new covenant was foremost for the Jews (Jeremiah 31:31). *Yov* (Job) was not Jewish, but a regenerate Gentile born-again from above. He lived outside the *Torah* given only to Israel, and though a Gentle he is not part of *Shaul's* meaning of *Fullness of Gentiles.*

The phrase *fullness of the Gentiles* does not even refer to those myriad Gentile believers who will come to faith during *The Great Tribulation* period and who will reside in the millennial kingdom, that is, Gentiles that the 144,000 Jews will reach with the Gospel. Myriad Gentiles will be saved in that period, although the phrase "fullness of the Gentiles" is a gathering of Gentiles from the time period sandwiched between the OT remnant of Israel and the inauguration of the millennial kingdom of Israel when Israel's Messiah, *Yeshua* will be enthroned. That 'sandwich' is the Church age, believers who are predominantly Gentiles.

The church has not always existed; it began in AD 33 at Pentecost. As *Yeshua* said He would do, He is building His church. It was not already built. In fact, the *Tanakh* or OT speaks nothing of a "church," but exonerates an ethnic nation called Israel. God's Israel is primarily ethnic. God's church is without ethnicity and is inclusive of all peoples. *Yov* was righteous as were his friends, but they were not Israel, and they were not the church. *Adam* and *Avraham* were righteous, but neither were Israel and neither were the church. Israel and the NT Church are clearly two entities as the Holy Scriptures teach (Romans 9:6; 1 Corinthians 10:32; Hebrews 12:22-24).

Biblical Israel (I am not referencing modern Israel since 1948) was and is an ethnic, political, earthly, visible, born-again, and regenerate Jewish nation. The Church is a universal, nonethnic, nonpolitical, spiritual, heavenly, and an invisible kingdom of Jews and Gentiles in this present era, the majority of believers being Gentile.

Israel began with *Yaaqov,* not *Avraham* or *Yitzhak. Yaaqov* became Israel and his physical descendants who were regenerate were the true Israel as *Shaul* (Paul) revealed in Romans 9. The Church began on *Pentecost* and is said to be, "one new man in Christ." This phrase suggests that the church did not already exist, for the church is a "new man." The church exists now and only for a moment more, until *the fullness of the Gentiles has come in.*

After the *fullness of the Gentiles* is complete God will rapture or seize His church. God will then return to His original plan for an ethnic, political, earthly, visible, and Jewish nation called Israel. A Jewish King will sit upon the Davidic throne and will rule the world from *Yerushalayim.* Israel will be that regenerate nation who will cooperate with Him and the New Covenant will be the Law rather than the obsolete old covenant (Hebrews 8:13). After all, the new covenant was foremost for Israel (Jeremiah 31:31).

Yeshua will be Israel's king Who will reign over the nations. The Jewish nation will be the dominate viceroys of the kingdom, and myriad Gentiles will come to faith by their evangelization. Those Jews and Gentiles saved during this new era will not be the Church. The Church will be ruling alongside *Yeshua* and *David* and the twelve Apostles in *Yerushalayim.*

The *fullness of the Gentiles* is a sobering reality. *Shaul*/Paul warned non-Jews of this present age or era that God has a limit. Of course! Did He not measure a *fullness* in *Noach's* day, in Lot's day, in Israel's captivity in Babylon? Let us be warned! Don't miss His count!

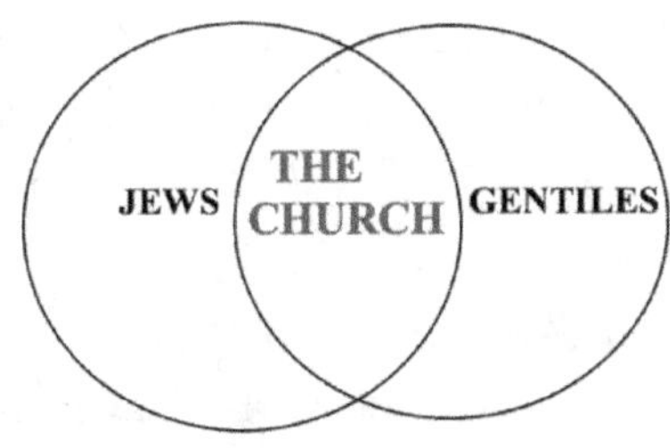

THE TIMES OF THE GENTILES

*"And they will fall by the edge of the sword, and will be led captive into all the nations; and Jerusalem will be trampled underfoot by the Gentiles until the **times of the Gentiles** are fulfilled"* (Luke 21:24).

The "times of the Gentiles" spoken of in the Gospel of *Lukas* is distinguished from the "fullness of the Gentiles" spoken of by *Shaul* in Romans. The *times of the Gentiles* has nothing to do with Gentiles being saved or a fullness or a number of the non-Jewish remnant. The *times of the Gentiles* is considered to be the period during which time the *goyim* [Gentile] nations of the earth have dominance over *Yerushalayim*. The best of scholars determines this era to have begun at the time of Babylon's siege of Israel, in 609 BC, 597 BC, and 586 BC and continues until the Second Coming of *Yeshua*.

Yeshua lived during the *times of the Gentiles,* the *talmidim* or disciples and the apostles lived during the *times of the Gentiles* as did the first church, and we are living in the *times of the Gentiles,* today. Yet, how can this be since *Yerushalayim* is not in the hands of Gentiles today, and Israel has become a Jewish nation separate from the *goyim* nations since 1948?

The *times of the Gentiles* will be complete when the Jewish people are back in their land (they are today), when Israel is an autocratic nation (they are today), and when Israel is ruled by a regenerate and messianic Judahite king from the lineage of David sitting upon the Davidic throne. This has not happened! Therefore, the *times of the Gentiles* continues until *Yeshua* returns. The *times of the Gentiles* continues until and after the *Rapture,* through the *Great Tribulation,* and until the *Second Coming* of *Yeshua* Who will return, first in judgment, then He will *aliya* or "go up" to His rightful Davidic throne in *Yerushalayim* for His millennial reign.

The *times of the Gentiles* will remain after the *fullness of the Gentiles* is complete, since the later has to do with a saved remnant of Gentiles believing in *Yeshua*, and the former has to do with the political rule or control of Jerusalem. They are not synonymous.

Israel has been back in their land since 1948 and they have autonomy or self-rule, however, modern-day Israel is not biblical Israel, an ethnic, political, regenerate, born-again, and righteous nation of descendants of *Yaaqov* dwelling in the land of Israel loving their messiah, *Yeshua*, and the Gospel of *Yeshua* streaming out of the Holy Land to the *goyim*. Biblical Israel are Hebrews who have wrestled with God and like *Yaaqov* their progenitor, are "made" Israel (Genesis 32).

There have been many periods when the Jews were a reunited people, living in the land called Israel, controlling *Yerushalayim* without Gentile interference. Yet, their control was only temporary because the Holy Land belongs to YHWH, it is His backyard, and the Holy Scriptures are clear than ungodly people including the Jewish people (especially the Jewish people) will not remain in His land without regenerate faith in *Yeshua*, God's Son, the Messiah, the savior, and the heir of all.

The Jews controlled *Yerushalayim* during the *Maccabean* period, 167-60 BC. The Jews controlled *Yerushalayim* for a space during the Jewish revolt against Rome, AD 66-70, and during the Second Jewish revolt against Rome, AD 132-135. Modern Israel has controlled *Yerushalayim* since the Six-Day War in 1967, although scripturally, modern Israel is in the land which belongs to *YHWH Elohim* the Landlord. During *the Great Tribulation* the *anti-Christ* (a Gentile) will come with his false prophet to dominate the world and to rule Israel in particular. The *antichrist* will be a Gentile just as *Antiochus Epiphanes IV* who ruled *Yerushalayim* during the intertestamental period, although the *antichrist* will be more ruthless than the *Antiochus!*

Zechariah says that in that day (contextually, in the last days when Israel is back in the land dwelling safely although without belief in their messiah, *Yeshua*) two-thirds of Israel will perish, and one-third will be saved. The one-third that will be saved are the remnant (Zechariah 13:8,9). Jews will flee from *Yerushalayim* due to the control of the land

and the city by the *antichrist*. Israel will no longer be autonomous, they will no longer be a nation, and the *times of the Gentiles* will continue.

Since 1948 Jews have returned to the land of Israel from the ovens of the Holocaust, and they have christened the land to be Israel. Modern Israel, however, is not regenerate, and therefore Modern Israel is not the spiritual remnant, for the nation does not believe in *Yeshua*! The majority of the nine million Jews living in Israel are not messianic born-again believers in *Yeshua*, and thus, they are not Israel (Romans 9). They are only in the land of Israel for a space of time for repentance, a time to recognize and believe in *Yeshua*. The *antichrist* is perhaps born and being groomed for the political arena. The *antichrist* will follow the likeness of Adolph Hitler, although he will be more sinister and demonic.

We must also note that modern Israel is considering a two-state solution, that is, dividing the holy city of *Yerushalayim*. Biblically, modern Israel will never fully control *Yerushalayim*, the city of God, until the Jewish citizens recognize the rightful king and messiah of Israel. His name is *Yeshua*! Any Jewish control of *Yerushalayim* is temporary until the *Second Coming* of *Yeshua*, and His reign will be for ten centuries, a millennium.

Therefore, the modern nation of Israel is not in the land to stay! The present political move to unite *Yerushalayim* for both Jews and Moslems (and Christians) is only another step away from the *theocracy* of *Yeshua* the rightful heir of His Father's land, city, and throne. Israel is God's vineyard, *Yeshua* is the Landlord's Son, and He is the rightful heir of His father.

It may hard to believe that modern Israel will be willing to negotiate *Yerushalayim*, although the Bible speaks of the *times of the Gentiles* when Israel will be forced to negotiate with the *goyim* in order to remain a nation among them. We are perilously close to this concession!

In the last of the last days (following the disappearance or *rapture* of the Church) *Yerushalayim* will be the pulpit of two messengers from

God who will speak God's Word. *Yerushalayim* will have these two messengers, *Moshe* and *Eliyah* (see Question 26) killed, just as ancient pagan Israel killed the LORD'S prophets, *"from Abel to Zachariah"* (Luke 15:31)! Last days Israel and Jerusalem will be so evil and corrupt that *Yerushalayim* is likened to Sodom.

"And their dead bodies {will lie} in the street of the great city which mystically is called Sodom and Egypt, where also their Lord was crucified" (Revelation 11:8).

Prophetically, *Yerushalayim* will one day be the holy city of *YHWH* just as it was historically. First, however, the *times of the Gentiles* must be fulfilled. During the *times of the Gentiles* (in which we are presently living until the Second Coming of *Yeshua* and His millennial kingdom and reign) the city of *Yerushalayim* may be autocratically controlled by the Jews -for a few years or decades- but the holy city will be trodden down. This is for certain, and it will be underfoot of the Gentile nations for a three and one-half-years (3 ½ year) interval.

"Then there was given me a measuring rod like a staff; and someone said, "Get up and measure the temple of God and the altar, and those who worship in it. Leave out the court which is outside the temple and do not measure it, for it has been given to the nations; and they will tread underfoot the holy city for forty-two months" (Revelation 11:1,2).

A peek into the political arena of the *times of the Gentiles* from the Babylonian captivity until the *Second Coming* of *Yeshua*, was given to the prophet *Dani'el* and recorded in his book. There are two important texts in *Dani'el* to be studied regarding the *times of the Gentiles*: Daniel 2:31-45 and Daniel 7:1-28.

The *times of the Gentiles* was likened to a great image (Daniel 2:31-45; 7:4-6) first revealed by the head of gold. *Dani'el* gave the inspired interpretation. Nebuchadnezzar and Babylon were that head of gold initiating the beginning of the *times of the Gentiles* (586 BC). The *times of the Gentiles* can be outlined by the following kingdoms.

The Babylonian Kingdom
The Medo-Persian Kingdom
The Greek/Hellenistic Kingdom
The Roman and (?) Kingdom
The Millennial Messianic Kingdom

The second era, the breast and arms of silver was the *Medo-Persia Empire* (539-333 BC). This kingdom was interpreted by *Dani'el* as bear-like (Daniel 7:5). Next, was the belly/thighs of bronze which was the empire that followed *Medo-Persian* rule. Historically, this was *Greece/Hellenism* (333-65 BC) seen by *Dani'el* as leopard-like (Daniel 7:6). Then, the legs of iron and clay appeared, which was the empire of Rome #1 that began in 65 BC. Rome came to an end, although the Roman "system" did not. In fact, the Roman empire is the very influence of the power of the Pope and Catholicism with its Replacement Theology, the dating of the Gregorian calendar, the celebration of Easter, the structure of the USA Senate and government, and other colossal factors of our world as we know it. Rome exists today via its system although it is obscure.

In the end days Rome #2 will appear, the feet of iron and clay. The picture is a one-world government which is the unity of Rome consisting of ten divisions (Daniel 7:7,24; Revelation 13:1; 17:3, 12-13).

The conclusion of the prophecy in *Dani'el* speaks of a great stone falling and crushing the entire image, from the head which was Babylon, to the empire of the last days, the one-world government soon to be actualized in our world. That great stone represents the new *messianic* millennial kingdom and rule of *Yeshua* that will completely annihilate the *times of the Gentiles* when myriad Gentile nations have ruled, controlled, dominated, and wrongly influenced *Yerushalayim* and Israel. *Yeshua* the Jewish Prophet, Priest, and King will rule, and there will never-ever again be, *"times of the Gentiles!"*

At the end of the *"time of the Gentiles,"* a new global one-world government will be installed with King *Yeshua* on the throne ruling with His twelve *talmidim* and His *kehillah* or Church. This rule will be a *theocratic* kingdom. This is the millennial kingdom and rule of *Yeshua*. This kingdom rule was prompted in God's original plan for Adam in the Garden in Eden. He as God's image was to rule the world from the holy land of Eden. Rebellion and sin wrecked God's plan, but God has no plan B. God's desire [Plan A] will be accomplished! We are going back to the beginning. Israel will one day be the seat for the greatest kingdom ever to rule the earth, a rule of strong love by *Yeshua,* the Son of God, the Second Adam, along with His Prime Minister, *Melek David* (King David), and His *Knesset* or Parliament, the Church. The *times of the Gentiles* given in the prophetic book of *Dani'el* (Chapter 7) can be outlined by the following Kingdoms.

The Babylonian Empire

The Medo-Persian Empire

The Greek/Hellenistic Empire

The Roman and (?) Empire
    United Kingdom
    Divided Kingdom
    Ten Nation Confederacy
    Anti-Christ Kingdom

The Messianic Kingdom

The Eastern Gate to the old holy city of Jerusalem. This wall is Turkish period although the wall sits on stones beneath which are Solomonic period. This picture was taken by the author from the Garden of Gethsemane.

Question 5

The Apostle Paul wrote, "all Israel will be saved" (Romans 11:26). Who is the "all Israel" whom Paul was referring?

Answer

The Apostle *Shaul* writes concerning the regenerate remnant of Jewish people in Romans 9:6, 27.

"But {it is} not as though the word of God has failed. For they are not all Israel who are {descended} from Israel…Isaiah cries out concerning Israel, though the number of the sons of Israel be like the sand of the sea, it is the remnant that will be saved."

Israel has always had a holy seed or *remnant* who have believed and who are being saved. In every age and dispensation and in every place under heaven, there have been Jews who have heard God, received the heavenly revelation, believed, and were and are being saved. Yet, *Shaul* writes of a time when "ALL Israel will be saved." There has never been such an ethnic cleansing.

There have been many interpretations of this verse. Replacement Theology erroneously suggests that *"all Israel"* is the church, born-again Jews and Gentiles who comprise a "new Israel of God." Nowhere in the Bible is the church called Israel. The allegorical interpretation of calling the Church, "Israel" is an invention of Roman [pagan] Catholicism. The Pope is the new High Priest of the new Israel. The cardinals and bishops are the new priesthood of the new Israel. The city of Rome is the new holy city of the new Israel, and the Vatican is the new holy place of the new Israel. Rubbish! This allegorical method of interpretation spread like gangrene, and protestant churches eventually began using the terminology and many still do. The "local church" became allegorized as the *sanctuary*. The city of the Christian became allegorized as Jerusalem.

I remember as a young boy watching men outside the church throw down their cigarette butts since it was time for church to start, and these cancer sticks weren't allowed in the sanctuary. The biblical truth is those puffing the cancer sticks were the sanctuary!

There are others who interpret *"all Israel"* in Romans 11:26 to mean "all ethnic Israel," that is, every Jew who has ever lived, those who are living and those who have died, all will be saved! This view is heretical. The unregenerate dead, Jews and Gentiles will not be resurrected to a second chance for salvation. Every individual makes his eternal choice of her/her destiny while he/she is living. *Yeshua* stated clearly to the Jews to whom He was speaking, that if they did not repent and believe, they would see *Avraham* and *Yitzhak* sitting in the kingdom, but themselves outside in a place of torment (Matthew 8:11,12). *Yeshua* wept for secular Israel who were without hope, for they were dead spiritually! He called them *children of the devil*, not because they were *Yehudim* (Jews), or *Parushim* (Pharisees), or *Tsaddikim* (Sadducees), but because of their determined choice of spiritual alignment. The devil was their master!

Some suggest the *"all Israel"* to be the Jewish masses on earth at the time alluded, that is, every Jew living in the last days will be saved. That is almost correct, although we must be exact for biblical prophecy says that two-thirds of last days Israel will be unbelieving and these will be destroyed, and only one-third will come through the fire. That one-third will be the remnant (Zechariah 13:8,9).

"It will come about in all the land," Declares the LORD, that two parts in it will be cut off {and} perish; But the third will be left in it. And I will bring the third part through the fire, refine them as silver is refined, and test them

as gold is tested. They will call on My name, And I will answer them; I will say, 'They are My people,' And they will say, 'The LORD is my God."

To help us correctly interpret the meaning of, *"all Israel shall be saved"* we must biblically and theologically define Israel. Who is Israel? *Shaul* wrote, *"not all who descended from Israel are children of Israel, nor are they all children because they are Avraham's descendants, but through Yitzhak your seed will be named"* (Romans 9:6,7). *Shaul* identified the true children of *Avraham* as those descendants of *Avraham* born of a supernatural miracle. Sarah conceived and gave birth because of a promise God made and by His miraculous intervention. Sarah and *Avraham* could do nothing. They were old and her womb was dead. The son, *Yitzhak* was the fulfillment of God's promise to *Avraham* and Sarah. He was a miracle child. He was supernaturally born! God moved in upon *Avraham* who was old and upon Sarah who was old and barren, and they did! They had a child because of God's supernatural intervention and work within them!

Shaul continues in Romans 9 further describing the "remnant" who are "all Israel." *Shaul* wrote,

"Though Revkah also conceived supernaturally as Sarah for she was barren, and the twins in her womb having done neither good or bad, moral or immoral deeds, Elohim loved Yaaqov and hated Esav" (Romans 9:10-13).

Shaul knew his readers would have great questions about a sovereign God Who would choose to have mercy on one person while hardening the other, without good or bad works to substantiate God's choosing. So, *Shaul*/Paul supported his apologetic of the sovereignty of *Elohim* by using metaphoric symbolism of a potter and his clay. The potter decides what he will make with the clay; the clay doesn't choose what it will be when it grows up. The potter decides to make one vessel for honorable use and another to perhaps collect dung. *Shaul* shows the sovereignty of *Elohim* over all vessels, for in the same chapter (Romans 9) he brings in the Gentiles.

There is a remnant of Gentiles that God has made as vessels of honor, and there is a remnant of Jews that God has made vessels of honor.

"Though the number of the sons of Israel be like the sand of the sea, it is the remnant that will be saved" (Romans 9:23-28).

It is always the *remnant* who are being saved. The *remnant* of the twelve tribes of Israel will believe and become regenerate believers born into the kingdom of heaven. This has always been the case. From the mass of world Jewry in the last days, it is the remnant that will come forth and comprise an everlasting nation of Israel. Two-thirds of last days physical and national Israelis will die in their unbelief, but the remnant third-part, will be saved.

During the horrendous and coming holocaust, the *Time of Yaaqov's Trouble* or *The Great Tribulation* that will occur in the last days, it is the remnant who will be saved from the grasp of the *antichrist*. These Jewish believers will form the "all Israel" that will be saved. *Yeshua* will be their king! In fact, *Yeshua* will be the King of the earth reigning from *Yerushalayim*.

During the millennial kingdom yonder in the not-too-distant future, every Jew on earth will be a believer, since the non-remnant will have died in unbelief during the *antichrist's* Holocaust. The remnant who will believe, are the "all Israel" *Shaul* speaks of in Romans 11:26-27. The "all Israel" are those Jews in covenant with their Messiah *Yeshua* whose ungodliness has been removed, their sins taken away, who are beloved by *Elohim,* and who will have wrestled with *Yeshua* Who will make them Israel, just as He made *Yaaqov, Y'srael* (Genesis 32).

Question 6

Isn't Modern Israel the Chosen People? God kept the Jews alive through the inquisitions, pogroms, and the Holocaust, and He brought them back to their land, Israel. Any nation that comes against Israel will reap the wrath of God. Do you agree?

Answer

Whose land did you say it was? Can Christians herald the new nation of Israel since 1948 as the resurrected and re-gathered "last days Israel" that is to return to the land, blessed by God, *olam v'olam* ("forever and forever")? Modern Israel is opposed to God's authentic King and Messiah, *Yeshua. Yeshua* is the only begotten Son of the Landlord. *Yeshua* is the divine King. *Yeshua* is Israel's messiah and savior, and *Yeshua* had quite a lot to say about who inherits His estate! It is His domain for He is the Heir, and He is to rule as King over His kingdom! That kingdom, is the land of Israel!

God has not covenanted the blessings and privileges of *Avraham, Yitzhak,* and *Yaaqov* to the physical descendants of the patriarchs (Romans 9). Most Jews today as in the day of *Yeshua* resist *YHWH,* refuse His New Covenant, disregard His Messiah, *Yeshua,* and snub their noses at Him, while continuing to live secular lives in opposition to God's moral laws. The religious Israelis have a form of spiritual service, although if they loved God's Law, they would come to recognize *Yeshua,* for that was/is the purpose of Torah, to be a tutor to lead Jews to God's Messiah and His messianic new covenant (Galatians 3:23,24).

Can modern Israel, living in noncompliance to God's decree concerning His Son and disregarding the Lordship of *Yeshua*, dictate the terms of their proprietorship as tenants in the land? Can Modern Israel claim ownership to the land of Israel according to political and/or national laws of military conquest, without regard to God's Son? When one considers the seriousness of *Yeshua,* it is not a hard question, really. The Bible is simple and direct concerning the only begotten Son of God, Who is the [only] way, truth, and life. The Son is the Landlord's true heir!

Zionists, both secular and religious claim the land belongs to the Jews, that the land is Israel's. Period. Fundamental Christians and Christian Zionists join that bias promoting Israel's entitlement to the land due to God's unconditional covenant made with *Avraham, Yitzhak, Yaaqov,* and *Yaaqov*'s dozen. The *Zionist* logic goes something like this. The Jews are descendants of the twelve tribes, they survived the inquisitions, pogroms, and the horrendous Holocaust, they are back in the holy land of Israel, God performed this miracle, therefore, Modern Israel are the heirs of the land. The unconditional aspect is lifted so high that they miss the conditional part for every individual participant. Jewishness is not enough to be an heir! *Yeshua* warned, one must be born again! A descendant of the patriarchs may inherit and enjoy the land only if he/she is truly a son or daughter of *Avraham* and with *Avraham's* faith. From *Adam* and *Havvah* to the New Jerusalem in Revelation 21, no one inherits the land of Israel or abides in it for every long without the spirit of *YHWHshua.*[3]

Evangelical prophecy connoisseurs interpret Israel's presence in the land today as the prophetic fulfillment of *Yekhek'el's* (Ezekiel's) vision of dry bones (Ezekiel 37) and other OT prophesies that speak of Israel's return to the land in the *acharit hayomim,* or last days. Those prophecies are true, and in the last days Israel has and will continue to return home as dry bones, but to receive the land they must receive

---

[3] Leviticus 18:24-30; 20:22-26; Deuteronomy 4:25-27, 40; 8:17-19; 11:11,12; Joel 2:28,29; Ezekiel 36:27; 37:14; Jeremiah 31:33; Isaiah 32:13-15; 41:1; 44:3; 59:19,20; 61:1.

His breath! Zechariah 13:8 says that two-thirds of last days Israel who return home will perish, and only one-third will come through the fire or judgment which will be the Great Tribulation. We cannot lie to Israel, comforting them by saying they are the chosen people of God, the land is freely theirs, nothing is required except being Jewish, so go and be blessed as the *Chosen People. Oy Vey*! It is a lie! *Yeshua* matters! Inheriting the land is conditional. Read the Holy Scriptures! Study history!

The Arabs also allege a legal inheritance to the land, advocating that Allah made His covenant with Ishmael, that Ishmael's birth order was preeminent to Isaac's, Esau's birthright was stolen by Jacob, and the land was first inhabited by their Canaanite predecessors before Israel's entry. The Israeli *Palestinians* who are Arabs claim that the land belongs to them due to tenure, and that the 84 percent majority Jewish Israelis of modern Israel are merely immigrants to Palestine since 1945, and the end of World War II and the Holocaust. Middle-Eastern Muslims argue the land belongs to Islam vis-à-vis Allah. But, Allah is another name for the god of this world, and his prophet *Muhammed* was a false prophet who is now in hell, the compartment of the underworld called *Sheol* in the Tanakh or Old Testament awaiting his being cast into the lake of fire (*Gehenna*) in the last of the latter days. Muslims need *Yeshua,* too!

Our Lord did not promise *Nahor* or his descendant, *Lot* or his two sons, or their seed, *Ishmael* or his twelve tribes, or *Esau* and the *Edomites,* or the boys of *Avraham* and *Keturah,* inheritance of the Promised Land of Israel. The Bible is clear. Neither does the Bible promise any blessing to the non-remnant of *Avraham, Yitzhak,* and *Yaaqov* except the "blessings" that rain upon every man. *Shaul/* Paul wrote warning every man (Galatians 4:22-31). It is the sons of promise that inherit the blessings and not the sons of the bondwoman, *Hagar,* and he was not talking about Jews and Arabs. *Shaul/*Paul was talking about the spiritual birth in contrast to those who born only in the flesh. Jerusalem and the Jews of *Shaul/*Paul's day were likened to *Hagar* in verse 25 (*present Jerusalem*), those not miraculously and supernaturally born as *Yitzhak*, but rather born naturally, by man's seed, the woman's womb, nine-months gestation, born in water of the flesh, and who walk in the flesh, fleshly —like Ishmael.

In Romans 9 *Shaul*/Paul is clear that it is the remnant who inherit the blessings, and "all Israel shall be saved" (Romans 11). The "all Israel" is the remnant Israel who are born again. God has been and now is gathering His remnant. This is what *Messianic Ministry to Israel* is about. We are gathering all that the Father has given to the Son. Those Jewish people the Father has NOT given to the Son do not get the land. The landlord remains the Lord of Israel and He has spoken concerning His heirs.

To answer this question more fully, I encourage you to obtain my book, *YESHUA'S YISRAEL: Do the Ancient Holy Scriptures Validate the Modern Jewish and Palestinian Claim to the Land of Israel* (see page 367 to order).

While completing my intern in Israel in 1997, I was visiting the Mount of Olives. An army officer was giving a lecture to her troops about Christianity, although it was actually, Catholicism. When she asked if there were questions, I raised my hand and asked if I might give the soldiers an explanation of Christianity since I was a Christian. She gladly invited me to share. I spoke of *Yeshua*, an Israeli, the son of David, the son of Jewish parents, the Jewish Messiah, with Jewish disciples [all of them], the entire first church being Jews, and myriad Jews have believed in Him from the 1st Century until today. When I finished the soldiers applauded; they enjoyed hearing about the Jewish *Yeshua*!

Question 7

Is the modern regathering of the Jewish people to Israel since 1948, a fulfillment of biblical prophecy?

Answer

Prophets of both the *Tanakh* (Old Testament) and the *Brit Chadasha* (New Testament) prophesied of a Jewish ingathering to happen in the last days. However, there is a chronological order of that ingathering given to us in the Scriptures. First, there will be a regathering of the Jewish people to the land of Israel, although they will come without salvific faith in *Yeshua*. Their return will be somewhat miraculous in that God will save a physical remnant of the Jewish people as He has always done throughout history. The prophecy of *Yekhek'el* (Ezekiel) likens the Jews coming to the land of Israel as *dry bones* in a valley (37:2) buried in graves (37:12), and the dry bones being myriad in number and very dry (37:2). The prophecy of Ezekiel 37 is one of resurrection. The global *dry bones* rise from the graves which are the nations, making *aliya* or going up to the land of Israel (Ezekiel 37). The *dry bones* that were skeletons will become an ethnic community with flesh and muscle, although initially they have no breath.

YHWH spoke to *Yekhek'el* the prophet, that he was to prophecy to the *Ruach*, the wind/breath/Spirit (*Ruach* in Hebrew can mean all three). *Yekhek'el* prophesied, the Spirit came and moved through the channel, and breath came into the former lifeless community of *dry bones*. *Yekhek'el* was given the meaning of this prophecy. The *dry bones* are the whole house of Israel (Ezekiel 37:11). The *dry bones* are not the church, and the dry bones are not the redeemed through the ages. The *dry bones* are the descendants of the twelve tribes of Israel. Their resurrection and regathering is supernatural, although they gather in unbelief. This is shown in Ezekiel 36:24 where they are gathered from all the lands and brought to their own land, yet in unbelief. Once in the land of Israel, God sprinkles clean water upon the dry bones and gives them a new heart. He becomes their *Elohim* (Ezekiel 36:25-28) and they become His children.

The Jewish people have been supernaturally preserved through the crusades, *pogroms*, inquisitions, and the horrific Holocaust, demonic attempts to dissolve world Jewry. The Jews have regathered to the land of Israel especially since 1948, just as *Yekhek'el* prophesied (Ezekiel 37). We may declare that the modern statehood of Israel since 1948 is the beginning of such a miraculous last-days resurrection, although the fulfillment of what *Yekhek'el* was given remains to be fulfilled in the future since the majority of Jews living in modern Israel are not believers. They have not been sprinkled with clean water (the washing of the Word), they are not free from idols, they are not regenerate, and they do not have God's *Ruach*, that is, His Holy Spirit. How do we know they do not? The Holy Spirit speaks of *Yeshua*. In fact, the Holy Spirit is the ghost of *Yeshua* (Matthew 28:20; John 20:22). *Yochanon the immerser* said that *Yeshua* coming after him would also be a baptizer, only He would immerse those coming to Him in the Holy Spirit. *Shaul* (Paul) said those without the [Holy] Spirit are not His (Romans 8:9).

Today, Jews continue to gather to the land of Israel from the nations of the world, but they gather in unbelief. Most Israelis today are like citizens of every other nation; they are secular atheists and/or agnostics. Many Israelis like many Gentiles are *Baal* worshipers. Many others are deceived by the cult of rabbinic Judaism, as Gentiles are deceived by cults and false religions. Many Jews are Buddhist, other Jews are seekers in mystic religions, and the majority of Jews like Gentiles do not embrace *Yeshua*. In fact, most Israelis today do not embrace *YHWH* of the Old Testament. For this reason, they are destined to inherit the coming *wrath of God*.

Of the present 9 million Jews in the land of Israel today, only about two-percent are believers in *Yeshua*. The biblical *Great Tribulation* will be necessary according to the prophet *Dani'el* (a contemporary of *Yekhek'el*) to cause Jewish people to come to Yeshua. *Dani'el* prophesied that God's coming wrath will force the Jewish *remnant* to call upon *Yeshua* for salvation. Therefore, modern Israel's resurrection to the land of Israel in modern times, and the revival of the ancient Hebrew language, the raising of the ancient *Magen David* or Star of David flag as the Jewish symbol, and the Jewish desire for a Temple are precipitous of the next steps of prophetic fulfillment. All of these things are installments of a coming revival in Israel.

Second, the Bible predicts the reestablishment of a spiritual nation of Israel to occur in the last days, although a spiritual nation does not yet exist! Modern Israel is a secular nation. Modern Israel does not embrace the biblical covenant, and Modern Israel is not the regenerative nation seen by *Yekhek'el* in chapters 36-38. The Holy Bible reveals that in the end of days, both old and young Jews will dance before God, and the *goyim* or nations having heard that God Almighty is with the Jews will grasp their garments and go up or *aliya* with them to the holy land of Israel (Zechariah 8:21-23).

The nation called Israel that exists today may be an impetus of the biblical regenerate nation of Israel that will one day exist in the millennial kingdom. Modern Israel is an embryo stage of that kingdom, the progeny of it. However, for now, Modern Israel is anti-*Yeshua*, and therefore, *antichrist*.

Third, Israel will soon resurrect a Temple in *Yerushalayim*, but it will be to Israel's demise (see Questions 8 & 9). There will be a re-instituted Temple of God with an Ark of the Covenant and the Levitical sacrificial system (Daniel 9:27; Matthew 24:15; 2 Thessalonians 2:4; Jeremiah 3:16-17). This is on the immediate horizon. There are many groups in Israel today who are pressing the Israeli government to realize the necessity in gaining ancient Israel's glory, and fame, things ancient Israel realized because Israel had a national, political, and spiritual focus among the nations. The hallmark of ancient Israel has always been the grand and colossal Temple. A Temple built in comparison to the ancient Solomonic Temple would most certainly rally Jews from around the globe to consider an ethnic reunion to the holy land, while also rallying Christians, Israel's best friends, to help.[4]

Precipitous to any temple in *Yerushalayim,* is the finding and uncovering, or the rebuilding and the presentation of the *Ark of the Covenant.* Such an image in the ancient land of Israel would unite Jews and Semite lovers globally. A religious fervor would ignite Jews and Christians and even mystics to have an interest in the historical, biblical, and prophetic relevance of the *Ark* thought by some to be a "biblical transmitter to God" as depicted in the movie, *Indiana Jones, Raiders of the Lost Ark.*

Just as important as the *Ark of the Covenant* in order to inaugurate the Temple, is the realization of an authentic red heifer. The rabbinic sage, Moses Maimonides is quoted in the *Mishneh Torah,* saying that only nine cows in history have fulfilled the mint condition requirements for a "red heifer," according to the scriptural book of Numbers and worthy for the ritual sacrificing. The tenth cow is to arrive according to Maimonides at the time of Messiah's arrival. The red heifer is necessary as a precondition for building the Temple since every Jew in the world is unclean by reason of presumed contact with death, and the ashes of the burned red heifer is the prescription for cleansing from impurity for one claiming he qualifies as High Priest. No one can ascend and approach God's presence in the Temple without ritual cleansing! All of this, of course, is the veneration of the Mosaic system which has become obsolete since *Yeshua* has installed the new covenant. According to the New Covenant, all believers are clean (John 15:3; Acts 10:15; 1 Corinthians 6:11; Hebrews 9:17; 10:22).

---

4 This is a very sad commentary, since believers in *Yeshua* should know that the Church, the body of Messiah, is His Temple. The *kodesh kodeshim* of God today is no longer a building made with human hands, but His Temple is His people, His Church, His born-again and redeemed people. The Holy Spirit now resides in us. For Christians to exalt a Temple in Jerusalem, made in the likeness of Solomon's Temple is apostasy, a "falling away" from the new covenant of *Yeshua.*

Fourth, the next step in the sequence of Jews coming forth from the mass of world Jewry to make up a last days remnant Israel which would fulfill biblical prophecy, is a colossal, universal, and catastrophic event that would shake the world and especially the Jewish world, causing world Jewry to fall out and immigrate home to Israel for security, patriotism, and preservation as a single nation in the only land on earth that is a refuge for them, the land called Israel. One such event that could cause a stampede of world Jewry to Israel, would be the *Rapture*, *Yeshua*'s snatching of His Church, a sudden universal disappearance of all Christians or *holy ones* or *saints* of the earth.

A global disappearance of Christian men and women who love *Yeshua* and who love the nation of Israel, will certainly cause global panic, hysteria, and a consolidation of the Jewish people to Israel. An event like the *Rapture* with the disappearance of millions of saints who love Israel, and are then missing would unite the Jewish people worldwide and they would return to the land of the Jews and in a very short time they would reinstitute Jewish autonomy of all the land of Israel including the Temple Mount which presently Israel allows the Muslims to control due to their golden Islamic dome which sits atop the lofty and holy mountain of Moriah.

Some Israelis will begin seeking the deep truths within the Holy Scriptures, and the Holy Scriptures will direct them straight to *Yeshua*. This is what the Holy Scriptures are supposed to do, since *Yeshua* is the major motif of Holy Writ. From this salvific revelation and regeneration will come 144,000 Jewish evangelists. Not all Jews will believe. In fact, two-thirds of last days Jewry will not believe, and many will attempt to reclaim the glory days of the Jews when *David* and *Sh'lomo* reigned and the Jewish Temple in the holy city was the wonder of the world. They will not recognize *Yeshua* as the Son of David.

Holy Writ is clear that a Temple will exist in *Yerushalayim* in the last days. *Yeshua* confirmed this in Matthew 24 as did the Apostle *Shaul* (Paul) to the Thessalonians (2 Thessalonians 2:4). A Jewish Temple is coming! The Jewish priesthood will be reestablished, and there will be an *Aaronic Cohen Gadol* or Aaronic High Priest. These things are on the immediate horizon for Israel. The ancient biblical Jewish *Levitical* sacrificial system will be renewed, while in the shadows the devil's *antichrist* will be politically groomed and will gain attention for his international global seat in world politics. He will then take center stage.

Model of the ancient Temple of Sh'lomo in Jerusalem

Dome of the Spirit (left) and Dome of the Rock (right)

Question 8

Will there be a Temple in Jerusalem in the last days? Isn't the Temple an OT edifice no longer needed under the New Covenant?

Answer

The Bible states clearly that a Temple will exist in Israel, in *Yerushalayim*, on the Temple Mount in the last days, during a time the Bible calls, *The Great Tribulation.*

Yeshua said that there would be a Temple in Jerusalem in the last days.

> *"Therefore, when you see the Abomination of Desolation which was spoken of through Daniel the prophet, standing in the holy place (let the reader understand), then those who are in Judea must flee to the mountains"* (Matthew 24:15-21).

The Apostle *Shaul* said that there would be a Temple in Jerusalem in the last days.

> *"Let no one in any way deceive you, for {it will not come} unless the apostasy comes first, and the man of lawlessness is revealed, the son of destruction, who opposes and exalts himself above every so-called god or object of worship, so that he takes his seat in the temple of God, displaying himself as being God"* (2 Thessalonians 2:3,4).

Dani'el the Prophet said there would be a Temple in Jerusalem in the last days.

"And he will make a firm covenant with the many for one week, but in the middle of the week he will put a stop to sacrifice and grain offering; and on the wing of abominations {will come} one who makes desolate, even until a complete destruction, one that is decreed, is poured out on the one who makes desolate" (Daniel 9:27).

The Apostle *Yochanon* said that there would be a Temple in Jerusalem in the latter days.

"And they said to me, "You must prophesy again concerning many peoples and nations and tongues and kings." Then there was given me a measuring rod like a staff; and someone said, "Get up and measure the temple of God and the altar, and those who worship in it." Leave out the court which is outside the temple and do not measure it, for it has been given to the nations; and they will tread underfoot the holy city for forty-two months" (Revelation 11:1,2).

The biblical prophets prophesied that Israel would rebuild a Temple in the last days, and for that to happen, Israel must be in possession of the *Aron haBrit haQadosh*, the holy Ark of the Covenant since the purpose of the Temple is to house the Ark which under the old dispensation is where God dwelt, between the *Cherubim*.[5] If we know the purpose of the first Temple we can ascertain the purpose for any succeeding Temple(s), including Messiah *Yeshua* Who according to His own words was Himself, the Temple of God.

Initially, the Tabernacle and then the Temple was built as a dwelling place for God among Israel.

"And let them construct a sanctuary for Me, that I may dwell among them" (Exodus 25:8).

---

[5] YHWH dwelt between the two Cherubim positioned on the Mercy Seat which was the lid of the holy Ark of the Covenant, and where the yearly blood of the *Yom Kippur* sacrifice was sprinkled by the High Priest. This motif actually began with the *Cherubs* stationed at the Eastern Gate of the Garden in Eden and where Adam and Havva, Cain and Abel and their brothers and sisters and families brought their sacrifices.

His manifest residence was between the two *cherubim* on the Mercy Seat which was the lid to the Ark of the Covenant. The Temple was built to house the Ark of the Covenant (2 Samuel 7:2; 1 Kings 6:19; 1 Chronicles 15:1; 22:19; 28:2,18).

"…the king said to Nathan the prophet, see now, I dwell in a house of cedar, but the ark of God dwells within tent curtains" (2 Samuel 7:2).

"Then he prepared an inner sanctuary within the house in order to place there the ark of the covenant of the LORD" (1 Kings 6:19).

"Now {David} built houses for himself in the city of David; and he prepared a place for the ark of God and pitched a tent for it" (1 Chronicles 15:1).

"Now set your heart and your soul to seek the LORD your God; arise, therefore, and build the sanctuary of the LORD God, so that you may bring the ark of the covenant of the LORD and the holy vessels of God into the house that is to be built for the name of the LORD." (1 Chronicles 22:19).

"Then King David rose to his feet and said, "Listen to me, my brethren and my people; I {had} intended to build a permanent home for the ark of the covenant of the LORD and for the footstool of our God. So, I had made preparations to build {it.}" (1 Chronicles 28:2,18).

It is very probable that modern Israel has already found the ancient ark and is waiting until the right political climate to reveal their archaeological treasure to the world. This will be the most monumental event in modern history! In fact, the Ark will connect Modern Israel to ancient history. It will literally connect Modern Israel with Biblical Israel. Modern Israelis will desire the experience that their patriarchal and biblical fathers had with *Elohim*. So, the discovery and unveiling of the biblical ark of the covenant may be an impetus for "revival" among Israelis.

If Israel has not found the Ark, or if Israel does not soon discover the lost biblical ark of the covenant, modern Israel will -for certain- build one! You, reader, may mark this down. Israel is going to have an Ark since the purpose of the Temple is to house the Ark, and the Holy Scriptures say that last days Israel will rebuild the Temple. The dimensions of the prototype are given in the Torah, and if the Ark is not discovered, it will be built!

The traveling Tabernacle of *Moshe* was in essence a traveling Temple. When the tent arrived 'home' to its prescribed holy location, *Yerushalayim*, it was to become stationary and permanent.

The traveling Tabernacle of *Moshe* was also a traveling *Gan Eden* which when it arrived to the Holy Land, gave way to the permanent Temple, built eventually by *Sh'lomo*. Both the Tabernacle and the Temple were built for the zenith purpose of housing the "holy" things of God. All together these holy things exhibited God's presence. Both the Tabernacle and the Temple housed the holy *ark of the covenant* which contained the holy *manna*, Aaron's holy *budding rod*, and the holy *tablets of Law*. In harmony these holy things rendered the tent to be the seat of God's dwelling (Exodus 25:8). God dwelt beyond the veil, in the dark, in the *kodesh kodeshim* or the "Holy of Holies," between the *Cherubim* on the *Kaporet* or Mercy Seat of the *Aron* or Ark of the Covenant.

The Temple was built so that God might "dwell" with Israel (Exodus 25:8). Of course, there is no place or space that can contain the uncontainable God. No place in this world or the worlds beyond ours can contain God. God is outside all He has created. Everywhere is before God! Therefore, since the Tabernacle and Temple could not contain God, the holy building with its holy place, the holy of holies, and all the holy vessels was for the manifestation of God Who dwelt among the people. The Holy Scriptures say that God dwelt between the *Cherubim* upon the Mercy Seat, meaning His presence was manifest there. If God said He was there, He was there!

A Temple to house God's presence was initially David's desire. King David was greatly ashamed that he lived in a beautiful palace while God dwelt outside in a tent. So, David pledged to build God a magnificent colossal house, and he was initially encouraged to do so by the prophet, Nathan sent from Elohim to encourage David. The Temple was David's conception, not *Shlomo's* even though the House of God came to be called *Shlomo's Temple*. The Temple was David's desire and dream. David initially received God's approval to build it, though his son *Sh'lomo* would build the Temple since David was a man of war, and the architect of the Temple must be a man of *Shalom* or peace. The Temple would dwell in *YeruSHALOM*.

The original site for the permanent structure called the Temple (2 Chronicles 3:1) was the threshing floor of *Araunah* the *Jebusite* (2 Samuel 24:18-25; 1 Chronicles 21:18-30). This piece of Real Estate is the *eretz* or land that King David insisted on purchasing and establishing by title deed. He did so! Interestingly, this geographical place was the same site where patriarch Father *Avraham* came decades earlier to sacrifice his son, *Yitzchak* (2 Chronicles 3:1; Genesis 22:2). The mount of *Avraham's* sacrifice of *Yitzchak*, became the mount of all Temple sacrifices, the place of *Sholomo's* Temple, the colossal wonder of the world!

The primary purpose for a Temple (past, present, and future) is to house the holy *Ark of the Covenant* and its *Mercy Seat* where God dwelt. To do so necessitates the finding and revealing of the Ark, or the rebuilding and presentation of the Ark of the Covenant. Is that possible? Yes! Someone has estimated that a temple like unto *Sholomo's* Temple built today would cost near $80 billion. The estimates go something like this:

gold, silver, and brass - $35 billion

jewels - $34 billion

vessels of gold - $2 billion

vessels of silver - $3 billion

robes and vestments - $11 million

silver trumpets - $1 ½ million

food for workers - $35 million

other - $millions

This would be some project. Could such a Temple be on our immediate horizon? Will a Jewish temple be built on modern Israel's Tempe Mount?

Modern Islam would never allow a Jewish Temple on the estate Mohammed is acclaimed to have ascended to heaven,[6] the estate of the golden dome that Islam hallows as holy. In fact, Islam built their religious mosque on Mount Moriah knowing it was precious to the Jews. The Muslim *Dome of the Rock* is the holy shrine of Islam and sits on *haKotel*, the Temple Mount. Some Israeli architects say not to worry for the Temple is claimed to have sat more toward the southwestern corner. Others, including the famous Hebrew University professor Dr. Kaufman believes the locale was the northwestern corner of the Temple Mount, the same Mount Moriah although 300 feet from the Dome of the Rock. The most common view held by the majority of Israeli archaeologists suggests that the Temple sat exactly where the Dome of the Rock sits. This view is creditable enough that Muslims continue to halt any archaeological digs and excavations underneath the mount upon which their dome sits. In fact, Islamic excavations often on purpose destroy evidence of Jewish history of the Mount where the Dome sits in order to erase the distinguished Jewish presence on the sacred mountain.

What we know with absolute certainty is that a Jewish Temple in *Yerushalayim* is going to exist and maybe sooner than later! For the Temple to be realized in modern Israel the following scenario or one similar will happen.

- Worldwide hysteria caused by the disappearance of Christian people around the world and/or an international crises causing hysteria.
- The United States, Israel's greatest ally to be greatly crippled by a catastrophic event, something like the rapture of the saints, and/or a nuclear attack, a super coronavirus or similar.

---

[6] Mohammed did not ascend to heaven, but descended to hell/hades if Mohammed did not repent and believe in *Yeshua* as the only way, truth, and life to God. It is highly unlikely he repented, and he died the way he lived, an unbeliever.

- Israel will be awakened, religiously.
- There will be an ongoing rebuilding of Israel, while new archaeological digs alert the world of Israel's posture and prestige (Psalm 102:14).
- There will be continuing skirmishes on the Temple Mount by Jews and Muslims (and others).
- The Ark of the Covenant is found and unveiled, or an Ark that has been constructed is revealed. If the Ark is found outside of Israel it would be purchased and returned to the Israeli government. If the Ark is found in Israel, the ark will be positioned as a hallmark to Israel's history, and may be an impetus to war in order to retain their preeminence among nations. After all, the Ark was a special order by God for Israel!
- The Ark of the Covenant is revealed to the Jewish world and then the nations.
- A qualifying one-year old red heifer will be ordained for the ritual cleaning of the Kohens or priests, that they may serve in the Temple proper. To qualify the red heifer [cow that has never had a calf] must be without defect or blemish, a cow never under a yoke, and two years yet not yet three years of age. The ashes of the red heifer are formed into a paste which applied upon the Jewish participants cleanses them so that they may offer their sacrifice. To Jewish unbelievers all of this is necessary since they will be following the old/obsolete covenant (Hebrews 8:13).
- There will be religious fervor of world Jewry and sudden Jewish fanaticism, screaming *"Temple! Temple! Temple!"* Tension will quickly escalate among 200 million Arabs and 950 million Muslims in the world against 9 million Jewish Israelis and 25-30 million Jews worldwide.
- Israel's *Knesset* or parliament will purchase or seize the Temple Mount for the rebuilding of the Temple.
- World War!

The Western/Wailing Wall with the Dome of the Rock in the background. The mosque sits on Mount Moriah where both Solomon's Temple and Zerubbabel's Temple once sat. This is the holiest place in Judaism and will one day host the most sinister human monster the world has ever known, the Antichrist.

Question 9

If the Temple is to sit upon the biblical and historical Mount Moriah, what will happen to the Islamic mosque, the Dome of the Rock located on Mount Moriah today?

Answer

There are several possible scenarios that would allow for an "end-times" Jewish Temple to exist in Israel on Mount Moriah which was the biblical Temple Mount. First, the *Aron haBrit* or Ark of the Covenant must be found, or an exact replica must be built, since the purpose of the biblical Temple was to house the *Aron* (Ark), in particular the *Kaporet* or Mercy Seat, the dwelling place of YHWH (between the two *cherubim*). The Ark of the Covenant is not in Ethiopia as rumored[7], and it is not in Egypt as the fanciful *Indiana Jones and Raiders of the Lost Ark* portrays. The Holy Scriptures speak of the Ark after *Shishak* of Egypt came and raided Jerusalem (2 Chronicles 12:9). The Ark is not on Mt. Pisgah -it never was- and it is doubtful that the Ark was ever taken outside the perimeters of the holy city of *Yerushalayim*. The Ark is not in the Vatican in Rome, it is not in Mecca, it is not in Babylon, and it is not in the Smithsonian.

---

[7] It is believed by many that in Axum Ethiopia a monk called "the keeper of the Ark" guards the Ark day and night at the Church of Saint Mary of Zion. It was supposedly stolen from the Temple by Menelik, the son of Sh'lomo and the Queen of Sheba (who supposedly had an affair) upon one of his visits to Jerusalem to see *Abba* (Daddy).

The Jewish Talmud May Have the Answer

The Jewish Talmud suggests that the Ark was buried under the Temple Mount by instruction of Good King Josiah when he learned of the impending invasion of Babylon. He supposedly dug a hole under the wood storehouse of the Temple (*Yoma* 53b). An "off-site" room or chamber may be referred to in 2 Chronicles 35:3, since the Ark was being moved from its permanent position in the Temple.

"And said unto the Levites that taught all Israel, which were holy unto YHWH, put the holy ark in the house which Solomon the son of David king of Israel did build; it shall not be a burden upon your shoulders; serve now YHWH Elohim and his people, Israel."

Maimonides wrote that *Sh'lomo* foreseeing the destruction of his Temple selected a cave near the Dead Sea, and there *Yosiah* the king hid the Ark (*Maimonides, Laws of the Temple*, 4:1). According to archaeologist, Leen Ritmeyer the Ark is buried directly beneath the Dome of the Rock, in a section of bedrock cut out in the dimensions that supposedly match the dimensions of the biblical Ark according to the book of Exodus. Another answer is that the Ark of the Covenant has been forever lost, purposed by God. If so, Israel will have to reconstruct the Ark, and the Jewish Holy Scriptures have the schematic for its construction.

Once the Ark of the Covenant is in hand (whether discovered or reconstructed) the Temple's furniture and ritual system needs to be in place. Israel has already constructed some of those things. On our trips to Israel we always take our teams to the *Temple Treasuries* to hear the plans for the coming Temple by *The Temple Institute* in Jerusalem. This organization and others are making preparations for a new Temple. Israeli architects, design engineers, archaeologists, and rabbis continue to meet to strategize and make plans. The coronavirus of 2020 has not thwarted the planning to build, but has actually accelerated the projection and development since for many (the orthodox) the Temple must be built and ready to receive the messiah when he comes, and the coronavirus pandemic is considered to be a messianic sign.

The Temple can be built in two to three years, though the décor could take up to fifteen years to complete once started. A 90-pound pure gold menorah sits encased just outside the institute in Jerusalem. I have photographed it on every occasion of my nineteen trips to Israel. A High Priest's crown has been made of 24-karat gold, and the Table of Showbread is designed, and even the bread recipe has been written. The pitcher, cup, flask, chalice, shovel, boxes, washbasins, trumpets, harps, and other tools for the Temple are said to be already designed and some of these have already been fashioned. The time for the Temple is now, according to many religious Jews.

There is also the need for a *Sanhedrin*. How can that be since the *Sanhedrin* or the council of 70 are supposed to be Judahites, and who among the Jews today can prove what tribe he is from? On October 13, 2004, seventy-one highly respected rabbis in Israel received special ordination as a *New Sanhedrin*, although they are self-appointed Judahites. The fact remains that no Jewish person living in the last two millennia has legal documentation to prove his Jewish tribal identity. Documentation doesn't exist! In AD 70 the Jewish Sanhedrin became extinct due to the fall of Jerusalem, the destruction of the Temple, and the annihilation of Israel as a people. The Romans seized and burned the holy city to the ground destroying everything. One of the last decisions the 71-member Sanhedrin council made as they sat in jurisdiction over Jewish affairs, was their condemnation of YHWH's Son, *Yeshua*! It was YHWH's Son, that the Sanhedrin handed to the Romans for crucifixion. He died by their decree! Afterward, they claimed no guilt to His death, of course, and rabbinic Judaism continues to insist until this day that "the Romans did it!" That's similar to saying Adolf Hitler didn't kill Jews, the Nazis did!

Another decision the ancient Sanhedrin made was their plot to have *Shaul*/Paul killed after he appeared before them. Their plot was found out and *Shaul* was taken to Felix for protection (Acts 22:30-23:10-33).

Purchase the Golden Dome from the Muslims

Once the Jewish state has the Ark of the Covenant or a replica of the Ark and the other furnishings, they may seek to purchase the golden dome from the Muslims. The Temple Mount itself already belongs to the state of Israel by right of conquest and statehood. Every inch of every mountain, valley, and terrain lying in the estate called Israel belongs to the nation of Israel. However, Israel allows Islam to control the Temple Mount because their religious Islamic mosque has been there for many decades, just as Israel allows the Catholic Church to control certain "holy" sites in Israel, because the Catholics did so before Israel became a nation in 1948. Israel is a sovereign autonomous nation, yet Israel does not force its autonomy. Israel makes concessions, yet Israel may decide to offer a handsome payment for the Dome of the Rock, rather than militarily seizing their rightful estate.

In 1967 the Muslim Council was offered $100 million for *Al Aqsa Mosque*, Islam's third holiest shrine that sits south of the golden Dome of the Rock. The offer was declined by the Muslims, of course. It is this author's opinion that Islam will NEVER sell their holy mosque since it is a symbol of Islam in the Middle East. The Dome is a religious rallying center, and Islam will NEVER sell their golden domed mosque in *Yerushalayim*, and they will certainly never sell their mosque to Israel whom they identify as the infidel and little Satan.

Move the Golden Dome from Mount Moriah

Another option for Israel to gain Mount Moriah is to move the Muslim *Mosque* off the Temple Mount and clear the way for the Jewish Temple. Since Israel is the rightful heir of the land and they have sovereignty of every square inch of *Yerushalayim*, Israel may decide to display their sovereignty concerning the mount where *Avraham* offered *Yitzhak* and where *Sholomo's* Temple once sat. If they choose this option, it will probably ignite a Jewish and Muslim *holy* war. This was perhaps what Israel's former Prime Minister, Ariel Sharon was testing when he walked on the Temple Mount on September 28, 2000. The Muslim Arabs went mad and a miniature holy war was stirred as Prime Minister Sharon showcased Israel's sovereignty over all the land, especially *Yerushalayim*, including the holy mount of *Moriah*.

Israel may soon decide to flex their sovereign muscle and show autonomy, saying "all of Israel and all of *Yerushalayim* is ours," while also attempting to display an act of kindness and peace to Islam, saying "the Dome has to go from here, but we will preserve it; where do you [Israeli Muslims] want us to move it?" Israel has the technology for such a house-moving, and Israel may soon dare to be bold and declare, "Islam has Mecca and Judaism will have Jerusalem -all of it!" Such a bold declaration will cause war. I do not consider this to be a viable option for Israel to gain the Temple Mount. Islam will NEVER negotiate such an order.

The Golden Dome is Destroyed

The destruction of the mosque is a very real possibility. There are Israeli zealots and terrorists just as there are Muslim terrorists. We remember the Jewish zealot who assassinated Israel's Prime Minister, *Yitzchak Rabin*. There are myriad Jewish zealots that would do the unthinkable in order to rid Israel of the blasphemous mosque on holy ground. The same spirit that killed *Yeshua* remains in the bosom of many Jews in Israel today. There are Jews who would murder Muslims, Christians, Jesus Christ, the Pope, Franklyn Graham, or you, in the name of their faith! They would especially do so to rid the Holy Land of faiths outside Judaism although their Judaism is a reinvented and cultic one since AD 90, and not the biblical Judaism of *Moshe, Yehoshua, Ezra, Nechemyah*, etc. Perhaps some brave and courageous Israeli soldier with the zeal of an ancient patriarch might decide that the Mount belongs to the God of Israel, and with the spirit of *Shaul*/Paul before he became a believer in *Yeshua,* will fight in his/her zeal for God's Mount to rid the land of the non-Jewish infidels. This is a very possible option.

The Dome of the Rock could be destroyed from within. The Muslims could destroy the mosque in the name of *Allah* and blame the sinister deed on the Jews or the Christians or both. Muslim terrorists and/or extremists for the purpose of inciting holy war against the Jews and America in the name of *Allah,* could attempt to eradicate the mosque for the higher purpose. This would also hurry up the coming Muslim messiah, *al-Mahdi* ("the righteous guided one"). This scenario could lead to real *Jihad* or holy war. This is a very real possibility as there are many zealous Muslims who would do anything to unite world Islam and incite *Jihad,* one of the five pillars of the Islamic faith. If demonized Muslims would fly jets into buildings they would most certainly shoot rockets into a religious shrine, even a mosque!

A zealous Christian could destroy the mosque on Mount Moriah. There are many fanatical "Christian" terrorists and extremists who wish to inaugurate end-times prophecy. Such a crusader may attempt to destroy the Muslim mosque in order to help Israel take charge of their property and have sovereignty of the mount that belongs to Israel. "Christian" fanatics are as myriad as Jewish and Muslim fanatics. There are myriad Christians today who would be enthralled to hear that Israel is building a Temple, and these would sell their possessions and many would move to Israel if they could help in the building of a new Temple in Jerusalem. Of course, these "Christians" are biblically ignorant of what this scenario will mean. To engage in rebuilding the OT model of the Temple is to reject *Yeshua* and His NT Temple that He initiated and is building today. His Temple is His Church, the holy people of God in whom God now resides. He has no other dwelling place! There are at this present time, myriad churches, believers, and pastors who blow shofar horns, attach *mezuzahs* to their doors, wear *tallits* to pray, fly Israeli flags over their homes and in their churches, and who augment the right of the Jews to the land of Israel, and they have forgotten the chief cornerstone of the Gospel, *Yeshua.* These

"Christians" do not evangelize the Jewish people since they do not wish to offend the Jews, and it is ironic that they are timid in evangelizing Jewish people since the Gospel is Jewish (Romans 1:16), and by the preaching of the Gospel [which is offensive] Jewish people are brought to salvation.[8]

The *Mosque* or Dome of the Rock could be destroyed in war. A stray or strategically guided rocket or projected missile could be launched toward the dome, or an unintentional rocket or bomb could obliterate the Dome and the Mount. Such would cause Jews and Muslims and Christians to convene, restructure the cosmetics of the Temple Mount, implicate Jewish sovereignty and autonomy, and might be the actual answer to the question of how this biblical estate can finally and actually be in Jewish hands.

The Jews and Muslims Could Unite for World Peace

Jews and Muslims may soon unite for world peace. The world of nations might insist upon peace in the Middle East, and a radical new-age peace negotiation could reform the Middle East. One or many nations, perhaps the United States of America may intervene in the Jewish and Muslim conflict in Israel and on behalf of world peace enforce peace for political expediency. The current sitting USA President as I write, is Donald J. Trump who recently announced an historical peace agreement between Israel and the United Arab Emirates. US President Trump met with the Israeli Prime Minister, Benjamin Netanyahu and Abu Dhabi Crown Prince, Mohammed bin Zayed. Both Israel and the UAE said they would continue their efforts to "achieve a just, comprehensive, and enduring resolution to the Israeli-Palestinian conflict." Egypt, Bahrain, and Saudi all praised the agreement, while initially Jordan was quiet. The Palestinian Authority

---

[8] Christians of this kind are of the *dual-covenant* faith, that is, Jews have a covenant relationship with YHWH based on the Mosaic covenant, while Christians have a covenant with *Yeshua* based on the New Testament.

called for an immediate retraction of the agreement. What is remarkable is that this agreement marks the 3rd formal peace agreement with Israel and the Arab world. The first was in 1979 between Israeli Prime Minister Menachem Begin and Egyptian President Anwar Sadat. The second agreement was in 1994 with Israeli Prime Minister Yitzhak Rabin with Jordanian Prime Minister, Abdul Salam al-Majali.

Perhaps some cataclysmic world-shaking event, the disappearance of the saints all over the world, or another event causing hysteria might incite Jews and Moslems to rally together. The uniting of world Jewry could launch a massive immigration to the land and a return to Judaism. This is a viable solution to the question of the Temple and the Dome.

The Golden Muslim Dome and The Jewish Temple

The sacred Mount Moriah could also become a place for two temples and two faiths. The city of *Yerushalayim* is presently divided, and if the mount could share two magnificent edifices, a golden domed Mosque for Islam and a golden cubed Temple for Judaism, that would be a universal display of authentic peace. Two shrines for two peoples who have been at war for decades now co-existing side-by-side on the holiest real estate in the world, would be a real visual of world peace. Sounds like a solution the *antichrist* would relish. Modern Jewry might readily embellish the idea. Islam? I don't think so. The God of biblical Judaism shared no place with an idol, although today's rabbinic Judaism is fake Judaism and thus may very well partner with another faith for terms of peace. Historic Israel did this with Rome; they allowed Herod to choose their High Priest. Annas was chosen by the wicked Romans who controlled him, and he became the "godfather" of the Jewish *mafia* who eventually had *Yeshua* crucified. Jews and Romans worked together to kill God's son, *Yeshua*. There was a sinister hate between Jews and Romans to be sure, but they worked in concert to murder God!

Modern Israel makes no claim to *Yeshua* and Islam only recognizes him as a quasi-prophet. Both agree about one thing, *Yeshua* is not God!

Divine Intervention for the Jewish Temple

Divine intervention could be the cause for the destruction of the mosque. This seems to be the most viable scenario that might cause the Temple Mount to fall into Jewish hands again and the Temple be erected. The Temple and its mountain have been destroyed myriad times in history by [super] natural forces. In AD 33 an earthquake rocked *Yerushalayim* and destroyed the colossal Temple. The veil of the Temple was torn from top to bottom, clearly signifying that God had intervened, and according to the NT book of Hebrews, a new and living way was given to man that he might come before God.

In AD 363 when Julian authorized the Jews to rebuild their Temple in *Yerushalayim*, an earthquake destroyed the Temple Mount. Was this a freak quake of Mother Nature or was it the wrath of Father God? In AD 638 the Muslims conquered *Yerushalayim* and in AD 690 they built the *Al Aqsa Mosque*. In AD 746 an earthquake destroyed the mosque in *Yerushalayim*, and in 1016 another earthquake caused structural damage to the Temple Mount. In 1033 an earthquake shook *Yerushalayim* and destroyed the mosque, in 1546 an earthquake shook the Temple Mount and caused damage to the whole city, and in 1927 an earthquake weakened *Al Aqsa Mosque* which in 1955 was strengthened by Moslem Arabs from the country of Jordan.

An earthquake is a very real possible scenario of the destruction of the Golden Dome in *Yerushalayim* since the holy city lies on a fault. The *HaAretz* newspaper recently ran an article, ***Israel is Hundreds of Years Overdue for an Earthquake*** citing Jerusalem to be lying on estate riddled with fault lines although none active. The earthquakes that have happened originated in the Dead Sea rift (*HaAretz*, February 13, 2019; *https://www.haaretz.com/israel-news/.premium.MAGAZINE-southern-israel-is-hundreds-of-years-overdue-for-an-earthquake-1.6933565*).

Muslim Mosque Conversion to Jewish Temple

Another scenario is the conversion of the Muslim mosque into a Jewish Temple. This could happen if the original *Ark of the Covenant* is found and moved into the mosque or into any building since any building that houses the Ark of the Covenant is spontaneously a Temple. The purpose of a Temple was to house God Who dwelt between the *Cherubim* on the Mercy Seat of the holy Ark of the Covenant. The Temple was ordained a sanctuary for this primary purpose. But, would world Jewry and especially religious Jews in Israel ever consider the present blasphemous Muslim shrine, worthy to be a Jewish Temple? Never! Not to speak of the 250 million Moslems worldwide? Would they allow their mosque to be a Temple for Jews? Never! Though suggested as a possible scenario, this is not a viable option or possibility for the last-days Temple. This will NEVER happen!

The Great Synagogue Becomes a Temple

The consecration of the Great Synagogue in *Yerushalayim* to be a Temple is a very real possibility. The Great Synagogue in *Yerushalayim* is Jewish, and it is visited and used by Jews every day. Jews from around the world come to visit the Great Synagogue. Anointing the world renown synagogue to be the *Temple* would be no threat to the Temple Mount, no threat to the Muslim mosque, no threat to Jew and Muslim relations, and it would not be a threat to cause holy war. The Great Synagogue sits on land that already belongs to Israel; it is not contested, and all Jews know its location. All that is needed for the Great Synagogue to become the Temple is the admission of the Ark of the Covenant to its the interior. Most Jews of the world are secular and they might think this to be an excellent idea. After all, the *Synagogue* is for Jews, and the Great Synagogue is already in Jewish hands. However, the orthodox Jews might not consent even though they are a minority among world Jewry. This might actually happen?

Question 10

How bad will things be in the last days before the Lord returns?

Answer

Yeshua spoke of horrendous times in the last days likened to the beginning of "birth pangs" (Matthew 24:1-8).

"Jesus came out from the temple and was going away when His disciples came up to point out the temple buildings to Him. And He said to them, "Do you not see all these things? Truly I say to you, not one stone here will be left upon another, which will not be torn down. As He was sitting on the Mount of Olives, the disciples came to Him privately, saying, "Tell us, when will these things happen, and what {will be} the sign of Your coming, and of the end of the age? And Jesus answered and said to them, "See to it that no one misleads you. For many will come in My name, saying, 'I am the Christ,' and will mislead many. You will be hearing of wars and rumors of wars. See that you are not frightened, for {those things} must take place, but {that} is not yet the end. For nation will rise against nation, and kingdom against kingdom, and in various places there will be famines and earthquakes. But all these things are {merely} the beginning of birth pangs."

There is today much religious deception, myriad spiritual quacks, mystical gurus, religious cults, cabalistic faiths, and strange sensational sightings. There are wars, military positioning for more war, threats of nuclear aggression, terrorism, nuclear testing, germ warfare, natural calamities [of all kinds], unpredictable weather patterns, forceful and destructive tornadoes, hurricanes, tsunamis, famines, pestilences, and our world is unstable and potently lawless. We are not going back to the "Mayberry Days" we once knew and relished!

With these *birth pangs* of the end-times caused by sin, are "birth plans" for a sinful kingdom, the reunited Roman Empire which will emerge as a ten-nation confederacy predicted for the end-of-days by the prophet, *Dani'el* in the *Tanakh* or Old Testament and *Yochanon* in the *Apocalypse* of *Yeshua* in the *Brit Chadashah* (New Testament).

"Then there will be a fourth kingdom as strong as iron; inasmuch as iron crushes and shatters all things, so, like iron that breaks in pieces, it will crush and break all these in pieces. In that you saw the feet and toes, partly of potter's clay and partly of iron, it will be a divided kingdom; but it will have in it the toughness of iron, inasmuch as you saw the iron mixed with common clay. {As} the toes of the feet {were} partly of iron and partly of pottery, {so} some of the kingdom will be strong and part of it will be brittle. And in that you saw the iron mixed with common clay, they will combine with one another in the seed of men; but they will not adhere to one another, even as iron does not combine with pottery" (Daniel 2:40-44).

"After this I kept looking in the night visions, and behold, a fourth beast, dreadful and terrifying and extremely strong; and it had large iron teeth. It devoured and crushed and trampled down the remainder with its feet; and it was different from all the beasts that were before it, and it had ten horns" (Daniel 7:7).

"The ten horns which you saw are ten kings who have not yet received a kingdom, but they receive authority as kings with the beast for one hour. These have one purpose, and they give their power and authority to the beast" (Revelation.17:12).

In the near-future civilizations and governments will no longer operate on their own, with their own economy, social forms and reforms, and elected officials. Nations already need nations, governments are presently dependent upon other governments, financial institutions work in concert with other financial institutions around the globe. We now live in a world that is internationally connected in order to survive, and whether we want to believe it or not, there are international mafias that dictate the world's movements. No one should believe that their President, Prime Minister, King or Queen, and their elected officials rule their country, without outside interception or interference!

Our world does not have a system of rule that will work for all nations, ethnicities, genders, religious faiths, and castes of peoples, a system of rule that is inclusive to everyone. Such a system is coming soon. However, it will not be God's rule! God's rule will one day be realized and it will be a theocracy; He will rule His millennial kingdom. His rule is quite a few years in the future.

Our world has been and is presently influenced by *the god of this world* (2 Corinthians 4:4). *Satan* is the Hebrew term for adversary. There is a spiritual war and a day is yet ahead when the world will be demonized enough to receive a man sent from *Satan* and energized by him, *BaalZebuv*, "Lord of the Flies" (Revelation 12). For now, the Church, the body of *Yeshua*, the redeemed are holding his power and his program at bay! The force restraining the complete rule of the ruthless and evil system of the god of this world, is the regenerative body of believers in *Yeshua*, the Church. We are the light of the world, we are the salt which flavors, preserves, cures, heals, and maintains the world. The Church is the aroma that gives this world a moral influence. The Church also is God's moral, civil, and legislative government. The zenith business of the Church is to rule, and one day we will rule the entire creation. For now, we the Church are a barrier, a hindrance to the full measure of lawlessness. We restrain evil by our presence.

According to the divine library the world at the end of days will be imploding with immoral character, pornography, premarital sex, extramarital sex, fornication, marriage and divorce, remarriage and divorce, militant sodomy, homosexuality, legislation of same-sex marriages, abortion, drinking, drunkenness, drugs, slander, mutiny in the home, disappearance of the family unit, churches rejecting the authority of qualified men as elders and deacons, insubordination of women, insubordination of children, insubordination of employees, crooked and deceptive employers…a reckless society. All of this can be summed up in one word. Lawlessness! Governments will endorse a norm of society that will behave lawless and immoral in reference to the biblical standard by which the Church governs everything. Such a government can be seen today as I write, in New York, California, and Portland, Oregon. Anyone opposing or speaking out against these or other immoralities will be held accountable by the state supported by the federal government, for hate speech.

As for the Church, our Lord *Yeshua* has only one people, one body, one building, one bride, one congregation or church. His beloved holy ones or *saints* are His people. Whether Jew or Gentile, male or female, whatever ethnicity across the earth, those who have been regenerated by the Holy Spirit of God (e.g. born-again) make up the *"one new man in Christ."*

"by abolishing in His flesh, the enmity, {which is} the Law of commandments {contained} in ordinances, so that in Himself He might make the two into one new man, {thus} establishing peace" (Ephesian 2:14-16).

This oneness is because of the unity we have in *Yeshua* since each one of us who is saved is regenerate and indwelt by the Holy Spirit of God Who lives within us. The Holy Spirit is not divided (Ephesians 2:15). We have unity because of Him! He, the Holy Spirit of *Yeshua* is what binds us together and to Himself! There is unity, although the scriptures are not suggesting we are uniform. We are not the same! The same *Shaul* who was inspired to write of the *one new man* to whom all the saved belong, also wrote to Timothy his pastoral epistles governing the qualifications for elders and deacons, forbidding women to pastor or have authority over men, based on the creation order and the corruption order.

"I do not permit a woman to teach or exercise authority over a man. For Adam was formed first and then Eve." (1 Timothy 2:12,13).

Because man was formed first, the woman is not permitted to teach or exercise authority over a man. The second reason *Shaul* was inspired to forbid women to teach or exercise authority over a man, was the corruption order.

"And it was not Adam who was deceived, but the woman who was deceived and fell into transgression" (1 Timothy 2:14).

The body of Messiah is the Church. Where two or three gather, there the Church exists. The Church is not a building! The Church is a community of Chosen people. Because of the creation order and the corruption order, man is to lead and govern and woman is to help him.

The Holy Scriptures teach that within this one body of Messiah, are two races of people, Jews and Gentiles, two genders of people, male and female, and two kinds of Christians, spiritual and carnal. *Shaul* addresses both races, both genders, and both kinds of Christians as either spiritual or carnal (1 Corinthians 3:1-3).

"And I, brethren, could not speak to you as to SPIRITUAL men, but as to men of flesh, as to infants in Christ. I gave you milk to drink, not solid food; for you were not yet able {to receive it.} Indeed, even now you are not yet able, for you are still fleshly. For since there is jealousy and strife among you, are you not fleshly, and are you not walking like mere men?"

Yeshua in His *Apocalypse* or disclosure to *Yochanon* on Patmos, describes seven types of churches that existed in *Yochanon's* day. These seven kinds of churches were literal churches while also they represented seven kinds of churches that would exist throughout the church age and in the last days (Revelation 2, 3). In these last days, there are churches/congregations of believers like the one that existed in *Ephesus,* churches that are strong in deeds, in perseverance, that test false theology, discipline, false teachers, and churches that will endure. Yet, these kinds of churches have left their first love according to *Yeshua* (Revelation 2:1-7).

Second, there will be churches existing in the last days like the church in *Smyrna*, churches God says that are in poverty, although rich spiritually. These kinds of churches will endure tribulation and will be faithful to death (Revelation 2:8-11). What a model for any congregation to desire. Third, there will be churches like the congregation in *Pergamum*, churches who hold fast the name of our Lord, yet they will allow false teaching like unto *Balaam* who tried to offend Israel (Revelation 2:12-17). Think of the churches today who believe in *Replacement Theology*, who like Balaam do not know the messianic plan of God concerning Israel.

In the last days there will be churches like the church in *Thyatira*, churches with love, faith, service, perseverance, and doing great deeds, but who will tolerate immorality, idolatry, and spiritual harlotry. My wife, Crystal and I were members of a church in Arkansas when we first married, and the pastor left his wife for a woman in Little Rock (which meant he knew her intimately and had been seeing her), divorced his wife, married the woman, the deacons ignored the adultery, and this man is still pastoring a church. *Oy Vey!* The churches like *Thyatira* are likened unto *Yezebel* of the Old Testament (Revelation 2:18-29).

There will be churches in the last days like the church of *Sardis*, churches that are dead, and whom Messiah *Yeshua* warns to wake up! They are to remember and repent. These churches will have a few who have not soiled their spiritual bodies (Revelation 3:1-6). In the last days, there will be churches like the church in *Philadelphia* who keep His word, who have not denied His name, who persevere, and who love their Messiah (Revelation 3:7-13).

Finally, there will be churches in the last days like the church at *Laodicea*, lukewarm, wretched, miserable, poor, blind, and naked. These Churches are warned to repent and be refined (Revelation 3:14-21), although the spiritual climate of the majority churches in the last days may be *Laodicean.*

"Beloved, while I was making every effort to write you about our common salvation, I felt the necessity to write to you appealing that you contend earnestly for the faith which was once for all handed down to the saints. For certain persons have crept in unnoticed, those who were long beforehand marked out for this condemnation, ungodly persons who deny our only Master and Lord, Jesus Christ" (Jude 3:2).

The Holy Scriptures also warn of the worst sin and the most horrid fate, the sin of apostasy that will occur in the last days.

"Now we request you, brethren, with regard to the coming of our Lord Jesus Christ and our gathering together to Him, that you not be quickly shaken from your composure or be disturbed either by a spirit or a message or a letter as if from us, to the effect that the day of the Lord has come. Let no one in any way deceive you, for {it will not come} unless the apostasy comes first, and the man of lawlessness is revealed, the son of destruction" (2 Thessalonians 2:1-3).

"But the Spirit explicitly says that in later times some will fall away from the faith, paying attention to deceitful spirits and doctrines of demons" (1 Timothy 4:1).

"For the time will come when they will not endure sound doctrine; but {wanting} to have their ears tickled, they will accumulate for themselves teachers in accordance to their own desires, and will turn away their ears from the truth and will turn aside to myths" (2 Timothy 4:3-5).

Apostasy is defined as a de-appreciation for the Gospel, a loss of conviction that the gospel is true, contempt for the promises of God, and the rejection of the true Christian faith which results in despising the things and the people of God. Puritan Scholar, John Owen described apostasy as the following. "Apostasy is the rejection of the Spirit of God which results in an open declaration of hatred for Jesus." Such a spiritual climate already exists. The *apostate* according to the Apostle *Shaul*/Paul is one who is and will be recognized by the following apostate characteristics:

- abandons or defects from the faith (1 Timothy 4:1)
- follows deceiving spirits (1Timothy 4:1)
- follows doctrines of devils (1 Timothy 4:1)
- hypocritical liars (1Timothy 4:2)
- lovers of themselves (2 Timothy 3:2)
- lovers of money (2 Timothy 3:2)
- boastful, proud, abusive, unholy (2 Timothy 3:2)
- lovers of pleasure (2 Timothy 3:4)
- deceitful workmen (2 Corinthians 11:13)
- men who pervert the Gospel of Christ (Galatians 1:7)

The Apostle *Kefa* or Peter describes the apostate as one who practices destructive heresies (2 Peter 2:1) and has shameful ways (2 Peter 2:2). *Yochanon* says these are deceivers (2 John 7), and *Yudah* (Jude) the brother of *Yeshua* says these are godless men (Jude 4) and Messiah-deniers (Jude 4). Apostasy is one of the signs to anticipate as we near the end-of-time and prepare for the great reckoning. Apostasy is a defection from the faith. Apostasy is the worse state into which a man can fall, and it has the most terrifying judgment. It is good that our Lord gave us the lists, beloved, and it is good that we examine ourselves as the apostles warned of the apostasy that will happen in the last days (Hebrews 6:4-8; 10:26-27). *Shaul*/Paul also warned,

"the Spirit expressly says that in the latter times some will depart from the faith by devoting themselves to deceitful spirits and teachings of demons, through the insincerity of liars who consciences are seared" (1 Timothy 4:1-2).

2 Timothy 3:1-8 identifies apostates as lovers of self, lovers of money, proud, arrogant, abusive, disobedient to parents, unholy, ungrateful, heartless, slanderous, brutal, treacherous, reckless, conceited, lovers of pleasure more than God, who appear as godly although without the power of God, burdened with sins, led astray by passions, and never able to come to the truth. The days prior to the Lord's return for His bride will be one of testing and sifting. False teachers are to arise (Galatians 2:4) and many will fall from truth led away by false prophets and severe trials (Luke 8:13; 2 Thessalonians 2:3).

From the Uttermost Back to Jerusalem Mission Team, 2018

THE SEVEN CHURCHES IN ASIA

HISTORICAL CHURCH	AGE (HISTORICAL/PROPHETIC)		TEXT	DESCRIPTION OF SPEAKER	PRAISE HISTORICAL/REPRESENTIVE	REBUKE	COUNSEL	WARNING/JUDGMENT	NEGOTIATOR
Ephesus "Desired"	AD 30-100	The Apostolic Church	2:1-7	Holds 7 Stars (right hand), Walks among 7 Candlesticks	Hard workig Persevering Sanctified & Pure Disciplinary Autonomous Enduring	Abandoned relationship with First love	Remember Repent Do	Light/Life (testimony) removed from place	Holy Spirit
Smyrna "Myrrh"	AD 100-312	The Persecuted Church	2:8-11	The First and Last, Was Dead and Is Alive	Poor in Temporals, Rich in Spirituals (Roman Catholic/Replacement Theo)	None	Not to fear suffering Be Faithful in Death	None - exhorted to be faithful in the 10 days	Holy Spirit
Pergamum "Thoroughly married"	AD 312-606	State Church (1st Reich of Constantine)	2:12-17	Possesses the Sharp Two-edged Sword	Took and held His name; Faithful;	Embrace: pagan anti-Israel theolo; Idolatry; Immorality	Repent, or else	War against with the Sword (Word of God)	Holy Spirit
Thyatira "Perpetual sacrifice"	AD 606-1520	The Pagan Church	2:18-29	Son of God, Has Eyes like flame of fire, Feet like brass	Deeds, Love Faith, Service, Perseverance, Immediate works are greater	Tolerate Jezebel who introduces pagan philosophy	They? Repent You? Continue True	They? Cast into Great Tribulation, Pestilence You? To see and know	Holy Spirit
Sardis "Those escaping"	AD 1520-1750	The Dead Church	3:1-6	Possesses the 7 Spirits and the 7 Stars	A few who are unsoiled, pure, worthy	Reputation but no life; Unfinished tasks	Wake up; finish the tasks; Remember; Repent	Tragic and fearful visit of Jesus upon them like a thief (Rapture?)	Holy Spirit
Philadelphia "Brotherly love"	AD 1750-1900	The Favored Church	3:7-13	Holy, true, Has the Keys of David: Opens, Shuts	Little power, Obeyed His Word; Have not denied His name	None	Continue true/hold fast	Loss of Crowns	Holy Spirit
Laodicea "People Ruling"	AD1900-Tribulation	Lukewarm Church	3:14-22	The Amen, Faithful and True Witness, Source of Creation	None	Tepid, Apathetic, Wretched, miserable, blind, naked	Pay the price of God's riches, purity, and sight	Repent or be abnegated, vomited	Holy Spirit

Question 11

Will the Last Days be like the days of Noah, and were the Sons of God who married the daughters of man, angels?

ANSWER

Khanoch, the Grandfather of *Noach* Walked with *Elohim*

Let's answer this question by examining the days just before *Noach*, with *Noach's* great grandfather, *Khanoch* or Enoch. Enoch is an English transliteration of *Khanoch* (חֲנוֹךְ) which means, "dedication." *Khanoch* was the firstborn son of *Yared* (Jared) who following *Khanoch's* birth, had "other sons and daughters" in obedience to *Elohim's* command to be fruitful (Genesis 5:19). *Moshe* was inspired to select and tell us of *Khanoch* or Enoch who walked with God, and how *Khanoch* was inspired to do so:

> *"and he walked Khanoch haElohim after he begat him, Methushelach."* (Genesis 5:22).

In Hebrew semantics, the verb "walked" appears before the noun *Khanoch*. Also, in the Hebraic text there is no "with" between *Khanoch* and *haElohim*. The English translations read "Enoch walked with God" adding the preposition, "with." The addition of this small preposition in the English translation might alarm Christians. Yet, this is the way translations work. Translations supply words that help make sense and that make the translation read semantically smoother. However, again, in the Hebrew text this preposition does not exist. The prepositions, "is" and "of" do not exist in Hebrew, nor does the indefinite article, "a." The preposition "with" is supplied in English translations to read *Enoch walked **with** God after he begat him, Methushelach.* The *Targum Onkelos* renders the reading, "*Enoch walked in the fear of Elohim.*" The *Jerusalem Targum* has it, "*Enoch served in truth before the Lord.*" These are all interpretative translations, of course.

As the Hebrew reader knows, the *aleph-tav* (את) combination is never interpreted, but is a pointer to the direct object in a sentence and the direct object is often considered by some to be a messianic marker in the Hebrew text. What follows the *aleph-tav* (את) is the pointer to the direct object in the sentence, is then, the direct object of the verb in the sentence.

Another consideration in the passage above is why the definite article "the" is associated with *Elohim*. In Hebrew the definite article "the" attaches to the noun; but, that is typical so it is not in question. The question is, why the definite article "the" is attached to *Elohim* or "God" to read *haElohim* meaning literally, "the Gods" and translated "the God." This is the first occurrence of *haElohim*, "the God" in the Holy Scriptures and it is applied in relationship to *Khanoch*. Perhaps the meaning could be as simple as the English translations have it, *Khanoch walked **with** the Elohim,* expressing a life of intimacy *Khanoch* enjoyed with his trinitarian God. In fact, so close was *Khanoch* to Elohim, that the man of *Elohim,* was [like] *Elohim.*

A very possible interpretation is, *Khanoch walked as the Elohim. Khanoch* was so reflective of *Elohim* in his life or walk, that the two were one, and to see and know *Khanoch* was to see and know *Elohim. Adam* was the image of *Elohim* and he had a relational walk with *Elohim* in the garden before his colossal fall. *Adam* was the monarch and sovereign of all things *Elohim* had created. *Khanoch* was a descendant of Adam and also a "new *Adam.*" Therefore, like the first *Adam, Khanoch's* close proximity to *Elohim* affected him to become like God. In fact, in apocalyptic writings, *Khanoch* is identified as *Metatron,* or "The Angel of YHWH." In the Jewish apocrypha and in early *kabbalah, Metatron* is the name *Khanoch*/Enoch received after his transformation into an angel.

Khanoch was like his patriarchal father, *Adam* the very image of *Elohim*. *Elohim* in the Hebrew can be translated as "gods" (אֱלֹהִים, *elohim*), the plural of *El*, "God" singular. In the Holy Scriptures man is sometimes proclaimed to be *Elohim* although man is never said to be YHWH. In the scroll of Exodus, the *"judges of the earth"* were said to be *Elohim* or God (Exodus 21:6). *Moshe* was said to be *Elohim* to his brother *Aaron* (Exodus 4:16), and *Moshe* and *Aaron* were *Elohim* to Pharaoh (Exodus 7:1). Later, in the *tehillot* or Psalms, the saints of the earth are noted to be *Elohim* (Psalm 82) which is the passage *Yeshua* referenced when He was questioned by the hypocritical unbelieving Jewish leaders for saying He was *benElohim* or son of God. His response was the following:

"is it not written in your law I said you are Elohim. If He called them Gods to whom the Word of God came, and the scripture cannot be broken, Say ye of Him whom the Father has sanctified…you blaspheme because you say I am the Son of God?' (John 10:34-36).

The *tehillot* or psalms proclaim all who are righteous to be *Elohim*.

Elohim, also included angels, as the New Testament book of Hebrews translated Psalm 8, suggesting that *Elohim* in the passage meant angels (c.f. Psalm 97:7).

Khanoch walked Elohim may indicate that Enoch spent time with heavenly beings as the apocryphal book of *First Enoch* suggests, depicting *Khanoch* interacting with the heavenly angels. In the Holy Scriptures we discover later in Genesis 5:24 that *Khanoch* was taken by *Elohim* without his having the demonic experience of death. *Khanoch* superseded the death experience. Two other Psalms reflect the power of such a godly man as *Khanoch* (Psalm 49:15 and 73:24).

Khanoch being raptured was perhaps the origin of the Jewish hope for life with God after dying.[9] The New Testament scriptures speak of *Khanoch* (Enoch) on several occasions. In the scroll of Hebrews, the

---

[9] See the Apocryphal book, *Wisdom* 4:10-14 which displays *Khanoch* as the example of a righteous man and his hope of eternal life.

author, *Shaul, Apollos, Priscilla,* or another, attributes *Khanoch's metatithemi,* that is, Enoch being "carried over" to the other side was due to his faith, and his disappearance from earth to heaven was in accordance to God translating him. However, before his translation he had the testimony that he pleased God.

During the intertestamental period *Khanoch* (Enoch) was a legendary hero[10] due to the stories that declared him to be the first wise man and the first recipient of Holy Scripture with revelations of the secrets of the universe promoting them to men on the earth. In Jewish tradition, he is known for his wisdom of science that he acquired from angelic guides. Jewish writings state that he received astronomical, cosmological, meteorological, and prophetic revelation, and to him was given the solar calendar. Further legend says that *Khanoch* was given prophecies by God to be spoken against the fallen angels, and apocalyptic revelations for the *eschatological* last days. *Yehudah* (Jude) the brother of *Yeshua* quotes *Khanoch* incorporating a slice of the Book of Enoch in his scroll (1 Enoch 1:9; Jude 14) that logically is positioned in the corpus of the Holy Scriptures before the last book in the Bible, the apocalyptic scroll of *Yeshua* (Revelation 1:1).

As mentioned above, *Khanoch* is often identified as the Jewish *Metatron* or divine one, suggesting *Khanoch* was the "Little YHWH," or "the angel of the Lord." Others have suggested *Khanoch* to be the messiah figure who is one day to return to the earth, since he did not die, and to appear with *Eliyah* (1 Enoch 37-71; 71:14-17; 2, Genesis 5:24; 3 Enoch). This would mean then that *Khanoch* is one of the two witnesses of Revelation 11:3-14.

Of all the Jewish books in the intertestamental period *1 Enoch* is one of the most important. We have the complete text in Ethiopic, sections of it in Greek, and important fragments of 1 Enoch in Aramaic discovered among the Dead Sea Scrolls in Qumran. 1 Enoch contains five books: *the Book of Watchers* (1–36), *the Similitudes* (37–71),

---

10 See *Ecclesiasticus* 44:16; 49:14, 16; *Jubilees* 4:14–26; 10:17; and 1 *Enoch.*

the *Astronomical Book* (72–82), *the Book of Dreams* (83–90), and *the Epistle of Enoch* (91–105).

The *Tanakh* or Old Testament says nothing more about *Khanoch* outside of Genesis 5 except for the inclusion of his name in a list of names in 1 Chronicles 1:3. Later *Enochic* literature demonstrates that *Khanoch* was a significant figure in early Judaism, and also in early Christianity. Apart from *Eliyah* who "went up" to heaven in a whirlwind (2 Kings 2:11), *Khanoch* is the only other figure in the Old Testament of whom it is said that he did not die (compare Genesis 5:24).

Khanoch, the Grandfather of *Noach* Walked with *Elohim* after he Birthed *Methuselah*

The Holy Scripture says that *Khanoch walked* [as] *the Elohim,* "after he birthed *Methushelach,*" and *Moshe* tells us *Khanoch* had other sons and daughters. So, an important question rises with consideration of what was so significant about *Methushelach's* birth? We are not told unless there is a hint or message in his name. Hence, the study of his name. מְתוּשֶׁלַח (M'thushelach):

- *"man of the javelin/dart"* (Smith, S & Cornwall, J (1998). The Exhaustive Dictionary of Bible Names; Easton's Bible Dictionary).
- *"man of the spear"* (Theological Wordbook of the Old Testament).
- *"man of Lakh"* (Wood, D.R.W.; Marshal, Howard, New Bible Dictionary).
- worshipper of *Shelakh* (anonymous source).
- *"he dieth and the sending forth"* (Jamieson, Robert; Fausset, A.R.; Brown, David): Commentary Critical Explanatory on the Whole Bible.
- *"when he is dead it shall be sent"* (Exhaustive Dictionary of Bible

Names).

- *"when he is dead it shall be sent* (The Companion Bible).
- *"when he dies, judgment"* (Henry Morris Study Bible).

To help us determine the correct interpretation, we might consider the significance of his years. *Methushelach* was 187 years old when he birthed *Lamech* (Genesis 5:25). *Methushelach* lived 782 years after birthing *Lamech* (Genesis 5:26) which means that *Methuselach* lived to be 969 years old. When *Lamech* was 182 and birthed *Noach* (Genesis 5:28) *Methushelach* was 369 years old (adding his age, 187 when he birthed *Lamech*, to the age of *Lamech* 182 when *Lamech* birthed *Noach* which puts grandfather *Methushelach* at 369 years of age when *Noach* was born). *Noach* was 600 years old when the flood came (Genesis 7:6) and *Methushelach* who was 369 years old when *Noach* was born was then 969 years old when *Noach* was 600 years old and when the flood came. *Methushelah* lived to be 969 years old and he died. The flood came when *Noach* was 600 years old. Therefore *Methushelach* died the year the flood came. Jewish legend says *Methushelach* died seven days before the flood. When *Methushelach* died, the flood [of judgment] came as is the meaning of his name.

It appears that Jamieson, Fausset, and Brown (above) have it correct! *Khanoch* walked [as] *the Elohim* of the earth <u>after</u> he birthed *Methushelach*, for father *Khanoch* knew his son's name was pregnant with prophetic meaning. *Khanoch* was not so pietistic or mystical or heavenly minded that his walk prevented him from being a husband, father, and having a family. He had other sons and daughters, and he did have a strong opposition and voice against apostasy and wickedness (Jude 14,15).

Khanoch, the Grandfather of *Noach* Was Translated

Khanoch was the seventh patriarch from *Adam* (Jude 14), and he lived 365 years as *the Elohim* or God of the world, and, God took him!

"For God took him," according to the Jewish *Pentateuch and Haftorah* is profoundly significant. The Hebrew suggests first, that "God took him" as God takes every man since God is the giver and sustainer of all living. To die is to be taken by God in whose presence there is life eternal for the elect and righteous ones. The New Testament, however, gives us more. Hebrews 11:5 says of *Khanoch,*

"by faith Enoch was translated that he should not see death; and was not found, because God had translated him; for before his translation he had this testimony, that he pleased God."

The scroll of Hebrews says that "he was translated," translated used three times in this one verse. Also, *Khanoch* was "not found," because God took him for he had the testimony that he pleased God!

If *Khanoch* was a preacher and prophet of the coming judgment, that is, the deluge, *Khanoch* lived to see demonic intercourse with humans, he preached concerning their abominable sin, and appointed the coming judgment against them since the coming deluge was due - in part or in whole - to fallen angelic-beings amalgamating with humans producing hybrid humans. *Khanoch* was raptured or seized by God just prior to God's premeditated destruction of the demonized world by a flood.

Could *Khanoch's* experience and rapture be a foreshadowing of the New Testament Church seeing another amalgamation of fallen angels with mortal women before the rapture of God's saints and then the great and final judgment to follow? *Yeshua* prophesied that the last days were to be like the days of *Noach.*

Like *Khanoch,* we should preach and prophesy while we live, all the while anticipating that we will soon be raptured just before God unleashes His wrath upon the world, only this time by fire?

Only two men in the OT or *Tanakh* lived and went to God without experiencing death, *Khanoch* and *Eliyah.* Both, were prophets to their dispensation, both walked with *Elohim* (or, walked as *Elohim*/God) the image of God to their world, both heralded the coming judgment, and both were translated. *Eliyah* is to return to the earth to preach again according to *Malachi* (4:5,6) and *Mattityahu* (17:11), and *Eliyah* appeared with *Moshe* and *Yeshua* on the Mount of Transfiguration. He is also to appear once more, as one of the two witnesses in the last days, and perhaps *Khanoch* is the other of the two witnesses of Revelation 11:3-12.

History of the Book of Khanoch/Enoch

The biblical New Testament book of *Yudah* (Jude) refers to Enoch's prophesy found in the scroll of *Khanoch* (Enoch), chapter one, verse nine. If *Khanoch*/Enoch, the seventh from Adam is the author, copies of the scroll of Enoch survived the deluge which means *Noach* had a copy of the *Book of Khanoch* aboard the ark. The scroll of *Khanoch* was secured by one of *Noach's* three sons, *Shem, Cham,* or *Yaphet* and was passed on to one of his sons. The Book of Enoch survived the movement of the peoples of the earth to the east, landing in Shinar, and was perhaps an impetus for the building of the *ziggurat* or tower in Babel, a cosmological museum (Genesis 11:1-5).

The scroll of *Khanoch* was preserved and found in the academies of Egypt where *Moshe* studied, and the book was surely known to him. *Moshe* perhaps carried a copy of the scroll of *Khanoch* when he led the Hebrews out of Egypt in 1445 BC. It is suggested that the scroll(s) of *Khanoch* existed in Hebrew a thousand years after Israel's exodus from Egypt.

The *Book of Enoch* appeared in Ethiopia due to events that occurred during the reign of King Manasseh of Judah, 695-640 BC (2 Chronicles 33:1-20; 2 Kings 21:1-18). Many Jewish refugees escaped to Egypt, and then on to Lake Tana in Ethiopia. The Ethiopian *Falasha* Jews translated the *Book of Khanoch* into *Ge'ez* and Greek and Aramaic versions also survived.

The standard academic view suggests the *Book of Enoch* was written by some slightly demented religious fanatic about 200-300 BC, although many disregard this view because of the author's inference of the days of Noach and the description of the angels with firsthand knowledge, and also because of the potently accurate prophesies.

In the mid 1700s a Scotsman, James Bruce returned from Ethiopia with three manuscripts of the *Book of Khanoch*. He gave one copy to the library at Paris, the second he brought home, and the third copy he presented to the Bodleian Library at Oxford by way of Dr. Douglas, the Bishop of Carlisle (Laurence, vii). The *Book of Enoch* was a mystery and has been kept shrouded, until the manuscript was eventually issued its first English translation and edition in 1821 by Dr. Laurence, Archbishop of Cashel, former Professor of Hebrew at Oxford. The work was translated into German in 1838, into Latin in 1840, yet the *Book of Enoch* gained its greatest applause when published in America in 1838 (Laurence, viii).

Yehudah (Jude), the brother of *Yeshua* and author of the inspired scroll of Jude speaks of *Enoch* as a prophet (1:14). Jude's quote of the *Book of Enoch* infers it to be antecedent to the Christian era. All of the church "Fathers" were knowledgeable of the apocryphal *Book of Enoch*, and many of them cite the work.[11] Origen (AD 254) assigned the *Book of Enoch* the same authority as the Psalms. Irenaeus assigned the *Book of Enoch* such authenticity it was analogous to the writings of *Moshe* (Moses), and affirms that Enoch although a man was God's messenger to the angels.[12] Tertullian, the famous theologian, held the *Book of Enoch* to be as sacred as the Psalms or Isaiah.

References to the *Book of Enoch* are contained in the cabbalistic teachings of the *Zohar*, a book of Hebrew traditions and philosophical commentary. Archbishop Laurence gives extracts from the *Zohar* which refer to important passages from the *Book of Enoch*, and states, "the authors of the Cabbalistical remains wrote their recondite

---

11 Justin Martyr, Clemens of Alexandria, Origen, Irenaeus, Tertullian, Eusebius, Jerome, Hilary, Epiphanius, Augustine refer to the *Book of Enoch*. All the Church "Fathers" agreed that the *Book of Enoch* was to be denied canonical inclusion to the Holy Scriptures (Tertullian dissented). Some of these even considered denying Jude to the canon since the book has a quotation of the apocryphal book.

12 "Against Heresies," iv.16.

doctrines in Chaldees and possessed a copy of the *Book of Enoch* written in Hebrew, "which they regarded as the genuine work of him whose name it bore."

Prophecy of the Last Days According to the Book of Khanoch/ Enoch

As to the question of the identity of the "sons of God," according to the Scroll of *Khanoch* or the *Book of Enoch*, the *malakhim* or angels, children of the heavens, saw the beautiful and comely daughters of Adam and lusted for them, and conversed about crossing over into the human domain to take themselves partners for cohabitation.

"One chief angel, Semyaza, their leader was fearful to do this great sin alone, and coerced the chiefs to swear an oath and bound themselves to that oath, and they descended in the days of Yared (Jared), Khanoch's father, on the summit of Mount Hermon."

The *Book of Enoch* reads almost word-for-word as Genesis 6:1-8, and it gives the names of the chiefs of the band of two hundred angels who defected from heaven: *Semyaza,* their leader, *Arakibal, Rameel, Akibel, Tamiel, Ramlel, Danel, Ezeqeel, Baraqel, Asael, Armaros, Batrael, Ananel, Zaquel, Samsapeel, Satarel, Turel, Yomyael, Sariel.*[13]

The Scroll of *Khanoch* says that these all with the others together took unto themselves wives, and they began to go in unto them and to defile themselves with them, and they taught them charms and enchantments,[14] and the cutting of roots, and made them acquainted

---

13 We are familiar with the archangels, *Michael, Gabriel,* and *Lucifer* the *Cherub* who fell. The myriad stars are known and named by God as are the myriad angels whom He created. In chapter 69 *Khanoch* gives another list of twenty-one names of the fallen watchers.

14 The God of Israel detests divination, witchcraft, omens, sorcery, spells, mediums, spirits, calling up the dead, etc. (Deuteronomy 18:9-12).

with plants.[15] The women became pregnant bare great giants, whose height was three thousand ells.[16] These giants consumed all the acquisitions of men, but when men could no longer sustain them, the giants turned against them and devoured mankind. The giants also began to sin against birds,[17] and beasts, and reptiles, and fish, and to devour one another's flesh, and drink the blood.[18] Then, the earth laid accusation against the lawless ones.[19] "The lawless one" is the identity of the *antichrist*, according to the Apostle (Paul), in 2 Thessalonians 2:3

Khanoch wrote that God's word to *Noach* was to "hide thyself" for He was to destroy the earth with a great deluge. The ark served many purposes and one was a hiding place for the holy ones from the damned; a hiding place for the righteous from judgment, a hiding place for the righteous from seeing the wrath of God. The *Book of Enoch* says that Enoch also was hidden (see 12:1), and perhaps to receive revelation from God.

The archangel, *Gabriel* was to proceed against the bastards and the reprobates, and against the children of fornication, that is, the children

---

15 God judged the deserting angels for physical sexual copulation with humans which caused the corruption of human DNA. The satanic attempt was certainly to hinder the coming "seed of woman," a pure human Who was to crush the serpent's head. God also judged the renegade angels and humanity because of sorcery, the secrets regarding the spiritual, mystical, and immaterial world.

16 An *ell* is thought by some to be the equivalent of the Hebrew cubit which is the measurement from the elbow to the longest finger of the hand, approximately 18 inches. Three-thousand cubits that equal 18 inches each is near 45 feet. This seems to be quite an exaggeration; perhaps the figure was corrupted. The tallest giant mentioned in the Holy Scriptures was Og, King of Bashan, near twelve feet in height.

17 The Jewish apocryphal *Book of Jubilees* speaks of the giants sinning with the birds.

18 The sin of drinking blood is mentioned in the Jewish apocryphal *Book of Jubilees,* "take heed with blood, take much heed. Bury it in the earth, and eat no blood, for it is the soul, never eat blood." (c.f. Genesis 4:10; cf. Enoch 8:4; 9:2).

19 "Lawless one" is a term for the *antichrist* (2 Thessalonians 2:3). Thus, the spirit of the *antichrist* was then prevalent.

of the Watchers.[20] The archangel, *Michael*[21] was sent to bind, the leader, *Semjaza* and his comrades who had united themselves with human women, and their punishment was to see the hybrid sons destroyed and incarcerated for 70 generations. From *Khanoch* to *Yeshua* was seventy generations (Luke 3:23-38). Perhaps these are the "spirits in prison" to whom Messiah *Yeshua* went into the bowels of the earth to preach His Gospel. These now await their final judgment and terrifying fate, sentenced according to the *Book of Enoch* to *Gehenna* [fire].

According to the *Book of Enoch* word came to *Khanoch* from heaven to deliver a message to the "watchers" in chains. Here is that message.

> *12:4 "Enoch, thou scribe of righteousness, go, declare to the Watchers of the heaven who have left the high heaven, the holy eternal place, and have defiled themselves with women, and have done as the children of earth do, and have taken unto themselves wives: "Ye have wrought great destruction on the earth:*
> *12:5 And ye shall have no peace nor forgiveness[22] of sin: and inasmuch as they delight themselves in their children.*
> *12:6 The murder of their beloved ones shall they see, and over the destruction of their children shall they lament, and shall make supplication unto eternity, but mercy and peace shall ye not attain."[23]*

---

[20] Called "bastards" and "children of fornication" meaning these descendants were not children of marriage, an institution of God; the apostate angels did not marry human women, but took them, that is, by force. This is what *Moshe* wrote in the Torah (Genesis 6:1,2).

[21] *Michael* the archangel was sent to *Semjaza* to bind him and his comrades who had defiled themselves with human women. Their punishment was to see their sons destroyed, themselves incarcerated for 70 generations (perhaps until Messiah came), the final punishment being cast into eternal fire.

[22] There was forgiveness if Israelis married foreign women although after judgment, like having their hair pulled out as Nehemiah performed (Nehemiah 13:25). However, there was/is no forgiveness for a sexual union between an angel and [human] women.

[23] Elohim did not spare the fallen ones who crossed the unforgiveable line of habitation, and He will not save them for all eternity. These "watchers" are forever damned, they will never have mercy or peace, and their only hope is to live in the present, for the future holds their being cast into *Gehenna* [fire] (see 2 Peter 2:4,5).

13:1 *And Enoch went and said: Azazel, thou shalt have no peace: a severe sentence has gone forth against thee to put thee in bonds.*[24]
13:2 *And thou shalt not have toleration nor request granted to thee, because of the unrighteousness which thou hast taught, and because of all the works of godlessness and unrighteousness and sin which thou hast shown to men.*
13:3 *Then I went and spoke to them all together, and they were all afraid, and fear and trembling seized them.*[25]
13:4 *And they besought me to draw up a petition*[26] *for them that they might find forgiveness, and to read their petition in the presence of the Lord of heaven.*

Khanoch brought the petition before God and His response to the fallen apostate angels is as follows.

14:4 *I wrote out your petition, and in my vision, it appeared thus, that your petition will not be granted unto you throughout all the days of eternity, and that judgement has been finally passed upon you: yea (your petition) will not be granted unto you.*[27]

---

[24] The binding of *Azazel* was done by the archangel, *Raphael* (see 10:4). "*And the angels which kept not their first estate, but left their own habitation, he hath reserved in everlasting chains under darkness unto the judgment of the great day*" (Jude 1:6).

[25] *Kefa*/Peter was inspired to tell us that these angels who sinned were cast down to hell, delivered to bindings or chains of darkness, and reserved for judgment (2 Peter 2:4,5).

[26] Requesting *Khanoch* to write a petition shows both his saintly and holy character and also his literary skill. Petitioning *Elohim* by letter may have been to show reverence to the majesty of God, although it may have been to proof a record of true sorrow.

[27] The answer to *Khanoch*/Enoch's letter is here given. The petition of the apostate angels will not be given, even unto eternity. The apostates may never reenter heaven, they would be bound for eternity (some interpret this to be endless reincarnation), they would see their offspring murdered, and any requests on behalf of their descendants/sons would be denied. In Chapter 15 God mocks their petition to Him being brought by a man, *Khanoch*/Enoch when they were to be interceding for men. There is no hope for the apostate, and this includes humans who defect from *Yeshua* (see book of Jude).

14:5 And from henceforth you shall not ascend into heaven unto all eternity, and in bonds of the earth the decree has gone forth to bind you for all the days of the world.

14:6 And (that) previously you shall have seen the destruction of your beloved sons and ye shall have no pleasure in them, but they shall fall before you by the sword.

14:7 And your petition on their behalf shall not be granted, nor yet on your own: even though you weep and pray and speak all the words contained in the writing which I have written.

14:8 And the vision was shown to me thus: Behold, in the vision clouds invited me and a mist summoned me, and the course of the stars and the lightnings sped and hastened me, and the winds in the vision caused me to fly and lifted me upward, and bore me into heaven.[28]

According to the Jewish *Septuagint*, which is a Greek translation of the Hebrew texts, the "sons of God" in Genesis 6 were "angels." The Jewish historian, Flavious Josephus agrees with the *Septuagint*, as does the Greek Historian, Eusebius. That is to say, those closer to the event believed and recorded in their journals of history that angelic beings defected from God and heaven to crossover a boundary that was forbidden by the creator; that boundary was the demarcation line of habitation. These beings did so in order to cohabit with human women. The result was a hybrid line of humanity that were called *Nephilim*, also called *Anakim* and *Rephaim*. The result was corruption of the human DNA and genome, perhaps on purpose to hinder the coming champion of Genesis 3:15, the Son of God Who must come as fully man, the seed of woman. We may deduce that when God sent the deluge there were only 8 pure humans untainted by demonic influence, *Noach, Mrs. Noach, Shem, Mrs. Shem. Cham, Mrs. Cham, Yaphet,* and *Mrs. Yaphet.*

---

[28] *Khanoch* was evidently escorted to heaven by a space craft (see Ezekiel 1:15-28). Elijah ascended to heaven in similar fashion. "*And it came to pass, as they still went on, and talked, that behold there appeared a chariot of fire, and horses of fire, and parted them both asunder; and Elijah went up by a whirlwind into heaven*" (2 Kings 2:11).

Later, the *Nephilim* or "giants" return. One was a very infamous giant or "fallen one" named *Goliath*, living among humans since he was a hybrid human, along with his four brothers. David slew *Goliath* (2 Samuel 17), *Abishai* slew *Ishbi-benob* (2 Samuel 15:17), *Sibbechai* the *Hushathite* slew *Saph* (2 Samuel 21:18), *Elhanan* slew *Lahmi* (2 Samuel 21:19), and David's nephew *Yonatan* slew the unnamed giant who had six fingers on both hands and six toes on both feet and was 6 cubits tall (2 Samuel 21:21).

We will indeed see an invasion of *Nephilim* before the Rapture and before the Lord returns to set up His kingdom, since *Yeshua* said the last days would be like it was in the days of *Noach*. Perhaps we are already receiving a visitation of such beings, although we are not spiritually intimate with God enough to discern and recognize them.

Can angels take on the form of man? Certainly! No question about it. Simply read the Holy Scriptures. Angels always without exception appear as [young] men, they eat (venison and cornbread), they are clothed, they were recognizable as men though sometimes unrecognizable as angels [while entertaining humans], and they can see, hear, taste, touch, and feel, just as humans do.

Yeshua answered the trick question put to Him about "whose wife will she be in heaven," when asked about a man who had multiple wives, saying that in heaven there is neither marrying or giving in marriage. Yeshua stated a fact. He was not answering a question concerning the delegated power, supernatural abilities, or the dark alchemy He had delegated to Seraphim, Cherubim, Watchers, Archangels, Angels, the Four Creatures, the Angel of the Lord, and other beings God created. He has delegated colossal powers to these beings; they even have the freedom to defect. Their defection, however, is eternal. There is no repentance and no forgiveness. Perhaps angels are still falling away.

Pagan Canaanite altar on *HarMegiddo* ("Mountain of Megiddo");
children were offered to the gods on such altars.

Question 12

The term, *rapture* does not appear in the Bible, so why is it preached as biblical truth?

Answer

The term *missions* is not in the Bible, but all believers affirm the biblical truth of missions. The term *trinity* is not in the Bible, but the majority of Christian believers embrace the triunity of *Elohim*. For example, *Elohim* is the plural form of *El* (singular) and both are found in the Holy Scriptures. *Elohim* being a composite-singular noun and title shows that there is plurality of the Godhead. Even Jewish theologians embrace the idea that *Elohim* encompasses the majesty of heaven, God and the angelic beings and all other. *Elohim* consists of the Father, the Son, and the Holy Spirit, all three compose the being of God. *Yeshua* is one of the *Elohim*. *HaRuach haKodesh* or the Holy Spirit is one of the *Elohim*, and Father God, *Avinu*, "our Father," is one of the *Elohim*. All three are *Elohim* and all three are *YHWH*. God is all three and God does not exist without the three. The composite-singular God is a trinity.

The word *rapture* is not found in the Holy Scriptures, although the eschatological event certainly is biblical. *Yeshua* is coming to snatch or elope with His bride (John 14:1-3; 1 Corinthians 15:51-53; 1 Thessalonians 4:13-18; 5:1-10; 2 Thessalonians 2:1-3; Colossians 3:4; Revelation 4:1).

"For if we believe that Jesus died and rose again, even so God will bring with Him those who have fallen asleep in Jesus. For this we say to you by the word of the Lord, that we who are alive and remain until the coming of the Lord,

will not precede those who have fallen asleep. For the Lord Himself will descend from heaven with a shout, with the voice of {the} archangel and with the trumpet of God, and the dead in Christ will rise first. Then we who are alive and remain will be caught up together with them in the clouds to meet the Lord in the air, and so we shall always be with the Lord. Therefore comfort one another with these words" (1 Thessalonians 4:13-18).

The passage above is one of the main texts that reveal the event called the *Rapture*. The English word *rapture* comes from the Latin word *rapto* meaning "to snatch." According to the passage in Thessalonians, our Lord *Yeshua* is to return from heaven, descend into our atmosphere and believers in *Yeshua* (the Church) will be "snatched," or "caught up," or *raptured* and taken to heaven. The Second Coming of *Yeshua* happens later, where the Lord descends to the earth, His feet touch the Mount of Olives, the mountain quakes and forms a rift, and He then ascends up the valley into *Yerushalayim* to take His seat on the throne of David. More on this later (see Question 28).

Lukas gives the account of the angel speaking to the *talmidim* or disciples at Bethany saying that in the same way they saw *Yeshua* ascend into heaven He would return (Acts 1:9-11).

"And after He had said these things, He was lifted up while they were looking on, and a cloud received Him out of their sight. And as they were gazing intently into the sky while He was going, behold, two men in white clothing stood beside them. They also said, "Men of Galilee, why do you stand looking into the sky? This Jesus, who has been taken up from you into heaven, will come in just the same way as you have watched Him go into heaven."

This is the return *Shaul*/Paul described in the passage of Thessalonians (1 Thessalonians 4:13-18). The Lord descends from heaven to remove His church, the saints from the earth, and we will be received up into heaven. Later, *Yeshua* returns descending to Jerusalem to take His seat on the Davidic throne, but His return then, is as a warrior to take care of business! That return will be His *Second*

Coming to rule as the *last Adam* over all the earth, and that return is nothing similar to "in the same way" *Yeshua* ascended in Acts 1:9-11.

The Greek word *Shaul* (Paul) uses in the Thessalonians passage concerning the rapture, "with a shout" describes an exclamation of decree. The voice of an archangel is then heard, perhaps repeating the cry, or some other exclamation. The archangel will probably be one of the seven archangels spoken of in the book of Enoch and known in Judaism, *Michael, Gabriel, Raphael, Uriel, Raguel, Saraquel, Remiel.* The Bible speaks only of *Michael* or *Gabriel,* so we may assume it will be one of these two.

The ancient *shofar* or ram's horn would sound three particular sounds, *teruach, tekiah,* and *shivarim.* Each one of these 'blows' had a unique tone and length, which signaled the Jewish people to do something, to assemble, to celebrate, to attack, or, that all was well. The *shofar* sound of the *rapture* will probably be the one for assembly or gathering.

The *rapture* or seizing of the saints from the earth will happen suddenly, without a sign or notice, and without time to prepare spiritually. Just as sudden as the phone rings or a bird chirps or an alarm clock sounds, the rapture will occur. One should study both the Hebrew and Greek term for the English translation, "suddenly." People in every walk of life will *suddenly* disappear. Fathers will be taken leaving behind mature yet unbelieving children. Wives will be taken leaving behind unregenerate husbands. Siblings will be taken leaving unbelieving brother(s) and sister(s). Some will be taken while sleeping leaving a spouse, sibling, or friend who will awake and discover their lover, brother, sister or friend gone. People at work, driving to work, driving home from work, resting, recreating, students going to classes, sitting in classes, people traveling, etc., will be taken, while myriad others, the vast majority of others will be left behind.

At the *Rapture,* there is a sequence of *aliya* or "going up!" Those who have died *"in Messiah,"* that is, Christians who have died, will "go up" first, out from their graves. Then, those whom *Yeshua* knows who are living, will be raptured or taken next. In the days of *Yeshua* and in the New Testament era, the protocol was [always] *"to the Jews, first."* The Gospel was *to the Jews, first* (Romans 1:16), and also, *tribulation and distress to every soul who does evil, to the Jews, first* (Romans 2:9,10). However, at the *Rapture*, the dead saints, the *holy ones*, whether Jews or Gentiles, males or females, who have died in Messiah, are first. Then, "those of us who are live and remain" will follow.

The dead in Messiah "going up" will experience their bodily resurrection. The passage in Thessalonians does not suggest that the "dead in Christ" are soul sleepers. In verse 14 *Shaul* states *that <u>God will bring with Him</u> all who have fallen asleep in Jesus*. Saints who have died are presently with the Lord, though not yet inhabiting their glorified bodies which will happen in the *Rapture*. Their physical tent will be raised, and translated. The body, soul, and spirit will unite in an incorruptible celestial body. The saints who come with *Yeshua* will unite to their resurrected bodies which are quickened and changed to an immortal and terrestrial body (1 Thessalonians 4:14). In 1 Corinthians 15:54 *Shaul* states that the perishable becomes imperishable, and the mortal puts on immortality.

"But when this perishable will have put on the imperishable, and this mortal will have put on immortality, then will come about the saying that is written, "DEATH IS SWALLOWED UP in victory."

Shaul says that the *Rapture* is a glorious hope for believers, and that we need not grieve at the death of a believing wife, husband, mother, father, son or daughter, sibling or friend. God will bring these holy ones with Him (verse 14). Their bodies will be raised, first and then the saints who are living will be caught up and all together we will meet in the air (verses 14-18). We will then forever be with the Lord. The *Rapture* is not an eerie event for the Messianic believer to dread. The *Rapture* is our prescription for peace and sanity, especially when grieving at the death of our loved ones. It is a message of comfort for the believer, not a message to invoke fear. *"Therefore comfort one another with these words"* (1 Thessalonians 4:18).

It will be the *"one new man in Messiah"* who will be caught up to be in reunion with *Yeshua*. The saints, both dead and living, will be caught up to meet the Lord. *Shaul* shares of the event called the *Rapture* in 1 Corinthians 15.

> *"Behold, I tell you a mystery; we will not all sleep, but we will all be changed, in a moment, in the twinkling of an eye, at the last trumpet; for the trumpet will sound, and the dead will be raised imperishable, and we will be changed. For this perishable must put on the imperishable, and this mortal must put on immortality"* (1 Corinthians 15:51-53).

Yeshua, the bridegroom will come for His bride and elope with her, out from this world, and "she" will be changed. The bride will be *raptured* and escorted to a mansion that her Lord has been preparing for her for the past two thousand years (John 14).

Our groom has been quite busy! First, *Yeshua* serves as our advocate or attorney, since we have an accuser, *Lucifer* who continually accuses us before the throne night and day (1 John 2:1). In this present life the believer has no peacetime, there is no lull from battle against the dark powers of this atmosphere. We are at war! So, we need the Lord as our advocate.

Second, *Yeshua* serves as our *Cohen Gadol* or "Great High Priest" before the throne of God (Hebrews 4:14-16). The covenant God made with Israel necessitated a High Priest and by God's design Israel's *Cohen Gadol* was to be of Aaronic descent. However, *Yeshua's* priesthood is not the order of Levi. *Yeshua* is of the tribe of *Yehudah* which the Torah or Law spoke nothing concerning a High Priest, and *Yeshua* is a High Priest of the order of *Melchizedek*. *Yeshua* has inaugurated a new covenant, a new *torah* or instruction, and a new priesthood (Hebrews 7:14).

Third, *Yeshua* is a bridegroom and has been preparing the home for His bride. The most beautiful picture we have of the *Rapture* is the visual of the Jewish wedding that *Yeshua* gave us that *Yochanon* recorded in John 14.

"In My Father's house are many dwelling places; if it were not so, I would have told you; for I go to prepare a place for you. If I go and prepare a place for you, I will come again and receive you to myself, that where I am, {there} you may be also. And you know the way where I am going" (John 14:1-4).

The Jewish beau would come to the home of his hopeful bride-to-be, and as culture prescribed he would pour a glass of [covenant] wine. If she drank the glass with him she was accepting his proposal of marriage. If she accepted his proposal, he would then say something like, *"I go now to prepare a place for you, and if I go to prepare a place for you, I will come again to receive you to myself, that where I am you also will be."* He would go and he would prepare a place for consummation of the marriage, the wedding chamber. Jewish tradition has it that the beau never knew the time for their elopement and he was dependent upon the Father who would instruct the son when it was time. *Yeshua* actually said these very words, the very words of a Jewish beau to His bride-to-be. We have them recorded for us in John 14.

The *Rapture* is *Yeshua* stealing His bride for the chamber; the *Rapture* is an elopement [back] to the honeymoon cottage or mansion. There in the bridal chamber our marriage will be consummated as we come to know Him fully.

The *Rapture* is the first in a continuing series of events that follow for the believer. The *Rapture* does not pertain to the unbeliever except to seal his fate and eternal destiny, since he or she has heard the gospel and rejected it. The unbeliever will be left behind to await his eternal fate.

Shaul wrote to the Corinthians that a trumpet will sound to rally the people of God to assemble, just as the *shofar* sounded in the days of ancient Israel to gather the people of God. However, this is the 'last trumpet,' perhaps speaking of the last colossal blow of the Great *Shofar* sound, the one-hundredth blow on the *Feast of Trumpets* (Leviticus 23).

The *Rapture* is not a new concept, but is described throughout the Holy Scriptures. In fact, there are eight raptures spoken of in the Holy Scriptures.

(1) *Khanoch* or Enoch the seventh from Adam lived sixty-five years and then became the father of *Metushelach* (Methuselah). After he begat *Metushelach* he walked with God. *Khanoch* walked with God for three hundred years and "he was not" for God "took him." The term rapture is not found in the text, but the meaning is clear; God literally "took him" (Genesis 5:24).

(2) *EliYah* knew that his time was nearing and asked his successor, *Elisha* what he might do for him. *Elisha* asked for a double portion of *Eliyah's* spirit. In 2 Kings 2:11 the author (perhaps Samuel) wrote that as they were going along, a chariot of fire appeared with horses of fire, which separated the two of them, and *Eliyah* was taken up to heaven by a whirlwind (2 Kings 2:11). He was raptured!

(3) *Yeshua* after His resurrection told *Miriam* not to touch Him for He had not yet ascended on high, but to go and tell His *talmidim* (disciples) to meet Him in the Galilee. For forty days He appeared to them and taught them. Acts 1 tells the story of His being "caught up" as His *talmidim* were watching and a cloud received Him out of their sight, and in like manor He would return (Acts 1:9-11). His Second Coming is not in like similitude of these words, but the rapture is!

(4) Philip was told by an angel to arise and go south to the road that descends from *Yerushalayim* to Gaza. He arose and went and met an Ethiopian eunuch of high prominence who served the Queen; he had come to *Yerushalayim* to worship. Philip was invited to join him in his chariot and as he read the scroll of Isaiah, Philip gave the Ethiopian the interpretation of Isaiah, that the sheep and lamb led to slaughter in the messianic prophecy, was *Yeshua*! Philip baptized the eunuch and as sudden as the eunuch came up from the water, Philip was *raptured* and transported to Azotus and the Ethiopian eunuch saw him no more (Acts 8:38,39).

(5) *Shaul*/Paul gave testimony of his being "caught up" to the third heaven (rabbi's say there are seven heavens). The Greek term

used in the verse is *harpazo*, the term used for rapture in 2 Corinthians 12:2-4. *Shaul* saw things he was not permitted to communicate upon his return to his natural state of mind.

(6) The *Apocalypse* or Revelation which is the book of *Yeshua* (Revelation 1:1) mentions two witnesses, and because of their miracles, it is thought by many (this author included) that these two witnesses are, *Moshe* and *Eliyah*. During the Great Tribulation these two witnesses will come from heaven to earth to herald God's word to a world that will disdain their testimony. These two witnesses will be killed and their bodies will be left lying in the streets of *Yerushalayim* for three days without burial. The world will be jubilant at their death, so much so, they exchange gifts. Suddenly, the two witnesses will resurrect and be *raptured* to heaven (Revelation 11:3-12).

(7) *Yochanon* uses the Greek term *harpasthe* which means "raptured" in Revelation 12:5 when he writes of the "male child" (Yeshua) Who was "caught up" to God and His throne.

(8) The Church will be *raptured* before the Great Tribulation and the Day of the Lord. This could happen at any moment, even while you read this page!

The *Rapture* is called a mystery in the scriptures (1 Corinthians 15:51-55). It is an event that is not overtly revealed, and it awaits the time to be disclosed. A mystery is something hinted, yet unrevealed. So, one must dig to discover its meaning and value. A mystery is meant to be discovered, but not by slack folk; only by study and prayer! One who does not believe in or accept the NT doctrine of the *Rapture* and has not made an attempt to study the concept, since the *Rapture* is a mystery, will not know of its appearance.

The scenario of the *Rapture* will unfold with an immediate disappearance of saints world-wide. Millions of the best people of earth, the light of the world, the aroma of Christ, the salt of the earth, will be taken, those who are truly the very best flavor of mankind. One of the nations if not the nation most affected by the *Rapture* will be the

United States. The United States will succumb to become a third-world country due to the disappearance of its saints.

It has been suggested that there is no prophetic event that has to happen before the *Rapture* can occur, that the *Rapture* could happen any time. That is not exactly correct; bible prophecy reveals that on the heels of the disappearance of the godly saints from this earth, world Jewry will stampede home to Israel. Israel has to be in place (as *Elisha* was in place to follow *Eliyah*). The *Rapture* necessitates Israel being a [resurrected] people, in their place, the land of Israel, and ready, even while not knowing it. Since 1948 Israel has been in her place. Israel is back in the land speaking Hebrew and flying the *Magen David* or Star of David which began for the most part, May 14, 1948. Perhaps the *Rapture* will be the final and colossal impetus that will cause world Jewry to go home -very fast- especially considering the fact that the saints who are now missing were the beloved friends of Israel.

In proximity to the *Rapture* will be an announcement of world peace by a false leader. He will certainly be needed for in addition to the already zenith problems the world will be facing and attempting to maneuver, will be the horrific question of the location of the millions of humans missing due to the *Rapture*! Consider the affect that the *rapture* or snatching of millions of people worldwide will have on our global economy, global governments, global business, the world's societies, myriad families, citizens of countries across the world, and the consequences of dealing with the affairs of those missing. Consider the emotional state of families, spouses, parents, children, and friends left behind of such a bizarre and haunting disappearance. The world will be absolutely traumatized with colossal hysteria -way much more than the coronavirus of 2020.

For the believer, the *Rapture* will be our home-going; we will be like a bride eloping with our groom. The *Rapture* will be a reunion with everyone we love, our family, friends, heroes of the faith, and especially *Yeshua*. The bridegroom will have descended from the mansion city to receive us. *Yeshua* will descend with a voice and we will be elevated to embrace Him!

The *Rapture* will happen in a micro-millisecond, in *"the twinkling of an eye,"* *Shaul*/Paul wrote in 1 Corinthians 15:51-53. The *Rapture* is the "blessed hope" that *Shaul*/Paul wrote to Titus (2:13).

"…anticipating the blessed tikvah (hope*) and the appearing of the kavod HaEloheinu HaGadol* and *Moshieynu, HaMoshiach, Yeshoshua* (glory of our great God and Savior, Messiah *Yeshua*)."*

Yeshua's talmidim, His followers, and the Church in the 1st and 2nd Centuries, anticipated experiencing the Rapture in their lifetime.

The *Shofar* or ram's horn is blown in Jerusalem to celebrate the *bar-mitzva* of a thirteen-year old boy, his right of passage from child to man (a *bat-mitzva* for girls at age twelve).

Question 13

What happens to the people who are *raptured?* Did they die? Are they dead? Do they return to die later?

Answer

Following the *rapture* of the saints by *Yeshua*, the bridegroom, the church will appear in heaven before what the New Testament calls the *bema* or *judgment seat* of Messiah. The Greek word *bema* literally means, "platform." The term *bema* was borrowed by *Shaul*/Paul from the Grecian Olympics where Olympians were rewarded for their victory. A *bema* was the elevated or raised platform on which they stood to receive their notice, reward, and applause. In churches and synagogues today, the *bema* is the elevated platform where the pastor, elder, rabbi, or priest stands and preaches or teaches. He stands behind a *migdal* or pulpit on the *bema* or elevated platform. The *Bema* is the Judgment Seat of Messiah where Christians will stand before the elevated throne of God and everyone will give an account of their deeds.

"For we must all appear before the bema seat of Christ, so that each one may be recompensed for his deeds in the body, according to what he has done, whether good or bad" (2 Corinthians 5:10,11).

The *Bema* or "Judgment Seat" of Messiah will be a personal, face-to-face (Romans 14:10,12) account of the believer's works (Romans 14:10-12; 1 Corinthians 3:12-15; 4:1-5; 2 Corinthians 5:10-11). The *Bema* will be just and fair (Romans 2:11; Colossians 3:25; James 3:1; Hebrews 13:17), exhaustive, thorough, and complete (1 Corinthians

4:5; Hebrews 4:13; 1 Corinthians 3:10-15), while gracious and kind (Matthew 20:13-15). The *Bema* will take place in heaven following the *Rapture* and our appearance before God (1 Corinthians 15:51-52; Matthew 16:27; Revelation 4:1), in the heavenly tabernacle (Revelation 4:2-5:14).

The Judgment Seat of Messiah is an accounting of our works and the reception of our rewards; it will be something like an awards ceremony, although it is a judgment, only without reference to sins since legally Christians are justified, without sin, and able to stand before God "just-as-if-I'd" never sinned. Our sins were dealt with upon the person of Messiah *Yeshua* when He hung on the cross. Our sins are what killed the Son of God. He died for all our sins, even unrepentant sins, so they are settled. At salvation we received a colossal trade. We received [freely] His life, His death, His burial, His resurrection, His ascension, and His throne. At salvation He received our sins which separated Him from Father God. Our judgment before God is not as a sinner, but as a son and regarding our obedience to Him. Many will suffer loss and some great loss for their life's investment.

The *Bema* judgment is not the same as the *Great White Throne* judgment where sinners who are without Messiah *Yeshua* will appear. The *Great White Throne* Judgment follows the *Second Coming* of *Yeshua* and His millennial Kingdom, and is the final judgment for the unregenerate. That judgment will be for every lost person and for every sin they have committed.

The *Bema* judgment is about works, exclusively. There are no sinners in heaven. Saints have no sins. All sins of all saints, small sins and horrendous sins, sins that caused illness and/or death, and "little white lies" were all were placed on *Yeshua* on the cross, nailed to His body on the tree, and they cursed Him. He was cursed because of our sins. In Christ there is no sin! Reader, do you understand the magnitude of this grace? He is your propitiation!

Because of Messiah's sinless life and His death as the sinful one, He obtained for us everlasting justification and propitiation. He absolved our sin and debt. In Him, there is no sin! This is not to say that the *Bema* judgment is jovial. In fact, this judgment will be terribly sobering since every believer will appear and stand before Messiah to give an account of their entire life that he/she lived after being saved. We will not be able to make amends, change the record, return to get it right, repair ourselves, nor repent of the wasted years.

The *Rapture* is the gathering of His holy-ones or saints for the purpose of appearing before the *Bema Seat* Judgment. To reiterate, the *Bema Seat* Judgment is not in reference to sin, since the believer's position is, *in Messiah* and we have *put on Messiah,* and *there is therefore no condemnation to those who are in Messiah Yeshua* (Romans 8:1). We are identified with Messiah and positionally seated in heaven with Messiah. God sees us through the crimson lenses of the cross of *Yeshua.* In God's eyes every believer is the image of His darling son and our Messiah, *Yeshua.* This is the *hope of glory* the Apostle *Shaul* was inspired to write about concerning who we are as believers in *Yeshua,* our new identity in Messiah. All our sins were put on Messiah upon the cross, and the believer is exonerated because *Yeshua* died in his or her place. The believer will be judged for obedience, disobedience, good works, bad works, little works, and slothfulness. We are accountable and we will give an account.

Hyper Calvinist often parade the sovereignty of God to a gross exaggeration saying that the believer in reality has no will, that we make no decision as humans uncharted by the sovereign God, and that we are always performing the Will of God since God is God. However, the Holy Scriptures say that every soul has an accounting and the judgment will be legitimate. There will be loss, colossal loss, because God's will in your life was not performed. Many will have chosen to live less than God's design, and they (you?) will be appalled and even alarmed at what could have been, yet, is not, due to lack of prayer, obedience, loving God, loving others, and more. You will tremble before *Yeshua* because He saved you, and you are in heaven, safe and loved, although with much regret. Perhaps, that will be the greatest grief. Our standing before the One Who loved us so much, and our small works for Him, in return.

The *Bema* judgment will be about our walk with our Lord; it will be exact, complete, just, and with eternal consequences. This judgment is no *kangaroo court.* It will not be a mere slap on the wrist, nor will it be a finger in your face. God will not bite His tongue, yet He will not condemn, for there is no condemnation in Messiah. You, dear saint, will not be charged with sin, but you will be charged with what could have been and is not, and what YOU could have been, but are not.

At the *Bema* there will be no prejudice, no partiality, no payoff, no exemption, and no escape from the account. There will be no pardon of the verdict of the judgment. All judgment, all reward, and all loss will carry over with us into eternity. These few short three score and ten years we live on earth has serious implications. How we live life now will impact our eternity! Get busy serving *Yeshua* for that matters more than anything else in your short life here, and is reflected in your eternal life and position to come.

Author, Reginald Lisemby blowing shofar for dramatic presentation at Long Hollow Baptist Church, Hendersonville, TN.

Question 14

If our sins were washed away by the blood of Yeshua and we are placed "in Christ" with no condemnation (Romans 8:1), why is there a judgment of believers?

Answer

The Judgment Seat of Messiah has nothing to do with the sins of the believer, for in Christ believers have no sin. *Yeshua* is our propitiation or appeasement. The Judgment Seat has everything to do with obedience as sons of God, our works, and reward and loss for the believer, and also eternal positioning. Here are the biblical reasons given for the *Judgment Seat of Christ*.

1.   The *Bema* judgment is a review (Romans 14:10-12; 2 Corinthians 5:10; 1 Corinthians 3:13; Matthew 12:36; 1 Corinthians 4:5; Hebrew 4:13). We will stand before *Yeshua* Who is the Judge of the universe and be recompensed how we treated our body, His temple. Our works for the Lord that we have done or not done since we came to believe and follow Him will be made manifest. Did we work? Did we do the work thoroughly? Did we do the work(s) for show, to be seen and/or heard by men, to be recognized and applauded, or were our work(s) for *Yeshua*, in His name and power, and our being led by His Holy Spirit? Are we guilty for judging a brother or a sister in *Yeshua*? If we judged others we may be judged with the same scrutiny. The works we did, and the works we did not do, will be in view. Were we faithful in all things, some things, a few things, or were we unfaithful, and how much so?

2.   The *Bema* judgment is for rewards (1Corinthians 3:14; 9:25; 1 Thessalonians 2:19; 2 Timothy 4:8; James 1:12; 1 Peter 5:4; Revelation 4:10,11). Those who competed in the game of life and exercised self-control will receive an imperishable wreath. Every saint receives a *crown of righteousness* for he or she has received Messiah and Messiah is our righteousness. Any righteousness we have is because of His residence within us. The flesh certainly cannot produce righteousness. Messiah *Yeshua* drew us, convicted us, birthed us, lives in us, seals us, secures us, guards us, protects us, keeps us, and gets us home. However, we are responsible for our walk with Him and in Him. For those who have persevered under trial, they will receive the *crown of life*. There is also the *crown of glory*. *Yochanon* says that myriad believers will cast their crowns before the throne and the very words with which we will praise YHWH are recorded in Revelation 4:11.

"Worthy art Thou, our Lord and our God, to receive glory and honor and power; for Thou didst create all things, and because of Thy will they existed, and were created."

The Bible mentions the *crown/wreath of glory* (1 Peter 5:4). *Shaul/*Paul writes of the *crown/wreath of incorruption* (1 Corinthian 9:25), the *crown/wreath of rejoicing* (1 Thessalonians 2:19), and the *crown/wreath of righteousness* (2 Timothy 4:8). *Yacov/*James speaks of the *crown/wreath of life* (James 1:12) as does *Yochanon* (Revelation 2:10). We receive these rewards, yet interestingly we will lay these rewards at the feet of *Yeshua*. We will abdicate all given us, for we know that Messiah is our all! Because He dwells within us, these crowns were won. We will have earned them, but only because He first loved and saved us!

Here are ways that we can prepare for the *Judgment Seat* of Messiah.

1.   **How we treat others** (Hebrews 6:10; Matthew 10:41,42). A cup of water given to a believer will be rewarded. It's not the water or the container, but the mercy and kindness we demonstrated to meet an

authentic need of a brother or sister. Inspired by the Holy Spirit *Shaul* wrote that if a brother will not work, he will not eat (2 Thessalonians 3:10). Giving handouts to those on the street corners asking for help may be disobedience to God's kingdom principles. One of God's kingdom principles is that everyone labors, even in eternity! Man was laboring before the fall, only without the curse. Slothfulness is of the adversary. There are, of course, authentically poor people, and there are times each one of us may be put in a place of real need and be forced to ask for help.

2.   **How we use our God-given talent and abilities** (Matthew 25:14-29; Luke 19:11-26; 1 Corinthians 12:4; 2 Timothy 1:6; 1 Peter 4:10). Just like *Yeshua,* we must work the works of God. We must see what God sees and do His will. We must use what God has given us. We are accountable. How has God gifted you, dear reader? What spiritual gift has He given you to use in this life? Beyond that, what talents do you have, and are you using those for Him and His kingdom, or for yourself, to be applauded by man? It will matter when we stand before our King!

3.   **How we use our finances** (Matthew 6:1-4; 1 Timothy 6:17-19). As believers under the New Covenant we are nowhere told to tithe or "tenth" since that would imply that we are only one-tenth dead and nine-tenths alive to use the remaining treasures for ourselves. We are not partially dead to self. We are dead to self. In most congregations, believers have been taught to "tenth" God, and with the other wealth by default we purchase boats, cars, cycles, a ski-trip, a vacation, another home. Tithing implies that we did not die with Messiah and remain under a legal contract to the OT tithe (under the OT Law, Israel was obliged to pay three-tenths of their wealth). Under the New Covenant ALL we are and ALL we have belongs to Messiah, and each one of us like Messiah, are accountable and responsible for ALL that we have and ALL that we give. Do not let anyone legalize your freedom nor let

you consider your life your own. "I died with Messiah, nevertheless I live, yet not I, but Messiah lives within me," said *Shaul*/Paul (Galatians 2:20). There is absolutely no new covenant rule than commands we are to tithe! However, we are accountable for our giving and accountable to God, not to an institutional non-profit organization or church where you are rewarded for you tax exempt giving. Many churches and conventions are big business! You get in their way, they will run over you. If you don't tithe, you don't become an elder, deacon, pastor, or other. We are accountable to God, for going to Him, discovering from Him where He is going, and what He is doing, and then joining Him by giving to His work! You must decide this for yourself. Beloved, our Lord is not into architecture, carpets, stain-glass windows, ceiling chandeliers, gyms, walking tracks, real estate, ball leagues, and everything else we are told by secular church leaders God has led them to build in His name. We can certainly do these things for outreach because of our love for God and as a strategy to reach man for God. You discover for yourself where God is going and what God is doing, and join Him!

4.   **How we accept mistreatment and injustice** (Matthew 5:11-12; Mark 10:29-30; Luke 6:27-28; Romans 8:18; 2 Corinthians 4:17; 1 Peter 4:12-13). Like *Yeshua,* our character is often tested. After regeneration, that is, being saved, our God does not take us to heaven, but He leaves us here on earth to form character, the character of our great God. This life is the only arena of testing, and the result carries with us into eternity. Think about the consequences of this life, beloved. After the ages that God has prescribed, He will create a New Heaven and a New Earth and we will live forever in a pristine eternity, and how we live now, in this life, and the character that is molded is what we take with us yonder to the future. How we live right now, dictates our position in the kingdom for eternity.

5.   **How we endure suffering and trials** (James 1:12; Revelation 2:10). In this life we will have tribulation. Messiah *Yeshua* told us so (John 16:33). As believers we are not exempt from suffering and trials. Some of our affliction is directly from Satan and the powers of darkness who have not only asked, but in some cases demanded of God the right to sift us. Can the dark powers make demands of God? Yes, but only because of God's spiritual laws that are in order and that we may have broken. There are rules of engagement in spiritual war which God has established and of which everyone must abide, including all the spiritual beings, Lucifer, and God, Himself! Lucifer and evil powers were rebels from perfection. So, they were exiled from heaven, although they return to heaven on occasions to give an account (Job 1:6). All created beings are responsible and accountable to God and all must and they do follow God's spiritual laws of combat. All spiritual beings must abide according to the rules of spiritual war since these are God's spiritual principles. *Shaul*/Paul warned believers to dress daily in the armor for battle, because we are at war. Satan walks about as a roaring lion *seeking whom he may devour*. Yes, he may devour! He doesn't need God's permission. He already has it. Believers, are the audience to whom *Shaul* was writing pertaining to spiritual war. Satan demanded to sift *Kefa*/Peter; he had the legal right to do so and *Yeshua* told *Kefa* that he was going to be sifted, and that He/*Yeshua* had prayed for him. Let us be careful to obey our Lord and not to be disobedient less we forfeit happiness, health, and even life in this world. We may also forfeit reward in the life to come.

It is also VERY IMPORTANT to know your authority in Messiah. Satan and the fallen ones have colossal power, but you as a believer if you are walking in obedience, have ultimate authority since every spirit is obligated to obey authority. In sports some players on the field may be bigger, faster, and stronger than the referee, yet the ref has absolute authority since he rules by the rule book! If you are living in disobedience to God, you are living on dangerous turf, and you will reap what you sow -more than you sow!

6.   **How we spend our time** (Psalm 90:9-12; Ephesians 5:16; Colossians 4:5; 1 Peter 1:17). Seize the day! Seize the planning of the day for your day will go according to how you plan or don't plan. Our mistake is not only failing to seize the day, but foremost failing to plan the day (the night before) and then working the plan to win! The majority of believers live the day as it comes, "playing it by ear," or "off the cuff." Beloved, we will give an account for idle words and idle time.

7.   **How we run the race God has given us** (1 Corinthians 9:24; Philemon 2:16; 3:13-14; Hebrews 12:1). The author of the scroll of Hebrews gives the metaphoric illustration that the Christian life is like a game of life. The Apostle *Shaul* likens the Christian or Messianic life to a race that everyone runs, and that we should run the race with not only the intent to finish, but with the intent to win! To win often times means we have to endure. There are winners and there are crowns. For such rewards runners go into serious training. Again, the race is according to rules, and there are rules for the runners who compete, rules for those officiating the race, rules for those watching the race, and even rules that govern winning. We are already in the race, and we are accountable for the race, and we are expected to win. So, run to win, as Dr. Erwin Lutzer, the pastor of Moody Church in Chicago, encourages us to do!

8.   **How effectively we control our fleshly appetites** (1 Corinthians 9:25-27). In Messiah we have the same appetites as when we were unregenerate, although we are told not to satisfy the old man by living in the flesh. We are to pursue our new appetites and fulfill them so that we may grow spiritually and become like Messiah. You may recall the occasion when *Yeshua* told His *talmidim*, "I have food you know not of." One of the biblical sins we seldom hear preached or taught is obesity. Obesity is a result of gluttony. How sad that so

many Christian pastors, teachers, deacons, elders, evangelists, musicians, singers, and leaders of Christian organizations and churches are obese, some grossly so. To be obese means one is undisciplined, and often such men and women are the ones a congregation looks to for leadership and guidance in their Messianic faith and walk. We are accountable for the Temple in which we live. We are accountable for letting the appetites of the flesh swell to absorb our attention, uglyfy the body we were given that belongs to God, and the result is often mega health issues.

9. **How many people we influence by our witness and win to Messiah** (Proverbs 11:30; Daniel 12:3; 1 Thessalonian 2:19-20). One of the reasons we are left in this evil godless world after being regenerated is to do the works of God and to influence lost souls. Our Lord wants us to be "in the world, but not of the world" (1 John 2:15-17). We are salt to flavor the world. We are light to enlighten those who sit in darkness. We are the aroma of Messiah to draw attention to Him. We are, each one of us, "living epistles" so that the lost may see and read Messiah in us and be saved. Our Lord gave *Yekhek'el* (Ezekiel) a simple command concerning a graveyard of dry bones. He was to speak to the bones, and it was because of his obedience that the bones moved, rattled, and came together. We do our part, God does His, and souls of men are saved!

10. **How much the doctrine of the *Rapture* means** to us (2 Timothy 4:8). The *crown of righteousness* is reserved or *laid up* (NASV) for believers. The righteous Judge, *Yeshua* will award believers this crown for loving His return. This does not mean that believers have to be constantly anticipating the appearance of our Lord every second of every minute of every hour around the clock, 24/7. It does means that we live around the clock, 24/7 in obedience and in anticipation of His return -as our bridegroom, as our King! There are many believers who

have an unsaved spouse, child, parent, sibling, or friend, and they are hoping for an additional 24-hour day so that their loved one might be saved. Believers should be living for and anticipating the coming of our Lord with the excitement that a bride has as she waits and longs for her groom's appearance, for he is coming perhaps in the night to steal her away and change her life forever. If you do not have a concept or perception of your Lord as a groom, you might ask God to give you a new and salvific imagination of *Yeshua*!

11. **How faithful we are to God's Word and to God's people** (Acts 20:26-28; 2 Timothy 4:1-2; Hebrews 13:17; James 3:1; 1 Peter 5:1,2; John 1:7,8). Faith is a gift from God Himself and every believer has been given a measure of faith, for it is by faith that we are saved. Faith comes by hearing, and hearing by the Word of God. Therefore, spending time with the Father in His Word is of colossal importance for this is what gives faith and grows faith. Faithfulness is a sign of spiritual maturity. *Yeshua* asked the question, "when I return, will I find faith?" God is His Word! God's Word was with God in the beginning, and God's Word became flesh and tabernacled among us (John 1:1). God's Word is *Yeshua*! Also, God's people are God! *Yeshua* said, "as you have done to the very least of these My brothers (that is, to believers), you have done to Me!" We as believers of Messiah are His body. He indwells us. Therefore, how I treat you as a brother or sister, is recognized as how I have treated *Yeshua*. How faithful are you to God's Word? How faithful are you to God's people? Is there someone you need to visit (face-to-face, phone, internet) and forgive, or ask for forgiveness? Do it!

12. **How hospitable we are to strangers** (Matthew 25:35-36; Luke 14:12-14). We need to remember that the Church, those who are saved (not members on a roll of a local institution) are the body of *Yeshua*. How we treat a brother or sister is regarded as our treatment of *Yeshua*.

Mattityahu records the words of *Yeshua* saying, He was hungry…He was thirsty…He was a stranger…He was naked…He was sick…He was in prison…, and the reply will be, when were You hungry…thirsty…a stranger…naked…sick…in prison…when did we see You in these conditions?" The answer given is that when the very least, the weakest, the lowest of believers are in these perils, *Yeshua* is in these perils, for He indwells His people and we are His body!

The other principle given in *Lukas*, is the principle of being hospitable to the poor, crippled, lame, and blind, those whom are least lovely and who are least invited to festive banquets. Being handicapped often means they will require more attention, more care, and often the handicapped may appear to be less lovely. To attend to people like that requires a special heart, *Yeshua's* heart.

13. **How faithful we are to our vocation** (Colossians 3:22-24). *Shaul* exhorts the believer to work his vocation -whatever he does- with his whole heart as though his employer or superior is the Lord, *Yeshua*. The believer should do this, since *Yeshua* is our Lord and as Lord, He has given us our vocations. The reward for faithfulness in our vocation will be from our Lord. In everything we do, we serve *Yeshua!*

14. **How we use our tongue** (Matthew 12:36; James 3:1-12). *Mattityahu* records *Yeshua's* warning, that every careless word spoken will be accounted for in the judgment. *Yeshua* said, "by your words you will be justified, and by your words you will be condemned." In context, *Yeshua* was talking to the "brood of vipers," those lost Pharisees in the religious sect of Judaism. Believers of Messiah have passed from death unto life and we are without condemnation, "there is therefore now no condemnation to those in Christ Jesus" (Romans 8:1). Yet, our words reveal our character. We want to appear before our Lord *Yeshua* with pure character!

The Holyland Model of the Temple in Jerusalem

Question 15

If Yeshua is Our Savior, Who is the Judge at the Judgment Seat?

Answer

The Judge at the *Bema* Judgement will be Yeshua. In the Apocalypse of *Yeshua* (Revelation) the apostle *Yochanon* gives us a peek into the throne room where each one of the redeemed will one day stand. In the book of Revelation, Chapter 4, following his description of and messages to the seven churches *Yochanon* was "caught up" to heaven by a trumpet. He was told that he would be shown what must take place "hereafter," that is, in the prophetic future. He was given privy to gaze into God's tomorrows. *Yochanon* was "in the spirit," no longer in the flesh, and he beheld a throne "standing" in heaven, and his attention was drawn to the one sitting upon the throne which was upon the *Bema*. There was a heavenly halo, a glory about the throne that *Yochanon* described, and around the throne on the *Bema* were twenty-four thrones for the *twenty-four elders*. *Yochanon* described those seated with white garments and golden crowns and out from the throne came flashes of lightning and sounds of thunder. There were seven Spirits of God, a sea of glass, and four living creatures crying,

"Kadosh, Kadosh, Kadosh, YHWH Elohim, Shaddai, Hu Hayah, Hu Hoveh, Hu Yehyeh" (Revelation 4:8).

The English translation is, *"Holy, Holy, Holy [is] YHWH God, the Almighty, Who was, Who is, and Who is to come.* The living creatures gave glory to God on the throne. Then the twenty-four elders fell down to worship God. They cast their crowns before Him, and proclaimed His worth! Saints at the *Bema* judgment will have crowns, and we will lay them at His feet (see Questions 13; 14). Perhaps the *twenty-four elders* in *Yochanon's* vision represent the redeemed saints? *Yochanon* wept, but he wept because no one was found worthy to open the special book sealed with seven seals. It was then that the Lion of Judah stepped forward and took the book and opened its seals, and then two special songs were sung. It is thought that *Yochanon's* rapture and his appearance in the throne room is symbolic of the rapture of Messiah's Church and our appearance before God at the *Bema* judgment (Revelation 5:1-14). In this prophecy *Yeshua* is the one on that throne. He will be the judge (John 5:22,27; Acts 17:31; Revelation 5:6-9; 2 Corinthians 5:10).

"For not even the Father judges anyone, but He has given all judgment to the Son…and He gave Him authority to execute judgment, because He is {the} Son of Man…For we must all appear before the judgment seat of Christ" (John 5:22,27).

"Because He has fixed a day in which He will judge the world in righteousness through a Man whom He has appointed, having furnished proof to all men by raising Him from the dead" (Acts 17:31).

I encourage you dear friend to read for yourself the apocalyptic scroll, *The Revelation*. The *Rapture* or catching away of Christ's Church sounds fictional although the Holy Scriptures tell us it is done "in the Spirit" (Philemon 3:21; 1 Thessalonians 5:23; Luke 24:39).

"…who will transform the body of our humble state into conformity with the body of His glory, by the exertion of the power that He has even to subject all things to Himself."

The Judge of all the earth will be the Lion and Lamb of Judah. *Kiss the Son less He become angry and you perish in the way* (Psalm 2:12).

Question 16

What is the *Marriage Supper of the Lamb?*

Answer

Our salvation by the sacrificial atonement of *Yeshua* and our relationship to *Yeshua* our Lord is likened in the Holy Scriptures as one of marriage (2 Corinthians 11:2; Revelation 19:7,8).

"For I am jealous for you with a godly jealousy; for I have betrothed you to one husband, so that to messiah I might present you as a pure virgin."

"Let us rejoice and be glad and give the glory to Him, for the marriage of the Lamb has come and His bride has made herself ready. And it was given to her to cloth herself in fine linen, bright and clean; for the fine linen is the righteous acts of the saints."

For the Jewish wedding there was the betrothal or pledge which was the engagement that *Yeshua* spoke of and recorded by *Yochanon* (John 3:29), *Shaul* (Romans 7:4; 2 Corinthians 11:2; Ephesians 5:25-33), and *Yochanon* (Revelation 19:7,8; 21:1-22:7). *Yeshua* is the bridegroom (Luke 5:34; John 3:27-29; Romans 7:4) and we, the redeemed NT believers, the Church, are His bride (Ephesians 5:25, 26; Romans 7:4). Our marriage to *Yeshua* will be consummated in heaven (Revelation 19:7-10). The host of the marriage supper is the Father (Matthew 22:2,3).

"The kingdom of heaven may be compared to a king who gave a wedding feast for his son. And he sent out his slaves to call those who had been invited to the wedding feast, and they were unwilling to come."

At the festival called "the marriage supper" we may assume the guests will be the Old Testament saints who were indeed regenerated by faith, although they were under the OT mosaic covenant and are not participants in the "Church" that began on the Day of Pentecost when the New Covenant began as recorded in Acts 2.

The Bible says that the Bride has made herself ready for this special occasion, and she has done so by being born-again and a regenerate co-partner with Him for eternity. There are things we must do after we believe and are saved. My mother, Sue Grice Lisemby wrote the following words to her song entitled, *It's Not Finished for Me.*

"It's not finished for me, this side of eternity. Millions slipping out at each breath that I take. They are going away, to a place without hope, forever to be, oh, it's not finished for me!"

As we have said above, our relationship with *Yeshua* is likened to marriage. Our groom *Yeshua* has paid the dowry, and with His father's permission, He has come and sought out the Bride. He has said, "I do." He has said, "I am not willing that any perish, but I am willing that all come to salvation" (2 Peter 3:9). Our relationship to *Yeshua* can be helped by an understanding the Jewish tradition of marriage.

THE JEWISH WEDDING
(2 Corinthians 11:2; Revelation 19:7,8).

The relationship a believer has to *Yeshua* is likened to the marriage of bride and groom (Romans 7:4).

KIDDUSHIN – The Public Aspect of the Marriage

- Arrangement (parents meet) - John 6:37
- Negotiation (dowry agreed upon) - John 3:16; 14:26
- Betrothal (proposal) - John 14:2,3
- Legal Contract (*Ketubah*) - Romans 7:4
- Waiting and Working - Ephesians 5:25-29; Revelation 2:4

It has been almost two-thousand years since the *Kiddushin*, and at any moment (perhaps, while you are reading this page) the Rapture will occur which will be the bridegroom coming to rapture and take His bride to the bridal chamber for the *Neshin*.

NESHIN – The Private Aspect of the Marriage

- Return of the Groom (from preparing the place) - 1 Thessalonians 4:16
- Elopement (stealing the bride) - 1 Thessalonians 4:17; John 14:2,3
- Bridal Chamber (revealing/disclosure) - Revelation 19:7,8
- Consummation (two will become one) - 1 Corinthians 3:14; 9:25; 1 Peter 5:4
- Marriage Feast (celebration by VIPs) - Revelation 19:6,7
- Presentation (disclosure to private VIPs) - Revelation 21:9

The marriage ceremony takes place in heaven following the *Bema* judgment and the bride will be dressed in white linen (Revelation 19:6-8) which represents our works. All wood, hay, and stubble has been burned away. The Bride of *Yeshua*, the Church, is in heaven and will later return with *Yeshua* at His Second Coming so that He may display her before the entire world. She will rule alongside the King for His millennial kingdom on the earth.

SUKKOT – The Purpose of Marriage

God is preparing us for eternal Kingdom living.

- The Purpose of Marriage
  Physical = to satisfy a physical need; for intimacy
  Soulish = to be and to gain a helpmate; to build up
  Spiritual = to populate the kingdom
  Theological = to display our relationship to Messiah
  Biblical = to demonstrate qualifiers for the kingdom

- Those Qualified for Ruling the Kingdom (1 Timothy 3:1-12; Titus 5:1-9).

- Those Not Qualified to Rule the Kingdom (1 Corinthians 6:9-11; Romans 1).

The Reward. All that we are learning and our obedience in this life is carried with us to the judgment seat for rewards. Our reward will be our office or position in the kingdom. Perhaps after the Bride (the Church) returns to the earth with *Yeshua* for His Kingdom rule, the Marriage Feast takes place. Placement of the Marriage Supper is difficult.

PREPARING FOR MARRIAGE

1. PRAY FOR YOUR PARTNER What if you are already married and your spouse is unfaithful? You have two options. See 1 Corinthians 7:11.

2. PREPARE YOURSELF FOR YOUR PARTNER AND YOUR CHILDREN Make a list of what you would like in a spouse! Then, you be that list. We are free to ask; we are free to choose, but the choice is forever in this life (Romans 7:2). If a spouse divorces for any reason other than sexual immorality and then remarries, he/she commits adultery (Matthew 19:9). If a spouse departs you are not enslaved to make it work out (Matthew 5:32; 1 Corinthians 7:15), although you are not free to remarry unless the spouse dies (1 Corinthians 7:39). You are to labor for reconciliation. If anyone marries one that is divorced, or if anyone divorced remarries someone else, he/she commits adultery (Matthew 5:32; Luke 16:18). The *talmidim* (disciples) thought this was harsh and questioned *Yeshua* about such a restriction (Matthew 19). *Yeshua* warned them of the severity of adultery and fornication.

3. PROCEED AHEAD but, do not seek marriage (1 Corinthians 7:27). Let God put you, dear sister, in "Boaz's field;" or let God put you, dear brother, at the providential place of meeting Ruth.

4. PURSUE LOVE (1 Corinthians 13:3-7).

Reggie & Crystal at Ein Gedi, Israel where *Shir HaShirim* or "The Song of Songs" was written by Sh'lomo.

Reggie Lisemby at Ein-Gedi, an oasis in the Judean Desert. Here David hid from Saul, the *Song of Songs* love story was written, *Jehoshaphat* sang, *Ho Du LaAdonai KiTov*, "Give thanks unto the Lord for He is good" when surrounded and outnumbered by pagan enemies, and the sweetest wine for the Temple rituals in Jerusalem, came from the orchards grown at this oasis in the desert.

Question 17

What is the *Seven-Sealed Scroll* for the Lamb-Lion in Revelation 5:1-14?

Answer

Yochanon described his being in the throne-room of the Lord in the *Apocalypse* called Revelation. In the right hand of Him seated on the throne was a *Seven-Sealed Scroll* that was brought forth. He was evidently intrigued that the scroll was in the right hand, the position of acceptance, admission, and strength. To be on His right, is to be for Him and with Him, and to be on His left, is to depart from His presence.

Yochanon then noted that the scroll was written on both sides, within and without, meaning it was full and important. It was sealed not with one but with seven seals. The hidden mysteries and/or counsels of Elohim are securely locked and hidden until time for disclosure, and only to be disclosed by One from Elohim.

In concert with the accolades, holy voices, sounds, lightning, thunder, angels, archangels, four living creatures, and twenty-four elders, a "strong angel" is identified by *Yochanon* as the one making a proclamation with a loud question, so, loud *Yochanon* took notice and scribed that he was "loud!" The question put to the attendees was this, "*Who is worthy to open the scroll, to break its seals?*" There was deafening silence! Everyone was anticipating, but no one could answer. There was no one present worthy to open that scroll! *Yochanon* wails! *Yochanon* is wailing in the Temple in heaven, the prototype of the earthly Tabernacle given *Moshe* and the Temple given *Sh'lomo*. *Yochanon* was wailing because he was in the presence of holy beings God had created in the beginning, and *Yochanon* was in the most holy place of all creation and yet there is no one in the room qualified to unlock the scroll. No one is qualified to unseal the seven seals and look within to read and/or understand its contents. That scroll is a highly important book! In fact, that scroll's value supersedes the value of every being in that room! Who is worthy enough only to unlock it?

A loud voice exclaims, *"Do not wail. Hinei* (Behold) *HaAryeh* (the Lion) *MaHaShevet Yehudah* (from the Tribe of Judah), *HaShoresh Dovid* (the Root of David) has won the *Nitzachon* (victory) and He is able to open *haSefer* (the scroll) and its *Sheva Chotamot* (seven seals).

What is paramount in that room? Two things! The book and the one worthy to open the book (Revelation 5:1-5). The Lion appears! The Lion of *Yehudah* has been "on the move" from Genesis 49 where *Yaaqov* (Jacob) predicted his fourth-born son, *Yehudah* (Judah) likened as a Lion to be the preeminent tribe among his dozen sons. The Lion moved through the *Torah*, through the *Neviim* or the prophets, through the *Ketuvim* or the writings, through the gospels, the epistles, and to the latter end of time in the Holy Scriptures. *The Lion from the Tribe of Judah* now comes forth as the only "overcomer," the only one who has prevailed and Who is worthy among all the beings in heaven and earth and below the earth, to open the hallmarked scroll.

In the vision given to *Yochanon* the Lion is mirrored by the Lamb. The Lion of *Yehudah* is also the Lamb of *Pesach* or Passover. Yet, the Lion is not tame, and the Lamb is not halcyon.

The Song of the Lamb is sung by the twenty-four elders whom many believe to be representatives of all the redeemed. However, since these existed among all the other beings *Yochanon* saw when he was caught up or raptured to the throne-room in heaven, and because elders existed in heaven as the prototype of the elders in Israel in the Tanakh or Old Testament, these are spiritual beings like the angels, archangels, cherubim, seraphim, etc. and they are 24 in number.

"And they sang a new song, saying, "Worthy are You to take the book and to break its seals; for You were slain, and purchased for God with Your blood

{men} from every tribe and tongue and people and nation. You have made them {to be} a kingdom and priests to our God; and they will reign upon the earth" (Revelation 5:9).

The angelic beings who are myriads of myriads and thousands of thousands in number, make a proclamation to the one seated on the throne. The picture is one of worship, worship, worship, and forever and forever!

"saying with a loud voice, "Worthy is the Lamb that was slain to receive power and riches and wisdom and might and honor and glory and blessing. And every created thing which is in heaven and on the earth and under the earth and on the sea, and all things in them, I heard saying, "To Him who sits on the throne, and to the Lamb, {be} blessing and honor and glory and dominion forever and ever. And the four living creatures kept saying, "Amen." And the elders fell down and worshiped" (Revelation 5:12).

Yochanon had initially wept over the absence of one worthy to open the scroll. However, out from that book are unleashed seven seals, seven bowls, seven trumpets, and three woes, all to do with the *Great Tribulation* which will be the most horrific, terrorizing, fearful destruction of mankind since creation. Having read the book and knowing what we know, we might would say to *Yochanon* if we could go back and speak to him, "don't open that book! For out of that book comes hell!"

What comes from the seven-sealed scroll is the wrath and judgment of God! To know the effects of the seals, bowls, trumpets, and woes one must read the Apocalypse of *Yeshua*, the book of Revelation. By-the-by, the Apocalypse of *Yeshua* is the only book in the entire compilation of Holy Scripture that says it is *Yeshua's* revelation (Revelation 1:1), it is endorsed by *Yeshua* (Revelation 21:16), anyone who reads, hears, and obeys its contents will be blessed (Revelation 1:3), and that it is prophecy (Revelation 1:3).

Cave 4 at Qumran where many of the Dead Sea Scrolls were found. Some of the scrolls were apocalyptic scrolls, similar to the New Testament Apocalypse, revelation of the sons of light and the sons of darkness. The Apocalypse or Revelation is the only book in the Bible said to be *Yeshua's* book (Rev.1:1), promising a blessing to the one who reads, hears, and obeys (Rev.1:3), and endorsed by *Yeshua* (Rev.22:16).

Question 18

Why would Jesus be returning twice, in the *Rapture* and at the Second Coming?

Answer

The Holy Scriptures speak of three visitations of *Yeshua* to our world not including His pre-incarnate appearances called *Christophanies* or *Theophanies* seen in the Tanakh or Old Testament. His first coming was His incarnation. *Yeshua*, the Messiah of Israel was forecast to come from the beginning, and in Genesis 3:15 which is the mother prophecy of His coming, He was foretold to be the coming champion of man. It was necessary for Him to be born of woman in order to redeem humanity. At the *Rapture*, *Yeshua* is coming in the air (1 Thessalonians 4:16,17) and believers will be "caught up" to Him [in the air]. At His Second Coming, *Yeshua* is coming to the earth to set up His millennial kingdom and reign sitting on David's Throne as King. He will rule for a period of one-thousand years (Zechariah 14:4; Revelation 19:11; Acts 1:11).

At *Yeshua*'s first coming, the swaddling cloth in which Messiah *Yeshua* was wrapped at birth was both a sign of the poverty of his genealogical descent, that is, poor parents from the tribe of *Yehudah*, and also a sign unto the shepherds that He was born to die since swaddling cloth was wide strips of mummy cloth for wrapping bodies for burial. In the *Rapture*, *Yeshua* will return for His church in the same *shekinah* or *kavod* that His *talmidim* saw Him ascend (Acts 1:8).

"They also said, "Men of Galilee, why do you stand looking into the sky? This Jesus, who has been taken up from you into heaven, will come in just the same way as you have watched Him go into heaven."

However, at His Second Coming His attire is *apocalyptic*; He wears a robe dipped in blood (Revelation 19:13).

"He is clothed with a robe dipped in blood, and His name is called The Word of God. He is clothed in a robe dipped in blood, and the name by which he is called is The Word of God."

When *Yeshua* came at His first incarnation, there were many who recognized Him, even when *Yeshua* was an infant. The shepherds in the field were told of His birth, and eventually the *magi* came although they were expecting a king on the throne. They recognized Him as did *Sh'meon* when *Yeshua* was only eight days old. *Anna* from the tribe of *Asher* also recognized *Yeshua* as a wee babe. Many others who were studious of messianic prophecy recognized Him at His incarnation or first coming. However, when *Yeshua* returns in the air to *rapture* or seize His church, He is coming as a bridegroom to steal His bride and to take us away to the bridal chamber. No one will see or know it until it is past (John 14:3; 1 Thessalonians 4:17; 2 Thessalonians 2:1). At His Second Coming, *Yeshua* is returning with us, His Church by His side (1 Thessalonians 3:13; Jude 14; Revelation 19:6-14), and we are returning with Him to take care of business, and then to rule for the one-thousand-year millennial kingdom (Revelation 20).

The title given to the Messiah by the angel *Gavriel* to *Miriam* at His first coming was *Immanuel,* a word formed from two Hebrew words, *El* meaning "God" (singular) and *immanu* meaning "with us" (Matthew 1:23). *Yeshua* was and is "God with us!" At his *Brit Melah* or circumcision *Yoseph* and *Miriam* spoke His name, *Yeshua* meaning "YHWH has come to save." *YHWH Elohim* came to save His people from their sins, and *Yeshua* is His name when He returns at the rapture (1 Thessalonians 4:14, 16). However, when the Lord returns at His

Second Coming, the Holy Scriptures say that He will have a name *"no one knows…"* (Revelation 19:12), and in verse 13, the passage reads, *"His name is called the Word of God"* (Revelation 19:13).

At His first coming, His incarnation, it was only those who had been enlightened by the Holy Spirit and believed, that saw *Yeshua* for Who He was. When *Yeshua* returns in the *Rapture, Shaul* or Paul writes to the Thessalonians that only believers will see Him descend and they will disappear unto Him as He claims them. The world will not see or know, except they will soon discover that Christians worldwide are missing. At His Second Coming, every eye will see Him (Revelation 1:7). When *Yeshua* came His first time, He came in peace. The *Messiahmas* story reads, "peace and good will toward men" (Luke 2:14), and saints were delivered from darkness. When our Lord returns to *rapture* His bride from this dark world, He comes with comfort and as a bridegroom, and His coming is to remove saints before His coming wrath (1 Thessalonians 1:5-9). In fact, His *Rapture* is an event that is comforting for the saved, according to *Shaul* in 1 Thessalonians 4. However, at His Second Coming, *Yeshua* is coming in wrath (Revelation 19:15; Jude 15) and the unsaved will experience His fury (Revelation 6:12-17).

Finally, the three appearances of *Yeshua* are contrasted by His attention. At His first appearing His attention was Israel. He told His *talmidim "go only to the house of Israel"* for they were the children to whom the dinner belonged; the others were likened to pet dogs (Matthew 15:26). When our Lord returns in the *Rapture*, His attention is His bride, the Church, the saved, redeemed, and regenerate Jews and Gentiles. At His Second Coming His attention will be His millennial kingdom.

Someone once said, the Holy Scriptures are about three things, He is coming, He came, and He is coming again! Here are biblical texts for study concerning both the Rapture and the Second Coming.

RAPTURE: John 14:1-3; Romans 8:19; 1 Corinthians 1:7,8; 15:51-53; 16:22; Philippians 3:20,21; Colossians 3:4; 1 Thessalonians 1:10; 2:19; 4:13-18; 5:9; 5:23; 2 Thessalonians 2:1; 1 Timothy 6:14; 2 Timothy 4:1; Titus 2:13;

Hebrews 9:28; James 5:7-9; 1 Peter 1:7,13; 1 John 2:28-3:2; Jude 21; Revelation 2:25; 3:10.

SECOND COMING: Daniel 2:44,45; 7:9-14; 12:1-3; Zechariah 14:1-15; Matthew 13:41; 24:15-31; Mark 13:14-27; 14:62; Luke 21:25-28; Acts 1:9-11; 3:19-21; 1 Thessalonians 3:13; 2 Thessalonians 1:6-10; 2:8; 2 Peter 3:1-14; Jude 14,15; Revelation 1:7; 19:11-20:6; 22:7,12,20.

CONTRASTS OF THE LORD'S COMINGS

FIRST COMING	RAPTURE	SECOND COMING
Descent out of heaven TO THE WOMB (Matthew 1:20)	Descends out of heaven IN THE AIR (1 Thess.4:16-17)	Descends out of heaven TO THE EARTH (Zec.14:4; Rev.19:11; Acts 1:11)
Clothed: SWADDLING CLOTH (Luke 2:12)	Clothed: SHEKINAH (Acts 1:8)	Clothed: HIS ROBE DIPPED in blood (Rev.19:13)
TO His Saints	FOR His Saints (John 14:3;1 Thess.4:17; 2 Thess.2:1)	WITH His Saints (1 Thess.3:13; Jude 14; Rev.19:6-14)
"IMMANUEL" (Mat.1:23)	"Y'SHUA" the Lord Himself (1Thess.4:14,16)	"No one knows His Name, (Rev.19:12); WORD OF GOD (Rev.19:13)
EYES of Believers expected Him	EYES of Believers expect and will embrace Him (1Ths.4:13-18)	EVERY EYE shall see Him (Rev.1:7)
Announcement: PEACE *"On earth peace among Men"* Luke 2:14	Announcement: TRUMPET *"come up!"* (John 14; 1 Thes 4:13-18; Rev.4:1)	Announcement: JUDGES and wages war (Rev.19:11; Jude 15)
"MY EYES have seen my Salvation:" SAVIOR (Luke 2:20)	OUR eyes on Christ Revealed BRIDEGROOM (Col.3:4)	HIS EYES as Fire: JUDGE (Rev.19:12); THEIR Eyes shall look upon Him pierced
From His Mouth salvation Good News; liberty to captives; healing	From His Mouth a shout (1Thes.4:16)	From His Mouth a sword to smite the nations (Rev.19:15)
He comes in PEACE (Luke 2:14)	He Comes with COMFORT (1Thes.4:18)	He Comes in WRATH (Rev.19:15; Jude 15)
Saints delivered from Darkness	Saved delivered from Wrath (1Thes.1:10, 5-9)	Unsaved to experience Wrath (Rev.6:12-17)
SIGNS to precede	NO SIGNS preceding (1Thes.5:1-3)	SIGNS to precede (Luke 21:11,15)
Focus on ISRAEL	Focus on His CHURCH (1 Thes.4:13-18)	Focus on the KINGDOM (Mat.24:14)
ISRAEL is judged	CHURCH is judged (Bema)	WORLD is judged (White Throne)

Question 19

What is *The Great Tribulation* mentioned in Matthew 24?

Answer

Following the disappearance of the "holy ones," the saints of God, the Church in the *Rapture*, the world will face the most horrendous time of upheaval, distress, tribulation, hysteria, and terror that man has ever experienced! This colossal panic will come upon the entire world, although it is designed against Israel. In fact, one of its many titles is *Yaaqov's* [Jacob's] *Trouble*.

Jacob's Trouble (Jeremiah 30:7)

"Alas! for that day is great, There is none like it; And it is the time of Jacob's distress, But he will be saved from it."

Yeremiyahu (Jeremiah) received the Word of YHWH to write in a book, the book we have that bears his name. YHWH promised to restore the fortune of both *Ysrael* and *Yudah*, the two confederacies. Israel in the north and Judah in the south will one day return as one people to the one land that God gave their forefathers. Together, this one nation shall possess His holy land. We may suggest that this has already begun. In 1948 the Jewish people began returning to the land of Israel although no Jewish person can legitimately document his or her tribal identity. Many make their claim to be of the Levitical tribe because their name is *Levi, Levitt, Leventhal,* or *Cohen,* etc. Yet, their proof is their word or the word of a parent. There are no records or legal documents from antiquity to the present proving tribal identity or the historical genealogy of any Jew, that is, with the exception of the Jewish Messiah, *Yeshua* from the tribe of *Yehudah! Yeshua*'s genealogy is given in the Jewish Gospel of *Mattityahu* and the Gospel of the Good Physician, *Lukas*. No records exist that extend back to the first, second, or third Temple periods to document proof of Jewishness. All records were destroyed when Rome destroyed the Holy City, *Yerushalayim* and the Temple. No Jew today has legal documentation for representation for tribal identity and inheritance.

There is also no scientific measurement in genetics that can prove relation to the twelve tribes of *Yaaqov*, since DNA requires a sample of the prototype tracer to an ancient tribal ancestor. None exists. DNA may prove that Jews are kin, Jews are very close kin, or that Jews are family or tribal. Yet, there is no authentic link to biblical tribal identity since there is no primitive DNA of a biblical ancestor.

The Jewish people today cannot prove their link to either of the two confederacies, *Ysrael* or *Yudah*. The northern and southern confederations split near 990 BC. Ten tribes in the north retained the name, *Ysrael*, while the two tribes of *Yehudah* and *BenYamin* took the name of *Yehudah* since this tribe was the largest tribe. Israel was the northern confederacy and Judah was the southern confederacy. Links to either of the two remain in obscurity as far as tribal identity, although collectively the Jews are returning to the land of Israel nationally as one stick. *Jew*, is an English translation of the Hebrew term, *Yehudi*. The *Yehudim* were and are descendants from the tribe *Yehudah*. However, are all Jews today from the tribe of *Yehudah*? Are there none from the other eleven tribes?

The prophesy of Jeremiah declares that there will be a time when *Yaaqov* (who in Jeremiah's day had long been dead) would hear the sound of terror and the sound of dread at a time when there will be no peace. A visual is given of every man being pale-faced, holding his lower stomach or groin as though he is pregnant and about to give birth like a woman. This day is horrific! There has not and there never will be another day like it. This is *Jacob's distress* or *Yaakov's trouble!* In Hebrew this day is *gadol haYom* or the great day of *ayt-TzaRah l' Yaaqov,* "time of distress to Jacob."

This tribulation eventually comes upon the entire world, but it is specifically designed for the nation of *Yaaqov,* the children of Jacob, the nation of Israel. Their trouble is likened to a woman in travail, although a pregnant woman delivering eventually has relief when the baby comes forth. This travail has no relief; things only get worse!

It is important to note that, *"Yaaqov, My servant"* will be saved! True remnant Israel will be quieted, given ease, and will be set free from fear. YHWH says, *"I am with you to save you!"* However, this will be after much travail, anguish, and distress, wounds that are incurable, injury that is serious, sores that cannot be healed, iniquity that is great, and sins that are numerous. Non-remnant Israel will be punished, pained, devoured, captured, plundered, and given as a prey. The prophet *ZecharYah* prophecies that two-thirds of those living in the land of *Israel* will perish, and only one-third will be saved. In context those who were his audience were Jews living in the land. Again, it is remnant Israel who will be rescued! YHWH will save *Yaaqov* (Jeremiah 30). *ZecharYah* confirms this.

"and I will bring the third part through the fire, refine them as silver is refined, and test them as gold is tested. They will call on My name, and I will answer them; I will say, They are my people and they will say, YHWH is my God" (Zechariah 13:9).

The Day of the LORD (Joel 2:1-3)

"Blow a trumpet in Zion, And sound an alarm on My holy mountain! Let all the inhabitants of the land tremble, For the day of the LORD is coming; Surely it is near, A day of darkness and gloom, A day of clouds and thick darkness. As the dawn is spread over the mountains, {So} there is a great and mighty people; There has never been {anything} like it, Nor will there

be again after it To the years of many generations. A fire consumes before them And behind them a flame burns. The land is like the garden of Eden before them But a desolate wilderness behind them, And nothing at all escapes them."

Ancient biblical Israel was signaled by a blowing of the *shofar* horn. There were typically three blasts made with the ram's horn, and the blast of the *shofar* mentioned in the passage of *Yoel* is the *teruach* or the long-extended blast, which was the sound of an alarm! The message for Israel in the last days is alarm, although modern Israel is not hearing God's warning from the majority of Christians today. Many Christians are "playing Jewish" by blowing *shofar* horns, wearing prayer shawls, relenting from Sunday the day of the Lord, the day of His resurrection, to keep the sabbath, parading through the holy land celebrating the modern state of Israel as the Chosen People of God (having no understanding what "chosen" means), and many embracing torah-observant Judaism, which is rabbinic Judaism and not biblical Judaism. From these claimants professing to know Yeshua, the Jewish people are not receiving the message of the cross which often is offensive since the Gospel implies a new covenant.

The natural and expected outcome of Old Testament Judaism was and is the Messianic or Christian faith. It was quite natural for Zachariah and Elizabeth, Mary and Joseph, Simeon and Anna, the wise men, Andrew and Peter, and all others who recognized *Yeshua* to have done so. He was and remains the expected summation of the Holy Scriptures; they speak of Him! *Yeshua* came, yet, how odd that Israel as a whole did not recognize their Messiah. As the Prophet *Yeremiyahu* prophesied, the Messiah brought and inaugurated a new covenant, "not like the covenant God made with Israel at Sinai" (Jeremiah 31:31). The New Testament supplanted the Old Mosaic Covenant God had made with Israel at Sinai. The book of Hebrews declares that the old covenant is now obsolete (Hebrews 8:13) since a new and better covenant has been given.

"When He said, "A new covenant," He has made the first obsolete. But whatever is becoming obsolete and growing old is ready to disappear."

The NT scroll of Hebrews also gives serious warning of the spiritual crime of Judaizing, a most serious transgression that causes apostasy. This was the reason that the author of Hebrews (*Shaul, Apollos,* or *Priscilla*) wrote the book. Misappropriating unbelieving Jews and the unbelieving nation of Israel as "chosen people" gives them false hope and security. Israel is certainly "the chosen people," although one had better know what "chosen" means biblically, and who "Israel" is, biblically (e.g. Romans 9). We had better not herald to Jewish people that being Jewish is celebrity with God. *Oy Vey!* The Holy Scriptures declare that only those Jews who recognize *Yeshua* are truly *the chosen people* and truly Jewish and are the remnant. We had better be very careful of celebrating modern Israel since 1948 as a spiritual virtue when only 1% of modern Israel are believers in *Yeshua.* Such teaching is anti-Semitic and borders on heresy; it is not the Gospel, but is a false Gospel! *Yochanon* the immerser and *Yeshua* the Messiah gave unbelieving Israel -who were their audience- absolutely no hope without believing in Him!

Yeshua is the point! *Yeshua* is the rock of offense. He remains an issue for Modern Israel and world Jewry who are on the precipice of another Holocaust if they remain in unbelief and do not turn or repent and believe in *Yeshua.* In fact, an eternal *holocaust* called *Gehenna* (Revelation 21:8) awaits all Jewish and Gentile unbelievers who reject *Yeshua* as they Lord, savior, and atonement for sin.

God told *Yesha'yahu* (Isaiah) *"get high up on a high mountain"* so that all could see him and everyone could hear his message to Israel (Isaiah 40:9). God's alarm was to sound on God's holy mountain of *Tzion* (Ezekiel 20:40). *Tzion* has been His holy mountain since before Adam when Lucifer watched over *Eden* and *Tzion* (Ezekiel 28:11-19). The message of alarm in the land of *Tzion* is for the inhabitants of the land, those dwelling in the land of Israel whom *Yoel* does not call "Israel" but "dwellers." In context, the message for Israel was to "tremble," for the dreaded dark *"Day of the Lord"* that the prophets had warned for millennia, has come upon you! It is a time to fear!

Yoel the prophet stressed that the coming *Yom YHWH* or Day of the LORD is *Yom khoShek*, a day of darkness, *afayLah Yom aNan*, a dark day of clouds, and *araFel k'ShaKhar*, a darkness like dawn. The prophet *Yoel* prophesied that the people living in the land of Israel will be a numerous and mighty people who will consider their real estate as *Gan Eden* before them, perhaps due to their hard work and their success in reviving the land to make it productive. However, it will become a desolate wilderness. This has happened before, of course, and it will happen again.

In Genesis 1:1 *Moshe* described a pristine universe that God had created. However, Genesis 1:2 describes a desolate wilderness, *tohu va vohu*. What happened to the world God made in the beginning described in verse one? In that pristine perfect beginning a sheriff *Cherub* named *Lucifer* decided he should be more than a constable. In his pride and sin, he exalted himself and led other angelic beings in mutiny. The result was the *Luciferian* flood and perhaps the "big bang," and for certain a colossal upheaval of God's original lighted creation. The further result was a chaotic, contorted, confused, and dark world, or, as the Hebrew has it, *tohu va vohu* meaning "without form, distorted, deformed, empty and void." In context, there was "darkness on the face of the [subterranean] deep." Genesis 1:1 describes that which our God created at the beginning. Genesis 1:2 described how the "heavens and earth" came to be something that was terribly wrong, so wrong that in the end God will create new Heavens and a new Earth (Revelation 21:1).

Israel was once exiled from their fruitful promised land because of their sin in God's holy land. They were first exiled to Assyria near 722 BC, and then later Judah the southern confederacy was exiled to Babylon (605; 597; 586 BC). The holy land of Elohim again became something akin to *tohu va vohu;* it became a wilderness, just as God had said! When the Jews returned to the land after seventy years in captivity, they began rebuilding their faith thanks to *Ezra,* and rebuilding the land and its holy city, *Yerushalayim* thanks to *Nechemyah* (Nehemiah) and the remnant.

When Israel was removed from that land again, this time by the Romans in AD 70 the land became *tohu va vohu*, a wilderness. In fact, the land was a desolate land until 1948. Following the Holocaust myriad Jews began to return to the land of Israel to find the land was swamp and desert; a pitiful place! The land was revived by the *chalutzim* or pioneers who had made *aliya* to *eretz* Israel. The deserts were made (and, are being made) fertile and the nation is something near a miracle. However, the *Day of the Lord* (Joel 1:15; 2:11; 2:31; 3:14) will be experienced by the people dwelling in His land because they are without His messiah, *Yeshua*. The present land of Israel once more will become *tohu va vohu*, a desolate wilderness!

The modern state called *Israel* is not the last-days millennial Israel where *Yeshua*, God's King of Kings will be dwelling on the throne. Modern Israel consists of Jewish people the majority of whom are not believers in *Yeshua*, in fact, the majority who do not accept *YHWH Elohim* of the *Tanakh* or the OT and His ways. Therefore, modern Israel will experience this coming horrendous "Day of YHWH," and through horrific darkness, Israel will be brought to their knees, made to look up, and the remnant will recognize *Yeshua* their crucified brother, and will run to Him for salvation!

The Great Tribulation (Matthew 24:21-29)

"For then there will be a great tribulation, such as has not occurred since the beginning of the world until now, nor ever will. Unless those days had been cut short, no life would have been saved; but for the sake of the elect those days will be cut short. Then if anyone says to you, 'Behold, here is the Christ,' or 'There {He is,}' do not believe {him.} For false Christs and false prophets will arise and will show great signs and wonders, so as to mislead, if possible, even the elect. Behold, I have told you in advance. So, if they say to you, 'Behold, He is in the wilderness,' do not go out, {or,} 'Behold, He is in the

inner rooms,' do not believe {them.} For just as the lightning comes from the east and flashes even to the west, so will the coming of the Son of Man be. Wherever the corpse is, there the vultures will gather. But immediately after the tribulation of those days THE SUN WILL BE DARKENED, AND THE MOON WILL NOT GIVE ITS LIGHT, AND THE STARS WILL FALL from the sky, and the powers of the heavens will be shaken."

The terrible "Day of the Lord" has another name, the *Great Tribulation* (Matthew 24:21-29). The "great tribulation" spoken of by *Yeshua* begins with false messiahs leading Israelis into error. In context there will be wars, talks of war, plans for war, international tension, war, and more wars. There will be crises, starvations, deprivations, shortages, famines, earthquakes, false spokesmen for God, anarchies, disorders, mayhem, and lawlessness, and this is not a descending list. All of these things will be happening simultaneously and perhaps with the same intensity. Society will become a love-less society and there will be a defection from truth. Amid all of this, there will be a contemporary repeating of the historical *Abomination of Desolation* committed by *Antiochus Epiphanes IV* near 165 BC of which the prophet *Dani'el* wrote. That historical *madman* entered the Temple of God in *Yerushalayim* and committed a blasphemous sacrifice of swine in the place where prescribed clean and innocent sacrifices were given. Antiochus desecrated the holy place of God.

The Apostle *Shaul*/Paul speaks of the *Abomination of Desolation* in his second writing to the Thessalonians that will occur again.

"one who opposes and exalts himself above every god or object of worship will take his seat in the temple of God displaying himself as God" (2 Thessalonians 2:4).

Shaul remembered the *Abomination of Desolation* spoken by Dani'el and he remembered the words of *Yeshua*, that another messiah-like character is coming in the future. This event is prophetic, and when it happens, the word from *Yeshua* to Israel is, "***run!***" Run for your lives to the mountains (Matthew 24:16). *Yeshua* stated that there would be *"woes"* to the women pregnant with children, and to the women nursing children in that day. He warned that it will be worse if this happens during the winter or on a Sabbath (Matthew 24:15-20). This distress *Yeshua* called *the great tribulation.*

All people have trouble, every person in every age, in every dispensation, under every empire has tribulation. In fact, *Yeshua* told His people, *"in this life you will have tribulation."* Life is full of troubles. However, the "great tribulation" *Yeshua* spoke of in Matthew 24 is a specific and unparalleled distress, because it will be the wrath of God! *Yeshua* quoted from the prophet *Dani'el.*

"Michael the great prince who stands guard over the sons of your people will arise. And there will be a time of distress such as never occurred since there was a nation until that time, and at that time your people, everyone who is found written in the book will be rescued" (Daniel 12:1).

The good news is that out from this *great tribulation,* the remnant of Israel will be delivered, those whose names are written in the Lamb's Book of Life. Again, this has always been true; there has always been and there will always be a remnant. However, this remnant will have had to endure the greatest distress upon the earth and humanity to be saved. The distress of *the great tribulation* will be so horrendous that *"unless the days are shortened no life would be saved, yet for the sake of the elect those days will be shortened"* (Matthew 24:22).

False Messiahs and prophets will continue to rise and speak magnificently, and energized by Satan they will demonstrate unbelievable and awesome miracles to warrant their authority. A great deceit is coming, so colossal that it could almost, if possible, mislead the elect of *Yeshua* (Matthew 24:24).

Indignation (Isaiah 26:20)

"Come, my people, enter into your rooms And close your doors behind you; Hide for a little while Until indignation runs {its} course. For behold, YHWH is about to come out from His place to punish the inhabitants of the earth for their iniquity; and the earth will reveal her bloodshed, and will no longer cover her slain."

The prophet *Yesha'yahu* (Isaiah) invites the people of Israel to enter their houses, close their doors, and hide! *YHWHshua* is coming out from His place to punish the inhabitants of the earth for their iniquity. Remember that *Dani'el* had warned of this time of terror and judgment coming upon Israel. This period of time is called *Yaaqov's Trouble* which we spoke of above. All the earth will reap the whirlwind, although it comes to the Jews, first. The visual is given to us of the "earth uncovering her dead of bloodshed" which is reminiscent of the slaying of *Avel* by his brother *Cayin*, and *Avel's* blood that cried from the earth for judgment.

In Hebrew the "day of judgment" is personified as YHWH coming full of fury! Isaiah 34:2 says that YHWH's indignation will be against every nation on the globe, "all nations," and His wrath will be against all the armies of every nation. YHWH will utterly destroy the world leaving a world-wide slaughter, and the corpses of those slaughtered will lie in the open sun and rot until the corpses give off their stench. The mountains will be drenched with blood, and only then, will the host of heaven appear as the sky is rolled up like a scroll. YHWH's wrath and indignation are shown as a lion roused from His den! *Yeshua* is no purring pussy cat. *Yeshua* is the roaring Lion of Judah, and He is not tame. He is coming to devour. He is the king of the beasts! Who dares rouse Him up?

The Day of God's Vengeance (Isaiah 63:1-6)

"For the LORD has a day of vengeance, A year of recompense for the cause of Zion (Isaiah 34:8) Who is this who comes from Edom, With garments of glowing colors from Bozrah, This One who is majestic in His apparel, Marching in the greatness of His strength? It is I who speak in righteousness, mighty to save." Why is Your apparel red, And Your garments like the one who treads in the wine press? I have trodden the wine trough alone, And from the peoples there was no man with Me. I also trod them in My anger And trampled them in My wrath; And their lifeblood is sprinkled on My garments, And I stained all My raiment. For the day of vengeance was in My heart, And My year of redemption has come. I looked, and there was no one to help, And I was astonished and there was no one to uphold; So, My own arm brought salvation to Me, And My wrath upheld Me. I trod down the peoples in My anger And made them drunk in My wrath, And I poured out their lifeblood on the earth."

The coming *Great Tribulation* has another name, a *day of vengeance, a year of recompense for the cause of Zion.* Beyond all the glorious titles and appellations of the Lord, He has also revealed Himself as a warrior!

"The Lord is a Warrior; the Lord is His name" (Exodus 15:3).

When the ark of Israel was taken up and Israel began their march, Israel would say, *rise up, O YHWH! May your enemies be scattered; may your foes flee before you* (Numbers 10:35,36). YHWH was the commander of that army, and He appeared with sword in hand to *Yehoshua* (Joshua 5:13-15). When *Yehoshua* asked the warrior are you for us or for them, the warrior answered, "no!" Wrong question! God takes no sides, not Israel's side, and not the nations side. The question is, "who is on the Lord's side?" That was precisely the character of *Yeshua's* preaching. The remnant of Israel joined *Yeshua;* the non-remnant rejected Him -

unto this day! The non-remnant is never for the Lord. They perish, the Jews first, and then, the Gentiles.

NT *eschatology* speaks of God returning with the saints to execute war on the unbelieving. *Yeshua* is riding a white horse, a sword in His hand, fire in His eyes, and He has come to slay the wicked (Revelation 19:11-21). This is the terrible *day of the Lord*, the *great tribulation*, the *indignation*, and *the day of His vengeance!*

Holy War is indeed *Elohim's* concept, not Mohammed's, not Islam's. The Lord God initiated holy war in Genesis (3:15), and He intends to initiate holy war in the future against Islam, Judaism, Christianity, Buddhism, Hinduism, against all religions and wicked people who have rejected His son, *Yeshua* as personal redeemer, and King.

In the Isaiah passage the following questions are asked: *Who is this coming and with garments in glowing colors? Who is this in red, and garments stained with wine?* The answer is given. The one coming is "majestic," "great," "strong," "righteous," and "mighty to save." *YHWHshua* is treading the wine trough, trampling man in His anger and wrath, with their blood splashing upon His garments likened to a Jewish man stomping grapes and his garments stained from the juices.

Can this be the gentle Lamb of God, the Lord and savior, the mild and meek lowly child in the manger? Yes, but He is only gentle, the Lord, the savior, the mild and meek lowly loving shepherd to His own sheep, to His children. He is loving and romantic only to His bride, His congregation. To those outside He is a warlord!

The Seventieth Week of Daniel (Daniel 9:24-27)

"Seventy weeks have been decreed for your people and your holy city, to finish the transgression, to make an end of sin, to make atonement for iniquity, to bring in everlasting righteousness, to seal up vision and prophecy and to anoint the most holy {place.} "So, you are to know and discern {that} from the issuing of a decree to restore and rebuild Jerusalem until Messiah the Prince

{there will be} seven weeks and sixty-two weeks; it will be built again, with plaza and moat, even in times of distress. Then after the sixty-two weeks the Messiah will be cut off and have nothing, and the people of the prince who is to come will destroy the city and the sanctuary. And its end {will come} with a flood; even to the end there will be war; desolations are determined. And he will make a firm covenant with the many for one week, but in the middle of the week he will put a stop to sacrifice and grain offering; and on the wing of abominations {will come} one who makes desolate, even until a complete destruction, one that is decreed, is poured out on the one who makes desolate."

In Babylonian captivity the prophet *Dani'el* was given a prophecy concerning seventy *shavout* or seventy "sevens." Hebrew, Greek, and English translators have chosen to translate the term *shavout* as "weeks" since a week is a unit of seven; this helps make sense of the text though Sunday to Saturday is not the literal meaning. No student of *Dani'el* considers the "seventy weeks" to be literally seventy weeks of seven days or 490 days. All that was written by *Dani'el* did not unfold and happen in 16 months. Were the seventy-sevens that were decreed upon the people of Israel and the holy city, *Yerushalayim*, seventy-sevens of days (490 days), seventy-sevens of weeks (490 weeks), or seventy-sevens of years (490 years)?

According to the text, the seventy-*shavuot* of days, weeks, or years will accomplish the following:

- To finish transgression
- To make an end of sins
- To make atonement for iniquity
- To bring in everlasting righteousness
- To seal up vision and prophecy
- To anoint the most holy

Israel was to discern the time frame in accordance to the prophecy given to them by the prophet, *Dani'el*. From the issuing of the decree to restore and rebuild *Yerushalayim* (which came by King Artaxerxes in 445 BC) until *Messiah the Prince* (*Yeshua*) would be seven-sevens or forty-nine years. *Dani'el* wrote that an additional sixty-two sevens would also occur; this is an additional 434 years. Together, 49 and 434 equals 483 years. Altogether, *Dani'el's* prophecy of seventy-sevens equals 490 years! One unit of seven is left (490 minus 483 equals 7). Bible scholars interpret the seventy-sevens as 490 years. Thus, there are seven years remaining to accomplish and fulfill that which *Dani'el* wrote.

The prophecy continues. After seven-sevens of years (7 X 7 = 49) and sixty-two sevens of years (62 X 7 = 434), that is, after the 483 years, Messiah would be cut off. Then, the people *of the prince who is to come* would destroy the city of *Yerushalayim* and the sanctuary, and its end would be with a flood; to the end war and desolations are determined. We know for absolute certainty that the seventy *shavout* are not seventy sevens of days, nor seventy-sevens of weeks, nor seventy sevens of months, since all prophesied by *Dani'el* did not happen historically in 490 days, 490 weeks, or 490 months. But, amazingly it began happening in years.

According to Nehemiah (2:1-9) the date of the return of the Jewish exiles to Israel was the 20th year of *Artaxerxes* reign which was 445 BC. In 396 BC, forty-nine years later, the OT canon was completed in the time called "the Restoration Period." The sixty-two *shavout* or years can be seen as what some call the "silent years" between Malachi and Matthew, 434 years with no prophet until *Yochanon the Immerser* appeared.

Sir Robert Anderson with the help of Greenwich Observatory in London, England through lunar calculations estimated that it was about 483 years from *Artaxerxes* decree which happened in Nisan 1, 445 BC, until Messiah *Yeshua's* entry into *Yerushalayim*, April 6, AD 32 when *Yeshua* was crucified or "cut off." Sometime later, a people came who literally leveled the holy city of *Yerushalayim* and completely destroyed the Temple and its sanctuary. This happened in AD 70 when the Roman legions came under their emperor, Titus.

The text of *Dani'el* continues that "he," whom many bible scholars believe refers to the *"prince to come,"* that is, the prince of Rome who is coming will make a firm covenant or accord or agreement with Israel for one *shavout* or unit of seven, that is, seven years. In the middle of that *shavuot* or the midst of the seven years which is 3½ years this prince will stop sacrifice and grain offering, and commit the *Abomination of Desolation*. This is the event and time *Yeshua* was referring in Matthew 24. If *Yeshua* spoke of this event as prophetic from His day, the prophecy of *Dani'el* is yet to happen.

The "he" in verse 27 who is to make a covenant with Israel for one unit of seven (seven years), and who is to break that covenant in the middle (3½) of the seven years, and who is to commit the *abomination of desolation*, is from the "people" of verse 26 who destroyed the city of *Yerushalayim*. We know from history that people was Rome. Thus, the prince of *Dani'el* 9:26 will be a Roman. We also know "the Roman" is yet to come, and he "the Roman" will be the *antichrist* who will do as his forerunner, Antiochus Epiphanes IV and commit the *abomination of desolation* spoken of by *Shaul*/Paul in 1 Thessalonians and *Yeshua* in Matthew 24.

Of the 490 years prophesied by *Dani'el* only 483 years have been realized in history. There is a unit of seven or seven years, the *seventieth seven of Dani'el* yet to be realized. This will be fulfilled in the future to complete *Dani'el's* prophecy of seventy-sevens.

The *Apocalypse* of *Yeshua* also called The Revelation speaks of seven years and in its midst, which is 1,260 days the devil's *antichrist* is realized (Revelation 13:5). He will have made a covenant with Israel, and will break that accord in the middle of that seven years.

It is important to note, that reinvented Judaism or Rabbinic Judaism since 90 AD "rezoned" the prophetic scroll of *Dani'el* in the OT or *Tanakh* placing *Dani'el* among the *Ketuvim* or the *writings* rather than the *Neviim* or the Prophets. Also, rabbinic Judaism recalculated the date of *Dani'el's* writing since his amazing prophecy points so directly to *Yeshua*. This is what a cultic faith like Rabbinic Judaism does with biblical truth that points so exactly to *Yeshua*. However, *Yeshua* solidified *Dani'el* to be among the prophetic writings (Matthew 24:15).

The End Time (Daniel 12:9);
The End of the Age (Matthew 13:40, 49)

"He said, "Go {your way,} Daniel, for {these} words are concealed and sealed up until the end time."

Dani'el was given many visions of which he wrote in his scroll. In Chapter 12 of his book, *Michael* the great prince of heaven who stands guard over the people of Israel will rise during a time of distress the like of which has never occurred nor will ever occur again. This is the period called the *Great Tribulation* which we discussed above. This *Great Tribulation* is also called *the end time.*

Dani'el was told to seal up his book until *the end time.* In context the scriptures say that many will be purged, purified, refined, while the wicked will act wickedly. The *Abomination of Desolation* (we spoke of earlier) is mentioned in context with this era, along with the abolishment of the sacrifices in the Temple that are ended after 1,290 days, or three and one-half years. *Yeshua* calls this period *the end of the age.*

"So just as the tares are gathered up and burned with fire, so shall it be at the end of the age…So it will be at the end of the age; the angels will come forth and take out the wicked from among the righteous" (Matthew 13:40,49).

The Great Day of Their Wrath (Revelation 6:17)

"and they said to the mountains and to the rocks, Fall on us and hide us from the presence of Him who sits on the throne, and from the wrath of the Lamb; for the great day of their wrath has come, and who is able to stand?"

In the scroll of Revelation are seven seals that are broken. When the first of the seven seals is broken the *antichrist*, "the prince to come" of Daniel 9:24-27 appears on his white horse with a bow although with no arrows (Revelation 6:1). Perhaps this speaks of a bloodless victory? The second seal is broken and then comes war. The third seal is broken and the black horse brings famine. The fourth seal is interpreted by many to be the pale horse of death; one-fourth of the earth dies by sword, famine, pestilence, and from attacks of wild beasts. The fifth seal is broken and underneath the altar, the souls slain as martyrs for God are seen. The sixth seal is broken and the earth reels from myriad convulsions of nature, galactical chaos, the sun becoming dark as night, a universal earthquake, every mountain and island moved from its place, cosmological disorder, stars falling from their orbit, the sky splitting as a scroll, and finally, the realization that this *Great Tribulation* is not by natural calamity, but is the wrath of God!

Yochanon the receptor of *Yeshua's apocalypse* (*Yeshua* is the author of the scroll) asks a rhetorical question, "*who is able to stand?*" (Revelation 1:1). This question is borrowed from Psalm 76:7, "*who may stand in Thy presence when once Thou art angry?*" This horrendous time of Tribulation is "The Great Day of Their Wrath." Whose wrath? The One on the throne and the Lamb!

The Hour of His Judgment (Revelation 14:7)

"and he said with a loud voice, "Fear God, and give Him glory, because the hour of His judgment has come; worship Him who made the heaven and the earth and sea and springs of waters."

"The great day of His wrath," "the end time," "the seventy-sevens," "*Yaaqov's* trouble," "the day of God's vengeance," "the indignation," "the Great Tribulation," "the Day of the Lord," and "the hour of His judgment" are all names for the same event that is coming upon this earth and its inhabitants. We need to know and remember Who is the Judge?

In context Revelation 14:1 tells us it is the Lamb standing on Mount Zion with one-hundred and forty-four thousand (144,000) Jews from the twelve tribes of Israel, who have His name and the name of His father written on their foreheads. There is harp music thunderous like the sound of many mighty waters. Those purchased from among men are found blameless. Then, an angel flies having an eternal gospel to preach to those who live on the earth, to every nation, tribe, tongue, and people.

"fear God and give Him glory, because the hour of judgment has come; worship Him who made the heaven and the hearth and sea and spring of waters."

Then comes the warning against taking the mark of the beast and the warning of worshiping him. This is the *hour of judgment.*

Messianic Ministry to Israel Mission/Study/Tour at Auschwitz-Birkenau Death Camp. The Holocaust was horrifically sinister and was indicative of the coming biblical *Great Tribulation.* Germany's Fuhrer, Adolf Hitler and his 3rd Reich ("kingdom") exterminated six million Jews by programs like, *Bloody Wednesday, Operation Blot-out,* and *the Final Solution.* The antichrist's kingdom will be the 4th Reich.

THE *SHAVUIM SHIVIM* OF DANIEL
(Daniel 9:24-27)

Gavriel instructs *Daniel* who is in Babylonian captivity of *Shavuim Shivim* or "seven seventy" decreed upon the people, Israel and the city, *Yerushalayim* (Daniel 9:24). A *sh'vuah* is a unit of seven and the meaning of the prophecy is seventy sevens (70 X 7). How do we know it is seventy sevens of years and not days or months? The Hebrew word *sh'vuah* is used in Genesis 29:26-28 translated "weeks" although years are meant. Also, all that is to happen (below) DID happen, not in days or months, but [exactly] in years. 490 years were determined for the beginning to the end of God's messianic plan.

The seventy sevens [of years] or 490 years is to accomplish the following: *to finish the transgression; *to make an end of sin; *to make *kapporah* or atonement for iniquity; *to bring in *Tzedek Olamim* or everlasting righteousness; *to seal up the *chazon* or vision and the *navi* or prophecy; *to anoint the *Kodesh Kodeshim* or the most holy. These are the articles of God's messianic plan in its entirety.

the first time period (9:25) + additional time period (9:25)

final time period (9:27)

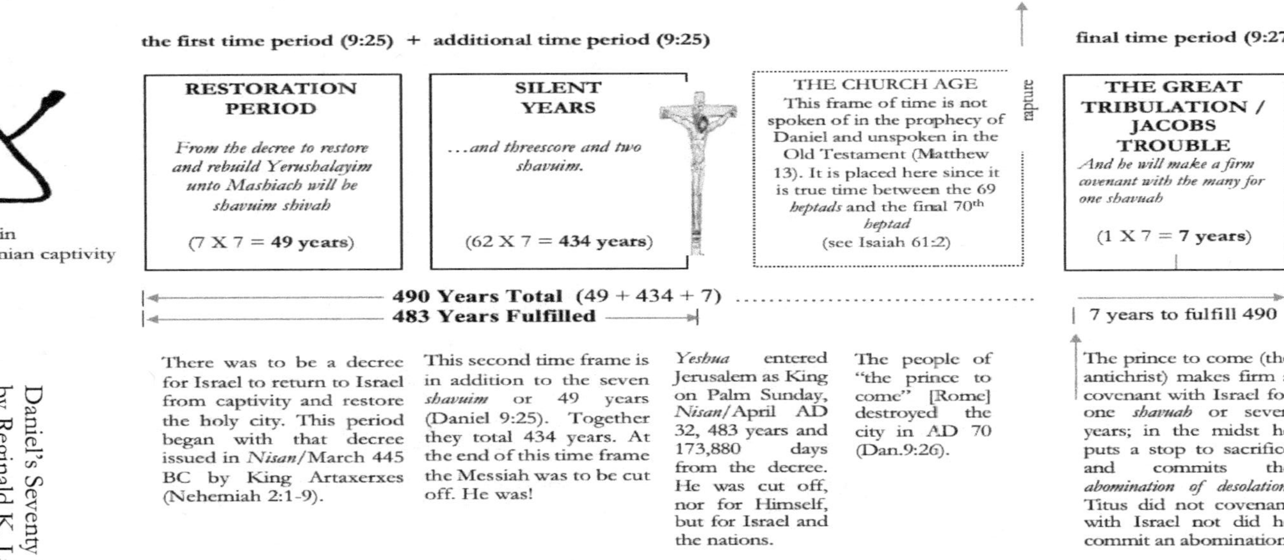

There was to be a decree for Israel to return to Israel from captivity and restore the holy city. This period began with that decree issued in *Nisan*/March 445 BC by King Artaxerxes (Nehemiah 2:1-9).

This second time frame is in addition to the seven *shavuim* or 49 years (Daniel 9:25). Together they total 434 years. At the end of this time frame the Messiah was to be cut off. He was!

Yeshua entered Jerusalem as King on Palm Sunday, *Nisan*/April AD 32, 483 years and 173,880 days from the decree. He was cut off, nor for Himself, but for Israel and the nations.

The people of "the prince to come" [Rome] destroyed the city in AD 70 (Dan.9:26).

The prince to come (the antichrist) makes firm a covenant with Israel for one *shavuah* or seven years; in the midst he puts a stop to sacrifice and commits the *abomination of desolation.* Titus did not covenant with Israel not did he commit an abomination.

Daniel's Seventy Weeks
by Reginald K. Lisemby

CONTRASTS OF TRIBULATION AND
THE GREAT TRIBULATION

TRIBULATION

Life has tribulation, troubles, trials, and distresses.

.ere is adversity upon everyone, from the world, the flesh, and the devil.

Tribulation comes upon the church from the world, evil men, and from Satan.

To the Church it is written *"in this world you will have tribulation."*

In our tribulation and trials, we have the lamb, Yeshua with us.

In tribulation we have peace.

Tribulation is to perfect our faith.

Tribulation and trouble are primarily against the church.

Tribulation is only while the church is present in this world and in this age.

This tribulation comes against the saints in the favorable year of the Lord (Isa.61:1,2)

There is distress, but we have Yeshua.

Tribulation is to perfect, to sanctify the Bride of Yeshua.

THE *GREAT TRIBULATION*

This is the *Great Tribulation* Mat. 24:21; Rev.7:14).

This is adversity from God; the Day of Wrath (Rev.6:17).

Great Tribulation comes upon the world by God.

The Church not appointed to this wrath (Rom.5:9; 1 Thes.1:9,10).

The *Great Tribulation* is the *"wrath of the Lamb"* (Rev.6:15, 16).

In the *Great Tribulation* there is no Peace.

The *Great Tribulation* is to judge.

This is *"Jacob's Trouble"* (Jer.30:7) designed in particular for Israel.

This tribulation is the 70th week of *Daniel* (Dan.9:27).

This tribulation is the "year of recompense…day of vengeance (Isa.61:2; 34:8); a day of wrath, trouble, distress, destruction, desolation, darkness, gloom, clouds, and thick darkness (Zep.1:14).

There is great distress due to the lack of being known of Yeshua.

The Purposes of Great Tribulation is
1) To make an end of wickedness: and wicked ones (Isa.13:9; 24:19,20)

2) To bring about a world-wide revival (Rev.7:1-17 cf. Mat.25:31-46)

3) To break the stubborn will of Israel (Ezek.20:34-38)

Names for This Period[29]

Yaaqov's Trouble (Jeremiah 30:7)

Seventieth Week of *Dani'el* (Daniel 9:27)

YHWH's Strange Work (Isaiah 28:21)

Day of Israel's Calamity (Deuteronomy 32:35)

The Tribulation (Deuteronomy 4:30)

The Indignation (Isaiah 26:20; Daniel 11:36)

Day of Vengeance (Isaiah 34:8; 35:4; 61:2)

Year of Recompense (Isaiah 34:8)

Time of Trouble (Daniel 12:1; Zephaniah 1:15)

Day of Wrath (Zephaniah 1:15)

Day of Distress (Zephaniah 1:15)

Day of Destruction (Zephaniah 1:15)

Day of Desolation (Zephaniah 1:15)

Day of Darkness (Zephaniah 1:15; Amos 5:18; Joel 2:2)

Day of Gloominess (Zephaniah 1:15; Joel 2:22)

Day of Clouds (Zephaniah 1:15; Joel 2:22)

Day of Thick Darkness (Zephaniah 1:15; Joel 2:22)

Day of the Trumpet (Zechariah 1:16)

Day of Alarm (Zechariah 1:16)

Day of the Lord (1 Thessalonians 5:2)

Wrath of God (Revelation 15:1-7; 14:10; 16:1)

Hour of Trial (Revelation 3:10)

Great Day of the Wrath of the Lamb (Revelation 6:16,17)

Wrath to Come (1 Thessalonians 1:10)

The Wrath (Revelation 11:18)

The Great Tribulation (Matthew 24:21; Revelation 2:22; 7:14)

The Tribulation (Matthew 24:29)

The Hour of Judgment (Revelation 14:7)

---

[29] Arnold G. Fruchtenbaum. *The Footsteps of the Messiah*. Ariel Ministries, 1982.

The old city of Jerusalem in the center. The new city of Jerusalem in the horizon.

Question 20

Will the Church be *raptured* before, during, or after the *Great Tribulation?*

Answer

The church in the New Testament Holy Scriptures is called the bride of messiah, the body of messiah, the temple, the aroma of Messiah, and a living epistle [of *Yeshua*]. The church/bride/building/epistle/body of *Yeshua* continues to endure much tribulation and even martyrdom because of who we are in Messiah. *Yeshua* said we would encounter very much grief and pain as He did, and because the world did not love Him, the world would not love us. Christians have suffered more afflictions, hardships, and more martyrdom in the twenty-first century, than in any era since *Yeshua*. However, our tribulations are of Satan, demons, the evil powers of darkness with whom we contend, and evil people their father being the devil. Our adversary and his legions are opposed to God and His people. As Christians we often make wrong choices, we walk "in the flesh" outside God's will, rather than seeking God's will and walking with Him in truth and light. So, we experience tribulation because our flesh is also our adversary. Third, because we live in a fallen and sin-cursed world, the world is also our adversary. The world in which we live is *antichrist*, it always has been! We will have tribulation! Yeshua said that we would (John 16:33).

However, the *Great Tribulation* is from God; it is the *Wrath of the Lamb*. Therefore, the bride/building/epistle/body of Messiah who are the Church, His *ecclesia,* are promised delivery from His coming wrath, since we are His people, we have no condemnation, and we have not been appointed to His anger (Romans 5:9; 1 Thessalonians 1:9,10; 5:9; Revelation 3:10).

Yeshua promised the church in Philadelphia that they would be kept from the hour of trial that is coming upon the whole world to *test* those who dwell on the earth (Revelation 3:10). No scripture in the Bible speaks of the church, the congregation of Messiah and the *one new man in Messiah*, as inheriting or experiencing God's wrath. The Great Tribulation comes directly from Him, it is His wrath (Deuteronomy 4:29-30; Jeremiah 30:4-11; Daniel 8:24-27; 12:1,2; Matthew 13:30, 39-42, 48-50; 24:15-31; 1 Thessalonians 1:9-10; 5:4-9; Revelation 4-18).

The church is not appointed to God's wrath according to *Shaul* in his first letter to the Thessalonians (1 Thessalonians 5:9) and will be removed by the *rapture* before His vengeance falls.

> *"For God has not destined us for wrath, but for obtaining salvation through our Lord Jesus Christ…"*

Enoch was raptured before the flood. *Noach* and his family were saved and protected from His wrath. *Lot* though vexed with the sins of the Sodomites, was brought out of *Sodom* before God's judgment fell. The firstborn of Israel were saved from the death angel by application of His blood on their dwelling. Israel's spies were saved in Jericho. Rahab's house was spared in Jericho, etc.

Question 21

If Israel is the chosen people of God, why is Israel to inherit *The Great Tribulation*, God's Wrath?

Answer

The *Rapture* precipitates the *Great Tribulation,* and the signing of a pseudo-peace accord by the *antichrist* with a nation calling itself *Israel* is what launches the *Great Tribulation.* The Holy Scriptures tell us that prior or in proximity to this international agreement, Israel will be religiously engaged in the ancient sacrificial system, although this will be to Israel's demise, since to resurrect the "old" covenant is to reject God's "new" covenant that He has made, His Son, *Yeshua,* being His final lamb, and His final solution for salvation of all people, the Jewish people, foremost. There is no other door, except *Yeshua* Who is the way, the truth, and the life. *Yeshua,* is the final atonement for sin. The Temple of God, His *kodesh kodeshim* according to God's new covenant, is the Church, His Holy Ones. The old covenant, the Mosaic covenant made at Sinai, is now obsolete (Hebrews 8:13).

Today as I write, religious Jews in Israel are thinking very much of a Temple. Religious Jews are studying and teaching the ancient art of Levitical sacrifice, and they are advocating archaeological digs to discover and recover the ancient Ark of the Covenant. Yet, their interest is in the old and obsolete covenant. The majority of Israelis like the majority of the world reject YHWH's son, *Yeshua* and His new and better covenant. To reject Yeshua is to reject God's only venue of eternal salvation, and thus, to remain forever lost and unregenerate.

Israel must be in submission to God's final Lamb, Messiah *Yeshua* Who is God's "new and living way." The Holy *Ruach* or Spirit of God is directing the Jewish remnant and the Gentile remnant, to *Yeshua*, YHWH's final sacrifice. The Holy *Ruach* is not directing Israel to the archaic and old system, for it is no longer in force. *Yeshua* is the fulfillment of all things! Israel's rejection of *Yeshua* and His Church is rejection of the Holy Spirit, and thus, committing the unpardonable sin. There is no pardon, no forgiveness for rejecting the one and only narrow way to heaven.

Orthodox and religious Jews are trying to reinstate the old covenant that according to Holy Scripture has become obsolete (Hebrews 8:13).

"When He said, "a new covenant," He has made the first obsolete. But whatever is becoming obsolete and growing old is ready to disappear."

The new covenant was not a fabrication by Gentiles. The old covenant made with *Moshe* was a temporary covenant, a *tutor YHWH* once mandated in order to lead Jews to *Yeshua* (Galatians 3:24,25). The new covenant of *YHWH*, unlike the old, is the everlasting covenant to which the old covenant pointed. The old covenant guides Jews to God's new and final covenant inaugurated by *Yeshua*, and to reject His covenant of atonement for sin is to miss the only way of eternal salvation. To reject the new covenant is actually to reject the old covenant, since the new is the culmination or goal of the old. *Yeshua* said that *Moshe* spoke of Him, so the natural outcome of knowing the old covenant is to anticipate, know, and inherit the new!

God favors His Son, *Yeshua* from the beginning. To insist that the *Mosaic* code is still in effect is to reject God's final sacrifice, *Yeshua*. To insist on the *Mosaic* code is to embrace another way of atonement for sin outside God's final Lamb, *Yeshua*. This is a very dangerous thing for the result is to forfeit the inheritance to God which results in eternal damnation (Romans 1:16). Rejecting *Yeshua* is a serious matter, for rejecting *Yeshua* is to reject God's eternal salvation from the damnable curse of sin. Israel's rebuilding of the Temple, their attempt to reincarnate the ancient Levitical sacrificial system, and their implementing the old ways of getting to God is a national statement that *Yeshua*, the messiah sent from God, is not for them.

Yeshua remains Israel's only hope for He is the only door to God (John 10:9), and He is the only way, the only truth, and the only life (John 14:6). For this reason, ministries like Messianic Ministry to Israel, Jews for Jesus, Friends of Israel, and other ministries exist.

The Levitical system of sacrifice is being taught in Israel today, and will soon be in operation. The *Ark of the Covenant* may be already unearthed, uncovered, and awaiting presentation. *Yeshua* Himself prophesied this would happen when He warned Israel of another *Abomination of Desolation* by the *antichrist* (Matthew 24:15; Daniel 9:27), as did *Shaul* (2 Thessalonians 2:3,4) and *Yochanon* (Revelation 11:1,2).

"Therefore, when you see the Abomination of Desolation which was spoken of through Daniel the prophet, standing in the holy place (let the reader understand), then those who are in Judea must flee to the mountains. Whoever is on the housetop must not go down to get the things out that are in his house. Whoever is in the field must not turn back to get his cloak. But woe to those who are pregnant and to those who are nursing babies in those days! But pray that your flight will not be in the winter, or on a Sabbath. For then there will be a great tribulation, such as has not occurred since the beginning of the world until now, nor ever will. Unless those days had been cut short, no life would have been saved; but for the sake of the elect those days will be cut short" (Matthew 24:15).

The *Abomination of Desolation* necessitates a Temple in Israel, a Levitical system of sacrifice, Levites ordering the rites and rituals, and articles to implement the system. What initiates the era called the *Great Tribulation* is the *Anti-Christ* who appears and at some point, signs a covenant of peace with Israel. Both prophets, *Dani'el* (9:27) and Ezekiel (38:8, 11) speak of this.

"And he will make a firm covenant with the many for one week, but in the middle of the week he will put a stop to sacrifice and grain offering; and on the wing of abominations {will come} one who makes desolate, even until a complete destruction, one that is decreed, is poured out on the one who makes desolate" (Daniel 9:27).

In concert with what will be happening in Israel, will be a revived and reunited Roman Empire that will emerge as a confederacy of ten-nations (Daniel 2:40-44; 7:7; Revelation 17:12).

"Then there will be a fourth kingdom as strong as iron; inasmuch as iron crushes and shatters all things, so, like iron that breaks in pieces, it will crush and break all these in pieces. In that you saw the feet and toes, partly of potter's clay and partly of iron, it will be a divided kingdom; but it will have in it the toughness of iron, inasmuch as you saw the iron mixed with common clay. {As} the toes of the feet {were} partly of iron and partly of pottery, {so} some of the kingdom will be strong and part of it will be brittle. And in that you saw the iron mixed with common clay, they will combine with one another in the seed of men; but they will not adhere to one another, even as iron does not combine with pottery. In the days of those kings the God of heaven will set up a kingdom which will never be destroyed, and {that} kingdom will not be left for another people; it will crush and put an end to all these kingdoms, but it will itself endure forever" (Daniel 2:40-44).

"After this I kept looking in the night visions, and behold, a fourth beast, dreadful and terrifying and extremely strong; and it had large iron teeth. It devoured and crushed and trampled down the remainder with its feet; and it was different from all the beasts that were before it, and it had ten horns" (Daniel 7:7).

"The ten horns which you saw are ten kings who have not yet received a kingdom, but they receive authority as kings with the beast for one hour. These have one purpose, and they give their power and authority to the beast" (Revelation 17:12,13).

Question 22

What does the term *antichrist* mean, who is the antichrist, and will we know when he appears?

Answer

In the last days the great world powers as we presently know them, the United States of America, Russia, and China will become subservient to another power, the revived Roman Empire.[30] This is a very possible scenario. Bible prophecy predicts a new power will arise and with it will be a new emperor who will ride a wave of chaos.

The future Fuhrer and his kingdom will be the Fourth Reich, as Adolf Hitler conducted the Third Reich. The *antichrist* will enter the stage upon a devastated and bewildered world, and with him will be his "abominable ten" leaders of ten nations of the world that together with the *antichrist* will rule the world in similarity of the ancient Roman Empire. These ten leaders are seen in the metallic image of Nebuchadnezzar's dread (Daniel 2:41-44), the ten horns of the beast of fury (Daniel 7:7), and the end-times government (Revelation 13:1; 17:12-14). The *antichrist* will work in concert with the obscene ten (John 5:43; 2 Thessalonians 2:3,4,8,9; Revelation 6:2; 11:7; 13:1; 14:9,11; 15:2; 16:2; 19:20; 20:10; Daniel 9:27; 11:45).

The *antichrist* is a man of many titles. He is called *antichrist* (1 John 2:22), the man of sin (2 Thessalonians 2:3), the son of perdition (2 Thessalonians 2:3), the lawless one (2 Thessalonians 2:8), the beast (Revelation 11:7), the man of earth (Psalm 10:18), the prince that shall

---

30 America will be crippled by a colossal event, perhaps something like the *coronavirus* or perhaps the *Rapture*. With the US economy in jeopardy and the disappearance of millions of American citizens, America will be devastated.

come (Daniel 9:26), the little horn (Daniel 7:8, 24-25), the king of fierce countenance (Daniel 8:23-25), the king (Daniel 11:36), the seed of Satan (Genesis 3:15), the idol shepherd (Zechariah 11:17), the bloody and deceitful man (Psalm 5:6), the Assyrian, the "rod of my anger" (Micah 5:5,6; Isaiah 10:5,6), the spoiler (Isaiah 16:4,5), and there are a few other titles for this sinister beast, the devil's son.

Bible Prophecy says that the *antichrist* will be energized by the devil although he will be held back or divinely restrained by God's power, His church (2 Thessalonians 2:7). At the appropriate time that God has decreed, the *antichrist* will rise and promote himself, and the conditions of the world will have been made so that he will be readily embraced, first by the European ten-nation confederacy or empire, and then by the remaining other nations of the globe, including Israel (John 5:43; Daniel 9:27). At a fixed time, the *antichrist* will commit the *Abomination of Desolation* that was committed by *Antiochus Epiphanes IV* and to which *Yeshua* referred in Matthew 24. The *antichrist* will sit in the Temple of God as god similar to Antiochus Epiphanes IV (2 Thessalonians 2:4; Daniel 9:27; Matthew 24:15), and he will be aided by the false prophet (Revelation 19:20; Revelation 13:12-15).

The OT Prophet *Dani'el*[31] says the *antichrist* will plant the tabernacle of his palace between the seas in the glorious mountain (Daniel 11:45) and that he will oppose and exalt Himself above all that is called God…*so that he sitteth in the Temple…showing himself that he is God causing the sacrifice and the oblation to cease* (Daniel 9:2). His dominion will be world-wide (Revelation 13:3,7,17), his duration will be forty-two months or 3½ years (Revelation 12:14; 12:6; 13:5), and he will act in concert with ten kings (Revelation 17:12-16).

The *antichrist* will have a relationship with Israel similar to the relationship Judas had with *Yeshua* (Psalm 55:11-14; Daniel 9:26-27; Psalm 41:9). Some bible students even consider the *antichrist* to be a reincarnation of Judas since Judas was said by *Yeshua* to be a devil (John 6:70), and both the *antichrist* and Judas are called "the son of perdition

---

31 *Yeshua* said he was a prophet in Matthew 24, and thereby his book is prophetic and not a writing in the *Kituviim*.

(John 17:12; 2 Thessalonians 2:3). The *antichrist* is also called "the beast" who ascends out of the pit, which means "the beast" had to be placed in the pit in order to be released (Revelation 11:7). Is the *antichrist*, Judas?

The *antichrist* will have intellectual genius (Daniel 7:20; 8:23; Ezekiel 28:3), political genius (Daniel 11:21; Revelation 13:1,2; 17:17), oratorical genius (Daniel 7:20; 11:36; Revelation 13:5), commercial /marketing genius (Revelation 13:17, Daniel 8:25; 11:26), and military genius (Daniel 8:24; Revelation 6:2; 13:4; Isaiah 14:16).

Religiously, the *Fuhrer* will be an atheist since "he will not regard the god of his fathers" or any god (Daniel 11:37). The *antichrist* will not be a Muslim mufti, a Jewish rabbi, a Jewish priest, or a cult member of a religious faith. The *antichrist* will be agnostic, rebelling against the laws of God, precepts of God, the rule of God, and against all things that pertain to God. In fact, at some point he will proclaim himself as *god* of the globe (2 Thessalonians 2:4), just as Antiochus Epiphanes IV did in history, a madman that the Jews nicknamed *Epimanes* or "madman."

The *antichrist* will enter the world stage during an era of fear and panic (Daniel 11:24) when comfort and consolation is needed. The *antichrist* will rise from among men (Revelation 13:1), a European of Roman descent (Daniel 9:27), and a Gentile (like Antiochus Epiphanes IV) who's doom is foretold (2 Thessalonians 2:8; Revelation 9:20; Revelation 20:10; Joel 3:9-14). His coming will be on a wave of peace (Daniel 11:24).

THE ANTICHRIST

TITLES

The Antichrist (1 John 2:22)
The Man of Sin (2 Thessalonians 2:3)
The Son of Perdition (2 Thessalonians 2:3)
The Lawless One (2 Thessalonians 2:8)
The Beast (Revelation 11:7; 13:1)
The Man of Earth (Psalm 10:18)
The Prince/Ruler that Shall Come (Daniel 9:26-27)
The Little Horn (Daniel 7:8, 24-25)
The Insolent King of Fierce Countenance (Daniel 8:23-25)
The Despicable Person (Daniel 11:21)
The Strong-Willed King (Daniel 11:36)
The Rod of My Anger (Isaiah 10:5)
The Idol/Worthless Shepherd (Zechariah 11:16,17)
The Assyrian (Micah 5:5,6; Isaiah 10:5)
The Spoiler (Isaiah 16:4,5; Jeremiah 6:26)

TRAITS

He will be a man (John 5:43; 2 Thessalonians 2:3,4,8,9; Revelation 6:2; 11:7; 13:1; 14:9,11; 15:2; 16:2; 19:20; 20:10; Daniel 9:27; 11:45).

He will deny both Father and the Son (1 John 2:22).

He rises from the "sea" interpreted as Gentile nations (Revelation 13:1; 17:15) from Gentile world powers (Daniel 7:7-8, 23-25; Revelation 13:7-8).

His dominion will be worldwide (Revelation 13:3,7,17).

His headquarters will be Rome (Daniel 9:26-27; Revelation 17:8,9).

He will rule by deceit (Daniel 8:24,25).

He will be received by Israel (Daniel 9:27; John 5:43).

He will sit in the last days temple of Israel (2 Thessalonians 2:4; Daniel 9:27; Matthew 24:15).

He will be aided by the false prophet (Revelation 19:20; 13:12-15).

He will have intellectual genius (Daniel 7:20; 8:23; Ezekiel 28:3).

He will have political genius (Daniel 11:21; Revelation 13:1-2; 17:17).

He will have oratorical genius (Daniel 7:20; 11:36).

He will have marketing genius (Revelation 13:17; Daniel 8:25; 11:26).

He will have military genius (Daniel 8:24; Revelation 6:2; 13:1-4; Isaiah 14:16).

He will rule the global economy (Revelation 13:16-17).

He will be [somewhat] religious (2 Thessalonians 2:4; Revelation 13:3,14,15).

He will be the instrument of God's wrath and vengeance, the rod of His anger (Isaiah 10:5, 24-25).

He will ride the wave of peace to gain control (Daniel 11:24).

He will make war with the saints (Revelation 13:7,8).

He will act in concert with ten kings (Revelation 17:12-16).

He will be Judas-like (John 6:70; 17:12; 2 Thessalonians 2:3; Revelation 11:7) and have a relationship to Israel similar to the relationship Judas had with Christ (Psalm 55:11-14; Daniel 9:26-27; Psalm 41:9).

He will insulate three peoples from his fury: Edom, Moab, and Ammon (Daniel 11:41).

He will claim to be God (2 Thessalonians 2:4).

His duration will be 42 months or 3 ½ years (Revelation 12:6,14; 13:5).

His appearance is being restrained by the Church (2 Thessalonians 2).

His doom is foretold (2 Thessalonians 2:8; Revelation 19:20; 20:10; Joel 3:9-14).

He is the son of Satan but counterfeits the Son of God/Son of Man:

- *Yeshua* is the Christ. He is the antichrist (1 John 2:22).
- *Yeshua* will set His mark on believers (Revelation 7:3,4; 9:4; 14:1; 22:4); the antichrist will set his mark (Revelation 13:15-18).
- *Yeshua* is the only begotten son of God (John 3:16); the antichrist is the son of perdition (2 Thessalonians 2:3).
- *Yeshua* was revealed in the fulness of time (Galatians 4:4); the antichrist will be revealed in his time (2 Thessalonians 2:6).
- *Yeshua* made a loyal covenant with Israel (Hebrews 8:8); the antichrist will make a false covenant with Israel (Daniel 9:27).
- *Yeshua* has a congregation/church; the antichrist will have a synagogue/congregation (Revelation 2:9).
- *Yeshua* has a bride (Revelation 21:2); the antichrist will have a whore (Revelation 17:1,16).

- *Yeshua* has His city, Jerusalem; the antichrist will have his city, Babylon (Revelation 17:5; 18:2).
- *Yeshua* was prophesied to come; the antichrist is prophesied to come.
- *Yeshua's* ministry was 3 ½ years; the antichrist will reign 3 ½ years, half of the seven-year Great Tribulation (Revelation 13:5).
- *Yeshua* was murdered and resurrected (Philippians 3:10; the antichrist will be killed and resurrect (Revelation 13:3,4).
- *Yeshua* had a prophet, Yochanon; the antichrist will have a false prophet.
- *Yeshua's* headquarters was Jerusalem; the antichrist focus will be Jerusalem (Daniel 8:24).
- *Yeshua* appeared with Moses and Elijah; the antichrist will be intercepted by Moses and Elijah.
- *Yeshua* was riding a white horse (Revelation 19:11); the antichrist will ride a white horse (Revelation 6:2).
- *Yeshua* was referred to as "which was, is, and is to come (Revelation 4:8); the antichrist is referred the same (Revelation 17:8).
- *Yeshua* cleansed the Temple, His Father's House (Matthew 21:13); the antichrist will sit in the Temple proclaiming it his house (2 Thessalonians 2:8).
- *Yeshua* has His army (2 Timothy 2:3,4); the antichrist has an army (Revelation 16:13-16).

Reginald. K. Lisemby

Question 23

Who are the *"false Christs"* Jesus spoke of in Matthew 24?

Answer

Let's first consider where the anticipation of a messiah originated? Some allege that *messianism* began in the *intertestamental* period. *"There is no evidence of true Messianism until the second century BC....It is on the threshold of the NT that we first encounter real Messianism"* (Becker, Meore 50, 87). However, during the intertestamental period (from Malachi to Mathew) while there was much Jewish literature, there was little or no messianic expectation. The *Apocrypha*, for example, is a pond of Jewish literature reflective of Jewish thinking that has to do with the business of living and surviving as a faithful Jew in hostile pagan environments, and there is no suggestion of any dramatic deliverance by a messiah figure (e.g. *Tobit and Judith*). *Sirach* and *Ecclesiastics* are books which emphasized the *Torah*, but they did not emphasize a messianic person coming to deliver Israel.

Messianism did not originate in the intertestamental period as suggested. In fact, a messianic hope already existed, although the hope was dwindling after the warning of the "minor" prophets. *MalaKhi, ZekharYah*, and *Chaggai* were called by *Elohim* to herald and exhort Israel to "keep looking!" (Malachi 3:1-3; 4:5,6; Zechariah 2:8-10; 9:9; 14:1-6; Haggai 2:3,9). Yet, by the time *Yeshua* came, messianic expectation was low.

There are some who say that *messianism* began after the return of the Jews from exile in Babylon. It is certainly true that messianic Judaism became more pronounced by 539 BC. The *targums* were written by the *meturgeman*, Hebrew scholars and teachers who translated the Hebrew into the vernacular language. The Hebrew tongue itself was being relearned, and there was great emphasis upon the return of the exiles to the land of Israel to await and anticipate the messiah's coming. *Dani'el* (Daniel), *Yechezqel* (Ezekiel), and *Zekharyah* (Zechariah) had a fully developed *Messianism* with Messiah as their focus. However, messianic hope did not originate in the post-exilic period.

Some say that *Messianism* originated as a logical conclusion of OT theology. But, the OT ended with "unexplained ceremonies, unachieved purposes, unappeased longings, unfulfilled prophecies" and unfinished inspiration (Zola Levit). Others suggest that *messianism* was never the emphasis of Judaism, that *messianism* was not so prevalent, but was a Christian interpretation of the OT scriptures. Numbers 24:15-19 does not refer to a Messiah, but to the supremacy of David and the tribe of Judah, they say. Hosea 11:1 is not messianic, and the seed of *Havvah* (Eve) in Genesis 3:15 was her near kin, not a faraway son or the messiah. They say, read Isaiah 7:14 and nothing is spoken of in that passage about a messiah. Christians supposedly reinterpreted this passages in their attempt to match *Yeshua,* the Christian hero to the old testament holy scriptures.

Here is our answer. First, the messianic design is God's plan, design, and story. It is not the Jews plan, and it is not man's plan. *Messianism* cannot be clearly understood without both the Tanakh or OT and the New Testament scriptures. The Tanakh is about *Yeshua* (Luke 24:27,44) as much as the New Testament. *Messianism* originated with GOD! To prove this declaration simply read and investigate the 300 plus messianic prophesies in the Old Testament of Tanakh.

Second, the messianic design predates creation. God was intentional. The *lamb was slain before the foundation of the world* (Revelation 13:8). *Messiah* (Hebrew) or *Christ* (Greek) was foreordained before the foundation of the world (1Peter 1:19,20).

Third, the messianic plan was not a new concept, nor was it a standby remedy for man's demise. Fourth, the Messianic design presupposes three axioms: (1) God intended a messiah prior to man's need; (2) God intended to accommodate man's sin which in His sovereignty He foresaw before the beginning; and (3) God intended to make the hallmark of His Holy Scriptures, the portrayal of His Messiah man must come to identify (Luke 24:27,44).

The Bible is a philosophy of history, not merely a recording of facts and names, but interpreting history toward a goal which is a person. That person is Messiah *Yeshua*! Messianic hope is centered in the house of David. Davidic descent is prominent in OT *Messianism*. God has a plan and it concerns three particulars.

(1) First, a messianic land is prominent. The Holy Land of God from Eden at the beginning, to Jerusalem in the middle of human history, to the New Jerusalem at the end, is zenith in God's messianic plan. There is a "nexus," a connecting link of the Garden of Eden, the Promised Holy Land of Israel, and Jerusalem in scripture (Genesis 13:10; 43:11; Isaiah 51:3; Ezekiel 36; Joel 2:3; Zechariah 14:8; Revelation 22:1,2). In the midst of the holy land was the *tree of life,* seen at the beginning in *Gan Eden*, in the middle of human history, the *Menorah* in the Holy Temple, and the *tree of life* again in the New Jerusalem at the end, as depicted in the scroll of Revelation.

(2) Second, along with the messianic land is a messianic people who are zenith in the messianic plan of God. The Bible begins (Genesis 1, 2) with the generation of the world, the fall and degeneration of the world (Genesis 3-11), the man and his posterity going east, *Avraham* in the east called back westward to a land, *Avraham* and his seed to be a blessing to the earth, and through *Avraham, Yitzhak, Yaaqov,* and his dozen the rest of the Holy Scriptures concern the regeneration of the world through the *Avrahamic Covenant* (Genesis 12:1-3; 15:7-21; 17:1-8; 26:1-5; 50:24; Exodus 2:24; Deuteronomy 4:31; 9:5; 2 Kings 13:23; Psalm 105:5-10; Jeremiah .31:31-37; Micah 7:18-20; Luke 1:67-75; Acts 3:25; Romans 9:4,5; 11:28; Galatians 3:8,9,17-18; Hebrews 6:13-20).

(3) Third, the messiah is colossal in God's plan. There is an intentional narrowing of focus of the seed we mentioned above! The coming seed will come from the race lineage of *Shem* (Genesis 9:25-27), the patriarchal lineage of *Avraham* (Genesis 12:1-8), the true heir lineage of *Yitzhak* (Genesis 21:12); the national lineage of *Yaaqov* (Genesis 28:3,4); the tribal lineage of *Yehudah* (Genesis 49:10), and the kingly lineage of *David* (Psalm 132:11).

The Jewish Holy Scriptures are pregnant with messianism and there are myriad messianic prophecies, more than 350 messianic prophecies, announcing His coming. Biblical history provides us with potent messianism. In every generation up until the time of *Yeshua*, there were those anticipating the coming son of man and seed of David. *Yeshua* is the Son of David, Son of God, Son of Man, and the Messiah of Israel. There is no other messiah.

However, as *Yeshua* prophesied there have been many *pseudo-messiahs* both in Israel and outside Israel. Below is a list of some of the known Jewish *pseudo messiahs*.

In Israel

Simon of Peraea (4 BC) a former slave of Herod the Great, he crowned himself king of the Jews and led a Jewish revolution; it was crushed, he was captured, and his head was severed (Josephus *Antiquities* 17.10.6).

Athronges the Shepherd (4 BC) is another insurrectionist and rebel along with his four brothers who were against Rome and Herod Archelaus. He was said to be of gigantic strength and stature (as was his brothers), but he was eventually defeated (Josephus Antiquities 17.10.7).

Judas of Galilee (AD 6) is mentioned in the writings of *Lukas* (Acts 5:37); this *Judas* who founded the Zealots (*Josephus Antiquities* 18.1.6;

20.5.2) led a tax revolt and violent resistance to the census imposed upon Israel by Quirinius of Rome. His movement was brutally crushed by Rome and he was killed, although his spirit continued to inspire his followers.

Menahem ben Judah was a descendant of *Judas of Galilee* (above) and a leader of the *Sicarii*. Using weapons captured by the Romans from the Jews upon Masada he aggressively took the Antonia Fortress in Jerusalem from the military of King Agrippa II in Judea. He was later captured by a competitor, the zealot rebel Eleazar. *Menahem* was judged as a tyrant, and he was tortured and killed. This grandson of *Judas of Galilee* may be one-in-the-same as *Menahem ben Hezekiah* mentioned in the Talmud (tractate Sanhedrin 98b), called "the comforter that should relieve."

Theudas (died AD 46) is mentioned in Acts 5:36 and in the writings of Josephus (*Antiquities of the Jews* 20.5.1). Leading his followers to the Jordan River he promised to divide the water by his word. He was overcome by the Roman Calvary who removed his head and took it to Jerusalem for display.

The Jewish Egyptian mentioned in Acts 21:38 brought his followers to the Mount of Olives promising that by his Word the walls of Jerusalem would fall. The walls did not fall, but the Romans came, and he fled (Josephus *War of the Jews* 2.13.5).

Vespasian (AD 70) claimed to be a messianic figure according to Flavius Josephus (Flavius Josephus, *Jewish War* 3.399-404 and 6.310-315).

Shimon Ben-Kosiba / **Simeon Bar Kokhbah ("son of the star")** a fierce military leader was acclaimed to be the Messiah by Rabbi Akiva about 130-135 AD. Israel was continuing to resist Roman domination while many Christians were leaving Israel remembering the words of *Yeshua*, that when you see Jerusalem being surrounded by its enemies, to get out. The messianic community did. In AD 70 Titus of Rome came and slaughtered 580,000 Jews. Realizing now would be a good time for messiah, a rabbi named Akiva began to promote Simeon bar Kokhbah as Israel's deliverer/messiah. The remaining true messianic (Christian) community in Israel disjoined themselves, and fled Jerusalem and Israel. In AD 135 Hadrian came from Rome and finished the scourge by plowing up the great city completely destroying the land. Bar Kokhbah died in battle.

Outside Israel

Moses of Crete (AD 448). There had been no messianic movement since the death of Bar Kokhba until Moses of Crete claimed he was the reincarnation of the ancient prophet of old who had returned to perform the same miracle of the past, to lead Israel through the sea once again. An interpretation alongside of a computation found in the Talmud, the messiah was expected to appear in AD 440 (Sanhedrin 97b) or 471 ('Ab.Zarah 9b) and coinciding with Roman invasions this Moses was the answer for many anticipating the messiah to appear. He certainly won over the hearts of the Jewish people in Crete, at least initially. On the day appointed for the great miracle of leading the Jewish people out of exile through the sea on dry-shod, the people disowned their possessions, obeyed his charge and they leapt into the sea. The sea did not open and many of his followers drowned while others were rescued by fishermen. There are two tales of his end, one is that this Moses drowned, and the other is that he fled and the wannabe Moses was never heard from again.

The Khuzistan Chronicle (7th century) a damaged chronicle of the history of Persia, written in Syriac lists an unknown messianic wannabe and claimant who rose to prominence alongside the Muslim conquest of Khuzistan. This "messiah" is said to have led the Jews in burning and destroying myriad Christian churches in Iraq and the coasts of Iran.

Ishak ben Yakub Obadia Abu 'Isa al-Isfahani of Ispahan (744-750). Known as *Abu Isa* he claimed to be the last of the five forerunners of the Messiah and that God had appointed him to free Israel. Having gathered a large number of followers, he rebelled against the caliph in Persia. He was defeated and slain at Rai. His followers claimed that he was inspired and as proof revealed the fact that he wrote books. In truth he was ignorant of reading and writing. He founded the first sect that arose in Judaism after the destruction of the Temple (Wikipedia).

Yudghan, called ***Al-Ra'i*** ("the shepherd of the flock of his people") lived and taught in Persia in the first half of the 8th century. He was a disciple of *Abu Isa* (above) who continued the faith after *Isa* was slain. He declared himself to be a prophet, and was regarded as a Messiah by his disciples. He came from Hamadan, and taught doctrines which he claimed to have received through prophecy. According to *Shahristani*, he opposed the belief in *anthropomorphism*, taught the doctrine of free will, and held that the Torah had an allegorical meaning in addition to its literal one. He admonished his followers to lead an ascetic life, to abstain from meat and wine, and to pray and fast often, in likeness of his master, *Abu Isa*. He held that the observance of the Sabbath and festivals was merely a matter of memorial. After his death his followers formed a sect, the *Yudghanites*, who believed that their Messiah had not died, but would return.

Serene (he also appears with the names, *Sherini, Sheria, Serenus, Zonoria, Saüra, Severus*). The Syrian was said to be born a "Christian" (720-723). He preached in the district of Mardin and proclaimed himself Messiah. The Zuqnin Chronicle reports that he proclaimed himself Moses "sent again for the salvation of Israel." Serene promised "to lead you into the desert in order to introduce you then to the inheritance of the

Promised Land which you shall possess as before;" he was more as a prophet like Moses than a Davidic "anointed one." The immediate occasion for his appearance may have been the restriction of the liberties of the Jews by the *caliph Omar II* (717-720) and his proselytizing efforts. Serene had followers even in Spain where the Jews were suffering under the oppressive taxation of their new Arab rulers, and many left their homes for the new Moses. These Jews paid a tithe to Serene. Like Abu 'Isa and Yudghan, Serene also was a religious reformer. According to *Natronai b. Nehemiah, gaon* of *Pumbedita* (719-30), Serene was hostile to the laws of rabbinic Judaism. His followers disregarded the dietary laws, the rabbinic prayers, and the prohibition against the "wine of libation." They worked on the second day of the festivals, they did not write marriage and divorce documents according to Talmudic prescriptions, and they did not accept the Talmudic prohibition against the marriage of near relatives. Serene was arrested, and brought before *Caliph Yazid II*, he declared that he had acted only in jest, whereupon he was handed over to the Jews for punishment. Natronai laid down the criteria by which Serene's followers might rejoin the synagogue; most of his followers presumably did so (Wikipedia).

Moses al-Dar'I (1127) was a teacher from Morocco. Convinced he was Messiah and would free the Jews in the Almoravid countries at Passover in 1127, he gained a very large gathering.

David Alroy (1147) a 12th century Messiah wannabe performed "miracles" and led a courageous uprising against the Moslem empire that commanded the eastern world. Alroy was born in Kurdistan and appeared in Persia about 1159 declaring himself the messiah. He led an attack to free the Jews from the Muslim empire, but failed to take the fortress of Amadiyah in the mountains of Azerbaijan. His head was severed (legend says by his own father-in-law) and sent to the Baghdad sultan as a prize.

Anonymous pseudo-messiah in Yemen (12th century) appeared in Fez as Muslims were attempting to convert Jews to Islam. He called upon Jews to unite, to divide their property with the poor to gain treasure in heaven, and was finally arrested by Muslim authorities and beheaded by his own will so that he might prove he was messiah by his resurrection. He is only known by the writings of Maimonides in the work, *Iggeret Teman* or the Yemen Epistle.

Abraham ben Samuel Abulafia (1240-1291) was the "prophet of Avila" in Spain, a cabalist (one studying *kabbalah* or mystic Judaism) he promoted himself first as the forerunner of Messiah, then as the messiah himself. He published a book, *Urbino* declaring that God had spoken to him, and that 1290 was the year for the messianic era to begin. One named Solomon ben Adret disclaimed him, condemned him, and led him to be persecuted so that he fled to Malta (1287). By 1295 he lowered his self-promotion and prophesied the messiah to appear. No messiah appeared.

Nissim ben Abraham (1295) said to be an ignorant Jewish prophet in Avila was visited by an angel that energized him to write the mystic work, *The Wonder of Wisdom*. Nissim's prophetic prediction was that on the last day of the fourth month, *Tammuz*, 1295 the Messiah was to come. This led to Jewish fasting and sacrifices and a congregation on the appointed day. The Messiah did not appear and in disappointment some of Nissim's followers converted to Christianity.

Moses Botarel of Cisneros (1413). After one-hundred years another messiah figure appeared, Moses Botarel who claimed by divine power to be able to compose all the names of God into one name of God. One of his followers was Hasdai Crescas; their relationship is spoken of by Geronimo de Santa Fe in his speech at the disputation in Tortosa.

Isaac ben Solomon Ashkenazi Luria and ***Hayim ben Joseph Vital*** in the 16th century initiated a messianic movement based on the

Kabbalah and its mystical visions and expectations. European Jewry sat up and listened attentively to the visions and dreams of these two messianic pretenders from Safed, a famed Jewish settlement in northern Israel. The two declared they had conjured up the spirits of dead rabbis, one telling them he was the messiah and he was coming soon. Luria (1534-1573) is considered the father of modern *Kabbalah* and considered himself the "suffering servant" of Isaiah 53 and the forerunner of the Messiah of David. Vital studied Kabbalah with Luria and after Luria's death understood that it was not Luria, but himself who was the messiah of David who would redeem Israel, but only when he could find ten righteous people. He [evidently] never succeeded.

Shabbetai Zevi (1626-1676) a *Kabbalist* from Safed misled many European Jews in the 17th century. With great charisma and influential teaching, he compelled them to follow him to Israel. However, this messiah was captured by the Muslims and he converted to Islam rather than die. His hypocrisy and shame utterly shattered faith in *kabbalah* for centuries.

Mordecai Mokia (1650–1729) a follower of Shabbethai Zevi remained faithful and claimed to be a messiah. He initially preached that Shabbethai was the true Messiah, that his conversion was for mystic reasons, and that he did not die but would soon reveal himself -within three years after his supposed death. Mokia pointed to the persecution of the Jews in Oran (by Spain), in Austria, in France, and to the pestilence in Germany as prognostications of his coming. He found a following among Hungarian, Moravian, and Bohemian Jews. Going a step further, he declared that he, Mordecai Mokia was the Davidic Messiah, and Shabbethai, was only the Ephraitic Messiah and because Shabbethai was rich, could not accomplish the redemption of Israel. He (Mordecai), being poor, was the real Messiah and yet also the incarnation of the soul of the Ephraitic Messiah, Shabbethai. Italian Jews heard him and invited him to Italy. He went there near 1680, and received a warm welcome in Reggio and Modena. He spoke of Messianic preparations that he must make in Rome, and hinted at having had to adopt Christianity outwardly. He was denounced to the Inquisition and was advised to leave Italy, so he returned to Bohemia, and then went on to Poland, where he is said to have become insane. From his time a sect began to form which still existed at the beginning of the Mendelsohnian era (Wikipedia).

Jacob Querido (died 1690), son of Joseph Filosof, and brother of the fourth wife of Shabbethai, became the head of the Shabbethaians in Salonica, being regarded by them as the new incarnation of Shabbethai. He pretended to be Shabbethai's son and adopted the name Jacob Tzvi. With 400 followers he converted to Islam about 1687, forming a sect called the Dönmeh. He made a pilgrimage to Mecca (c. 1690), and he died during the pilgrimage. After his death his son Berechiah or Berokia (c. 1695-1740) succeeded him (Wikipedia).

Miguel (Abraham) Cardoso (1630–1706), born of Marano parents, Miguel may have been initiated into the Shabbethaian movement by Moses Pinheiro in Leghorn. He became a prophet of the Messiah, and when the latter embraced Islam he justified this treason, saying that it was necessary for the Messiah to be reckoned among the sinners in order to atone for Israel's idolatry. He applied Isaiah 53 to Shabbethai, and sent out epistles to prove that Shabbethai was the true Messiah. Miguel even suffered persecution for advocating his cause. Later, he considered himself the Ephraitic Messiah, asserting that he had marks on his body, which were proof of this. He preached and wrote of the speedy coming of the Messiah, fixing different dates until his death (Wikipedia).

Lobele Prossnitz (Joseph ben Jacob) (early 18th century -1750). He taught that God had given dominion of the world to the "pious one," i.e., the one who had entered into the depths of Kabbalah. Such a representative of God had been Shabbethai, whose soul had passed into other "pious" men, like Jonathan Eybeschütz and into himself. Prossnitz pretended to be a prophet and gave his prophetic herald that he could and would call the Shekinah to appear at midnight. A large crowd gathered to see his miracle, when he was exposed behind a curtain, robbed in white, with the Tetragrammaton YHWH written on his chest. He was excommunicated by all rabbis of Moravia, yet he proclaimed himself as Yoseph ben Yaqov, the Messiah son of Joseph. He was never taken seriously and died in Hungary among non-Jews.

Isaiah Hasid, a son-in-law of the Shabbethaian, Judah Hasid who lived in Mannheim, he secretly claimed to be the resurrected Messiah, although publicly he had abjured Shabbethaian beliefs. He was a proven fraud who nevertheless attained some following amongst former followers of Shabbatai. He was later excommunicated along with Moses Meir Kamenker by the rabbis of Frankfurt, Germany because they condemned the Talmud and proclaiming adherents to the Talmud did not believe in the God of Israel.

Jacob Frank (1726-1791) in the 18th century claimed to be the reincarnation of King David, the patriarch Joseph, and Sabbatai Zevi all in one man. He claimed that salvation would happen through a mixture of Judaism, Christianity, and Shabbataism which he called the religion of Edom. His purpose was to uproot rabbinic Judaism, and he was forced to leave Podolia. This messiah wannabe willfully followed his sinful inclinations and promoted his nihilistic philosophy living in wealth until his death in 1791.

Eve Frank (1754-1817) the daughter of Jacob Frank became *the holy mistress* and leader of the sect of her father. She is the only woman in Jewish history declared to be a Jewish messiah. Eve declared herself to be the incarnation of the *Shekinah*, the feminine side of God, as well as the reincarnation of the Virgin Mary. She became the object on a sub cult in Czestochowa, her followers keeping statutes of her in their homes.

Shukr Kuhayl I (19th-century) was a Yemenite pseudo-messiah who revealed himself as a messenger of Messiah during a time of political turmoil in Ottoman, Yemen. He divorced his wife, became a traveling "preacher," inscribing messianic formulas on his hands, and correcting the passage of Isaiah 45:1 from "Thus said the Lord to Cyrus, His anointed…" to read, "Thus said the Lord to Shukr, His anointed…." The Jews of Yemen almost exclusively believed his claims. Shukr was killed by the Islamic Imam of San'a' Yemen who deemed Shukr as a threat. Shukr's son, Judah nor his sister mourned for Shukr for they expected his resurrection.

Judah ben Shalom (Shukr Kuhayl II). In 1868 Judah ben Shalom appeared claiming to be the deceased Shukr Kuhayl. He led a very significant messianic movement of both Yemenite Jews and Yemenite Arabs.

Rabbi Menachem Mendel Schneerson (1902-1994) was the more recent messianic hope. His followers waited for him to announce his messiahship though he never openly declared himself messiah, nor did he correct those who said he was. He was the spiritual leader of the *Chabad Lubavitch* (ultra-Orthodox) movement in New  York city. Schneerson healed and restored fertility to barren women and was also able to avoid family tragedies. He never set foot in Israel for under Jewish tradition the messiah will arrive only when the era of redemption comes. At his death at the age of 92 following a stroke a myriad of Hasidic Jews who claimed to have the supernatural and prophetic powers of Schneerson gathered to await his resurrection by turning to Isaiah 53 and predicting his ascension up to Jerusalem. Shortly after his death a bill was introduced in the U.S. House of representatives by Congressmen Charles Schumer, John Lewis, Newt Gingrich, and Jerry Lewis to bestow upon the Rebbe the congressional

Gold Medal. The bill passed and both houses with unanimous consent so honored the Rebbe. Some of Schneerson's followers still await his return as Messiah.

Other false messiah's recognized by religious Jews (listed in the Jewish Encyclopedia) Include:
- Asher Lemmlein (1502 A.D.)
- Reubeni and Solomon Molko (1525 A.D.)
- Mordecai Mokiaḥ (1680 A.D.)
- Moses Luzzatto (1707 - 1747 A.D.)

Traits of Jewish Pseudo-Messiahs

How can Jewish people embrace false messiahs when they have the Holy Scriptures, learned rabbis, and a history of evil men and cultic counterfeits deceiving the nation of Israel? Below are traits of those who deceive so that we may know how not to be deceived. *Yeshua* said in the last days false messiahs would be plentiful and would deceive many (Matthew 24:4,5, 23-24).

1. WATCH for men/women who are ambitious for themselves. While it is true that God always raises leaders, be careful of those who promote themselves, and of those who want to be seen and heard. Someone has said that wanting to be a leader and attempting to be so, is a good sign that person is not qualified. Promotion of our personal ambition is an arena of devilish pride.

2. BELIEVE the truth. Do not allow feelings, emotions, experiences, or circumstances to dictate what you believe. Dr. John McArthur speaks of a "truth war." The Holy Scriptures must be our truth.

3. KNOW the messianic prophecies. There has always been, there is today, and there will be tomorrow great lack of biblical knowledge of the Holy Scriptures, especially the messianic prophecies concerning the Messiah.

4. EXAMINE the teachings. In *Shaul's*/Paul's day there was something called *Gnosticism*, an esoteric "knowledge" available to the spiritual few; these 'few' held God's secrets and everyone needed then to listen to this select "messiah" person or group. *Shaul*/Paul purged the church of such individuals, groups, cults, and movements.

5. UNDERSTAND that God has given no fixed calculation of time to His programs. We may know in some cases that we are in the season of a prophesied era, but we never know the day or hour. Fixing dates is always characteristic of cultic movements.

6. PRAY. Most people who are deceived, from Adam until today, are deceived due to a lack of a strong relationship with *Yeshua*/God. Prayer is literally our strength!

Author, Reggie Lisemby worshipping *Yeshua* at Sepphoris or Zippori, not far from Nazareth. Sepphoris was once a seat of Rabbinic Judaism. "Here, Crystal and I saw a live performance depicting the sorrow of the village concerning the death of the Rabbi. We assumed the play was about *Yeshua*; after all, his father Yoseph and He perhaps both worked here as carpenters. The famous rabbi, was Akiva, one of the constructors of Rabbinic Judaism and who despised Yeshua. Rabbinic Judaism is a Baal in the land of Israel. At the end of the drama we wept with grief!"

Question 24

How long does *The Great Tribulation* last?

Answer

In the *Apocalypse* are seven seals that contain seven judgments (Revelation 6:1-17; 18:1-5). The context of the seven seals is of the *antichrist* and the contract he makes with Israel. The *antichrist* goes forth making conquests initiating a World War, and amid the famine that occurs with one-fourth of the earth's population consumed, believers in *Yeshua* rise out from the horrendous tribulation, and myriad Jews will be saved to become evangelists to the world. One hundred-forty-four thousand Jews from the twelve tribes of Israel are sealed (Revelation 7:3-8) while simultaneously a government rises from the ten horns, described elsewhere as ten toes and ten kings (Daniel 2:41-44).

With the seven seals, are seven trumpet judgments. Six of the seven trumpet judgments occur with one-third of the remaining earth's population destroyed. One-third of the sea will be destroyed, one-third of the fresh waters will be destroyed, one-third of the heavens will be destroyed, a world blackout occurs, and also occurring, will be a global invasion of beings from the underworld, demons to torment human beings (Revelation 9). The creatures from below the soil will come out as though from hibernation. After this, there will be a second invasion of demons, and one-third of humanity living at that time will be killed by them. Nothing like this has ever happened before, ever! Only in fiction books and movies do such horrific things happen. It is understandable why even today some "educated" believers step away from a literal interpretation of the *apocalypse*. Yet, when we examine the coronavirus, the living virus that invaded the globe in the year 2020, called "the invisible enemy" by the United States President, Donald J Trump, a global life-changing event, we can comprehend that apocalyptic things are already occurring.

A literal interpretation of the *Apocalypse* of *Yeshua* is considered Christian novel, but it is not fiction, it is not history, it is prophetic and the fulfillment will be real and horrific.

The first half of the *Great Tribulation* is comprised of the following: world-wide wars; world famine; convulsions of nature; blackout; ten kings arise; a shift of world power to Europe; instability of world governments and economies; sinister Middle East wars with a focus upon Israel; a power grid inaugurated by a world leader; perpetration of political promises and lies worldwide with intrigue and flattery; a covenant with Israel; the *antichrist* making conquests; 144,000 evangelists from the twelve revived tribes of Israel; ministry of the two witnesses, *Moshe* and *Eliyah*; ecclesiastical Babylon; one-half of the earth destroyed; one-half of salt water destroyed; one-half fresh waters destroyed; one-half heavens destroyed; blackout II; invasion of demons to torment; blackout III; a recurring invasion of demons to torment; one-half humanity destroyed. *Oy Vey!* God have Mercy!

The one-hundred-forty-four-thousand Jews will know that the *antichrist* is more than a mere man and that he is energized with sinister power (Daniel 8:19-23). The one-hundred-forty-four thousand Jews will also know the seat of the *antichrist* will be in Rome that sits on the seven hills which biblical prophecy foretells (Revelation 17:8-9), and they will discern the person of *antichrist* because of his genius, flattery, and persuasiveness. He will be a demonic and deceptive leader.

The 144,000 Jewish believers from the twelve tribes of Israel will be akin to last day *Apostle Pauls*. They will see the international approval rating of the beast although the *antichrist* will rule by deception and lies, and they will interpret him for who he is, when he brings himself to the table talk with Israel for Middle East peace. The *antichrist* will then suddenly make the same historical *abomination* as Antiochus Epiphanes

IV. The *antichrist* will proclaim himself to be god (Daniel 8; Revelation 17:8,9; Daniel 7:20; 8:24, 25; 9:26,27; 2 Thessalonians 2:3,4).

"The beast that you saw was, and is not, and is about to come up out of the abyss and go to destruction. And those who dwell on the earth, whose name has not been written in the book of life from the foundation of the world, will wonder when they see the beast, that he was and is not and will come" (Revelation 17:8).

"And the meaning of the ten horns that were on its head and the other horn which came up, and before which three of them fell, namely, that horn which had eyes and a mouth uttering great boasts and which was larger in appearance than its associates. I kept looking, and that horn was waging war with the saints and overpowering them. As I looked, this horn made war with the saints and prevailed over them...." (Daniel 7:20,21).

"His power will be mighty, but not by his own power, And he will destroy to an extraordinary degree And prosper and perform his will; He will destroy mighty men and the holy people. And through his shrewdness He will cause deceit to succeed by his influence; And he will magnify himself in his heart, And he will destroy many while they are at ease. He will even oppose the Prince of princes, But he will be broken without human agency" (Daniel 8:24, 25).

"Then after the sixty-two weeks the Messiah will be cut off and have nothing, and the people of the prince who is to come will destroy the city and the sanctuary. And its end will come with a flood; even to the end there will be war; desolations are determined. "And he will make a firm covenant with the many for one week, but in the middle of the week he will put a stop to sacrifice and grain offering; and on the wing of abominations will come one who makes desolate, even until a complete destruction, one that is decreed, is poured out on the one who makes desolate" (Daniel 9:26,27).

"Let no one in any way deceive you, for it will not come unless the apostasy comes first, and the man of lawlessness is revealed, the son of destruction, who opposes and exalts himself above every so-called god or object of worship, so that he takes his seat in the temple of God, displaying himself as being God" (2 Thessalonians 2:3,4).

Heaven's two witnesses, *Moshe* and *Eliyah* will begin their three-and-a-half ministry during this first three and one-half years.

"Leave out the court which is outside the temple and do not measure it, for it has been given to the nations; and they will tread underfoot the holy city for forty-two months. And I will grant {authority} to my two witnesses, and they will prophesy for twelve hundred and sixty days, clothed in sackcloth. These are the two olive trees and the two lampstands that stand before the Lord of the earth. And if anyone wants to harm them, fire flows out of their mouth and devours their enemies; so, if anyone wants to harm them, he must be killed in this way. These have the power to shut up the sky, so that rain will not fall during the days of their prophesying; and they have power over the waters to turn them into blood, and to strike the earth with every plague, as often as they desire" (Revelation 11:2-6).

During the first three and one-half years of the total seven years, a Jewish Temple will be erected in Israel, meaning Israel has developed and returned to the old Mosaic system, rather than considering *Yeshua* and His new covenant and His *Melchizedekian* priesthood which does not include *Moshe, Aaron,* and the Levitical system. Israel will embrace the old covenant and reject *Yeshua* and His new covenant, the covenant He made foremost for Israel (Jeremiah 31:31). Therefore, Israel will be without a savior and without atonement.

The two witnesses, *Moshe* and *Eliyah,* will appear, dressed in haircloth, a sign of mourning, and they will prophesy for 1,260 days (Revelation 11:3) which is 42 thirty-day months, or three and one-half years. We must consider the two witnesses to be *Moshe* and *Eliyah* since the author of Revelation (*Yochanon*) intends for us to do so. The author describes the two witnesses by the two miracles the two witnesses performed in the *Tanakh* or OT (Revelation 11:5,6). *Yochanon the Immerser* came as we remember the forerunner of *Yeshua* in the spirit of *Eliyah*, but the *apocalypse* predicts an actual appearance of *Eliyah* the prophet, as *Malachi* prophesied, and as the Gospels foreshadowed. *Eliyah* and *Moshe* appeared with *Yeshua* on the Mount of Transfiguration and their talk was of the coming kingdom (Matthew 17:3). The disciples present and watching were so awe struck by the appearance of the three with their prophetic discussions, they wanted to build them temples!

The two witnesses will perform miracles known in biblical history (Exodus 7-11; 1 Kings 17) for the purpose of (1) validating their claim to be from God, (2) proving their ministry to be Jewish, and (3) winning the right to be heard by the Jewish nation (Revelation 11:5). However, the Jewish nation of Israel will reject their preaching since the two witnesses will be preaching the kingdom of *Yeshua* Whom Israel continues to reject. Simultaneously, the *antichrist*, perhaps requested by the Jewish nation, will execute the two witnesses, *Moshe* and *Eliyah*, and their dead bodies will not be allowed burial, but will lie in the street of Jerusalem for three and a half days, after which to the awe of the entire world they resurrect and are *raptured* in similarity of the *rapture* of the church earlier (Revelation 11:11,12).

With the ascension of the two witnesses back to heaven, Jerusalem will immediately experience a colossal earthquake of a magnitude 5 or higher, and one-tenth of the city of *Yerushalayim* will be swallowed. Seven thousand Israelis will die (Revelation 11:13), the same number of the remnant believers in *Eliyah's* day (Romans 11:4).

The Mid-Point of the Great Tribulation

The Bible speaks of a strong angel coming down from heaven clothed with a cloud, his face like the sun, his feet like pillars of fire, his right foot on the sea, his left foot on the land, with "a little book" in his hand. He roars like a lion then seven peals of thunder are uttered. This strong angel lifts his right hand to heaven and swears. *Yochanon* is told to go and take the book out of the hand of the strong angel standing on sea and land. *Yochanon* is then told after taking the little book, to eat it. What? He does! The taste is sweet, although *Yochanon* experiences a sick stomach, for his stomach is made bitter. From his nausea *Yochanon* is told to prophesy concerning many peoples, nations, tongues, and kings (Revelation 10). All of this takes place between the horrific 6th trumpet judgment with the second woe (Revelation 9:14), and the final 7th trumpet judgment and the third woe (Revelation 11:14,15).

At the mid-point of the Great Tribulation there will be an invasion of the enemies of God and Israel into the land of Israel. God will decimate them (Daniel 11:40-45; Ezekiel 38, 39).

"At the end time the king of the South will collide with him, and the king of the North will storm against him with chariots, with horsemen and with many ships; and he will enter countries, overflow {them} and pass through. He will also enter the Beautiful Land, and many {countries} will fall; but these will be rescued out of his hand: Edom, Moab and the foremost of the sons of Ammon. Then he will stretch out his hand against {other} countries, and the land of Egypt will not escape. But he will gain control over the hidden treasures of gold and silver and over all the precious things of Egypt; and Libyans and Ethiopians {will follow} at his heels. But rumors from the East and from the North will disturb him, and he will go forth with great wrath to destroy and annihilate many. He will pitch the tents of his royal pavilion between the seas and the beautiful Holy Mountain; yet he will come to his end, and no one will help him. Now at that time Michael, the great prince who stands {guard} over the sons of your people, will arise. And there will be a time of distress such as never occurred since there was a nation until that time; and at that time your people, everyone who is found written in the book, will be rescued" (Daniel 11:40-45).

It is at this time that the *antichrist* will break the covenant he made earlier with Israel. The *antichrist* and Israel will have been in league together, even agreeing on the murder of the two heavenly witnesses, *Moshe* and *Eliyah*. The *antichrist* now invades Israel and he will extend his kingdom by plundering Egypt, Sudan, and Libya whose armies God will have destroyed in the land of Israel (Daniel 11:42-43; Ezekiel 38-39).

Following his victory, the *antichrist* will commit the *Abomination of Desolation* spoken of by *Yeshua* (Matthew 24:15), *Shaul* (2 Thessalonians 2:4), and *Yochanon* (Revelation 11:2). The Jewish Temple and its rituals that Israel will have embraced (rather than *Yeshua*'s messianic new covenant and new covenant temple) will be raided by the *antichrist*. In the same prophetic context, the *antichrist* will be violently killed and there will be no one to rescue or help him (Daniel 11:45). His wound will be fatal (Revelation 13:3).

The fatal wound of the *antichrist* will be healed, and he will resurrect (Revelation 13:12)! Now, the *antichrist* who is the seed of Satan will perform wonders, causing the world to be in awe of him. The world will believe him to be god, with no regard, of course, of Yeshua Whom *Moshe* and *Eliyah* had spoken of earlier, and of whom the Church had been worshipping for two-thousand years.

The world will begin to worship the *antichrist* due to his divine behavior, performing great signs, making fire descend from the heavens in the presence of mankind, and deceiving those dwelling on the earth (Revelation 13:14). These worshippers will make an image of the beast that had been mortally wounded, but has come to life (Revelation 13:14; 17:8).

"And he deceives those who dwell on the earth because of the signs which it was given him to perform in the presence of the beast, telling those who dwell on the earth to make an image to the beast who had the wound of the sword and has come to life."

"The beast that you saw was, and is not, and is about to come up out of the abyss and go to destruction. And those who dwell on the earth, whose name has not been written in the book of life from the foundation of the world, will wonder when they see the beast, that he was and is not and will come."

It is at this time that the god of this present domain of darkness, the invisible spirit who has been up until this time continually coming before God in heaven as the book of Job depicts, is finally cast down from heaven. The devil is God's devil, and God has been allowing Satan to be our accuser, night and day accusing us to the Father, and also tempting, testing, sifting, wrestling, fighting, warring, and even killing believers for God's divine purpose of conforming us to the image of His precious Son, *Yeshua*. The body of Christ is disciplined by our adversary. Having been cast down from heaven, he goes about to kill for he now knows his time is short. In a rage, he goes forth to make war on Israel and the saints of the earth (Revelation 12).

For those living on earth at that time (the Church will already have been raptured) God has prescribed three important helps for believers to overcome the devil (Revelation 12:12). Believers may be greatly harmed and even killed, and if a Christian compromises and suffers loss, it will be the benefits and rewards that salvation brings that he will forfeit.

The foe comes viciously, as a lion (he counterfeits the Lion of Judah) roaming the earth seeking to devour, as *Kefa* depicted Satan in his first epistle (1 Peter 5:8-10). The believer will overcome Satan by acknowledging his victory according to (1) the blood of the Lamb, that is, the believer's atonement is not by works, but the divine-human blood God has shed for man's sins; (2) the Word of God that has become the believer's Word, that is, the believer's testimony, and (3) letting go of the pleasures of living, loving not life until death (Revelation 12:10-12).

"Then I heard a loud voice in heaven, saying, Now the salvation, and the power, and the kingdom of our God and the authority of His Christ have

come, for the accuser of our brethren has been thrown down, he who accuses them before our God day and night. And they overcame him because of the blood of the Lamb and because of the word of their testimony, and they did not love their life even when faced with death. For this reason, rejoice, O heavens and you who dwell in them. Woe to the earth and the sea, because the devil has come down to you, having great wrath, knowing that he has {only} a short time."

According to *Yochanon* the *antichrist* will blaspheme God, and the False Prophet of the *antichrist* will perform great signs and wonders (Revelation 13:5, 11-15).

"There was given to him a mouth speaking arrogant words and blasphemies, and authority to act for forty-two months was given to him. And he opened his mouth in blasphemies against God, to blaspheme His name and His tabernacle, {that is,} those who dwell in heaven. It was also given to him to make war with the saints and to overcome them, and authority over every tribe and people and tongue and nation was given to him. All who dwell on the earth will worship him, {everyone} whose name has not been written from the foundation of the world in the book of life of the Lamb who has been slain. If anyone has an ear, let him hear. If anyone {is destined} for captivity, to captivity he goes; if anyone kills with the sword, with the sword he must be killed. Here is the perseverance and the faith of the saints. Then I saw another beast coming up out of the earth; and he had two horns like a lamb and he spoke as a dragon. He exercises all the authority of the first beast in his presence. And he makes the earth and those who dwell in it to worship the first beast, whose fatal wound was healed. He performs great signs, so that he even makes fire come down out of heaven to the earth in the presence of men. And he deceives those who dwell on the earth because of the signs which it was given him to perform in the presence of the beast, telling those who dwell on the earth to make an image to the beast who had the wound of the sword and has come to life. And it was given to him to give breath to the image of the beast, so that the image of the beast would even speak and cause as many as do not worship the image of the beast to be killed."

The False Prophet introduces and enforces what the Bible calls the *mark of the beast* (Revelation 13:16-18) and with that system in place, the *anti-Christ* will dominate the world (Revelation 13:4,5,15-18). Satan's two beasts, the *antichrist* and the *false prophet* are his chief means for making war against Israel and the world. Everyone is caused to receive this *mark of the beast* and only with this insignia will man be able to buy or sell, do business, make any transaction, in short, to survive.

Yeshua gave to *Yochanon* the *gematria* or the numeric value of the beast's name so that he may be identified. The beast will have a name and it will be possible for some, perhaps studied and enlightened Jewish believers to identify and recognize the beast by using the Hebraic numerical value of his name.[32] His number **for those who have wisdom** *being the number of a man, six hundred and sixty-six* (Revelation 13:15-18).

The Jewish people living in Israel will be forced to flee the country of Israel and find solace somewhere outside the land of Israel. It is believed that *Petra* in Jordan may be the haven of refuge for divine protection (Matthew 24:16-20; Revelation 12:15-17).

"then those who are in Judea must flee to the mountains. Whoever is on the housetop must not go down to get the things out that are in his house. Whoever is in the field must not turn back to get his cloak. But woe to those who are pregnant and to those who are nursing babies in those days! But pray that your flight will not be in the winter, or on a Sabbath."

"And the serpent poured water like a river out of his mouth after the woman, so that he might cause her to be swept away with the flood. But the earth helped the woman, and the earth opened its mouth and drank up the river which the dragon poured out of his mouth. So, the dragon was enraged with

---

32 Hebrew *alephbeit* and numeric values: *aleph* (1); *beit* (2); *gimel* (3); *dalet* (4); *hey* (5); *vav* (6); *zayin* (7); *chet* (8); *tet* (9); *yod* (10); *kauf* (20); *lamed* (30); *mem* (40); *nun* (50); *samekh* (60); *ayin* (70); *peh* (80); *tzade* (90); *qoph* (100); *resh* (200); *shin* (300); *tav* (400).

the woman, and went off to make war with the rest of her children, who keep the commandments of God and hold to the testimony of Jesus."

A literal interpretation of Revelation 12:15-17 is that Satan will cause a duplicate flood as in *Noach's* day in order to destroy Israel, although the flood will be localized and confined to Israel, and not global. With God's help the earth will open and swallow the waters. This will be done by an earthquake. Some interpreters see this flood metaphorically as political and military.

The *antichrist* will indeed gain political control over the ten kings of the Roman Empire, but shortly after he does so, only seven kings submit. So, the three noncompliant kings are killed (Daniel 7:24; Revelation 17:12-13).

The mid-point of the Great Tribulation is comprised of the following:

o World War

o antichrist killed

o Satan cast down to the earth and no longer access to heaven

o antichrist raised by Satan

o three kings are killed and seven kings submit to him

o ecclesiastical Babylon destroyed

o two witnesses (*Moshe* and *Eliyah*) killed

o seven-year covenant broken

o *abomination of desolation*

o false prophet

o the mark of the beast (666)

o persecution of Jews begins

The Last Half and End of the Great Tribulation

During the final three and one-half years there will be world-wide antisemitism and God will enter into judgment against the nations for their hate of Israel (Joel 3:2), myriad who are now messianic believers.

"I will gather all the nations And bring them down to the valley of Jehoshaphat. Then I will enter into judgment with them there On behalf of My people and My inheritance, Israel, Whom they have scattered among the nations; And they have divided up My land."

It is during this time that there is a deafening silence, a dramatic pause in heaven. Perhaps the lull is for a review, or perhaps the silence is to contemplate the dreaded expectation of what's coming. Then, the final last trumpet, the seventh trumpet is unleashed (Revelation 8-9). One-third of the remaining earth is charred, one-third of the remaining seas are turned to blood, one-third of the remaining sea life is destroyed, one-third of the world's sea vessels are destroyed, one-third of the remaining fresh waters of the earth are poisoned, and one-third of the remaining cosmological planets and stars and luminaries in the heavens are darkened. Locusts from hell are loosed; these are beings that sting like a scorpion while tormenting man for five months. Yet, man is unable to die. The appearance alone of these horse-scorpions from hell is a nightmare (Revelation 8, 9).

Yochanon heard a loud voice from heaven saying, *"Go and pour out the seven bowls of the wrath of God into the earth.* These are the bowl judgments (Revelation 16:1-21). Malignant sores, scorching heat, men gnawing their tongues because of pain, and then an invasion of a great army takes place, an army from "the rising sun," that is, China. Some interpret the invaders as a demonic invasion which brings the horrendous tribulation to an end.

"they are the spirits of demons, performing signs, which go out to the kings of the whole world to gather them together for the war of the great day of God, the Almighty…and they gathered them together to the place which is Hebrew is called Har-Magedon" (Revelation 16:12-16).

Babylon that had risen earlier will now be destroyed (Revelation 17-18), and the *Armageddon* campaign will have begun (Revelation

16:16). As for *Yerushalayim* it will have become so perverse by this time it is called *Sodom* in the apocalyptic scroll (Revelation 11:8). The following events occur during the last half of the Great Tribulation:

- o pestilence of malignant sores
- o salt water destroyed
- o fresh water destroyed
- o scorching heat of the sun increased
- o blackout III
- o invasion of China
- o world war/Armageddon
- o the two witnesses, *Moshe* and *Eliyah* murdered
- o *Yerushalayim* now called *Sodom*

The tribulation will be horrendous. In fact, *Yeshua* said there has never been nor will there ever be [in the future] such a horrific thing (Matthew 24:21).

The wrath of God is poured out upon the earth, and, again, to the Jews, first. He will shake the entire earth with a Holocaust that supersedes Hitler's. Lands, oceans, seas, rivers, drinking water, planets, stars, sun, moon, man, beasts, and birds will be affected. The *perfect storm* of judgment happens as the wrath of Satan which was unleashed earlier, and the wrath of the Lamb, which is now being poured out, both come together for torment and misery, and there will be absolutely nowhere to run, hide, or be secure.

The Second Coming of *Yeshua* is near!

Malakhi's words to the Jews in his prophetic scroll were something akin to this observation. "You just think you want the Lord to come!" He is coming, and He is coming in His wrath!

Jewish man praying at the Western/Wailing Wall in Jerusalem. There are three dominant prayers prayed here: (1) peace of Jerusalem, Israel, and the world; (2) a new Temple, and (3) the Messiah's coming. It is terribly sad that these prayers prayed today, are not the will of the Father, YHWH today. His Messiah, *Yeshua* has come and *Yeshua* has been and is being ignored and rejected, His Temple is His beloved followers of *Yeshua*, Who are His congregation/church, and He sees to it, that there will be no peace in Jerusalem until His son and Messiah, *Yeshua* reigns as king.

Question 25

Do the sun, moon, and stars predict the Rapture or the Second Coming of Jesus?

Answer

The stars are in essence suns, very similar to our own sun although so very far away they appear as tiny twinklers in the night sky. The star nearest to us is *Alpha Centauri* and is the size of our sun. By observing *Alpha Centauri* we can see how the sun would look if it were the same distance from us, that is 4.3 light years. How far is that? The distance of stars from earth is easier measured in *light years*, the distance that light travels in a year at the speed of light which is 186,000 miles per second. Think of the distance that light travels in just 1 minute based on that speed (1 minute is 60 seconds; 60 sec X 186,000 miles per second = 11,160,000 miles that light travels in 1 minute).

A *light year* is quite amazing. *Alpha Centauri* is 25 trillion miles from earth. The light you see tonight or any other night when you step outside and look up into the night sky (if you are able to see the heavens), left on its journey 2 million years ago or longer, which suggests then, that "the beginning" where God created *the heavens and the earth* (Genesis 1:1) was truly the very beginning, perhaps millions of years before Genesis 1:2. In the "beginning" the heavens and earth were created as God does by default, pristine and pure. Genesis chapter one and verse two describes a horrific sight: chaos; confusion; distortion; deformity; emptiness; darkness (*tohu vaV'ohu*), the result of the Luciferian fall and flood.

God's inspired author, *Moshe* begins his narration of the re-creation of the earth. God brought up from the dark seas, the land which remained a major motif in the Holy Scripture all the way to the end, until the *New Jerusalem* in Revelation. This re-creation given in Genesis happened near six thousand years ago. It has been six thousand years from Adam until this present day as I write and as you read this book.

As for the stars, astronomers tell us that there are 10,000,000,000, 000,000,000,000,000,000 stars (that's 10 with 27 zeros) in our own galaxy. More fascinating than that, is that according to the biblical psalmist, God knows the stars, every one, and He has named them and numbered them (Psalm 147:4).

"He counts the number of the stars; He gives names to all of them."

The prophet Isaiah also tells us that God has each star of the gillion, trillion, billion, million of them named (Isaiah 40:26).

"Lift up your eyes on high and see who has created these stars, the one who leads forth their host by number, He calls them all by name...."

Stars are colored; the hotter ones are whiter or bluer, and the cooler ones are orange or red. There are also dark stars, those too cool to give off enough light to be detected by infrared photography. During our days in Chicago while attending the Moody Bible Institute completing our *Jewish and Modern Israel Studies,* Crystal and I and the children enjoyed many perks of the big city. During a Christmas season in the windy city, we made a visit to the Adler planetarium. Founded by a Jewish astronomer of the same name, Adler planetarium has a computerized Zeiss projector that has the extraordinary ability to "rewind" and "fast forward" the map of the stars. In the planetarium's domed theater astronomers can choose dates from the remote past and recreate historical night skies with astonishing accuracy. Adler has recreated in a special sky show known as 'The Star of Wonder,' the sky that the *magi* might have seen between 4 BC and 2 BC. In August of the year 3 B.C. Jupiter known in Hebrew as *Tzedeq* meaning "righteous," the planet that supposedly represented kingship, coronation, and the birth of kings, passed very near Venus the brightest planet which is said to signify "new life." Months later, three new conjunctions took place between Jupiter, Venus and the star Regulus, a planet in the constellation of Leo. Some cosmologists think that this threesome star convocation may be the same constellation that *Yoseph* saw in his dream and told his father *Yaaqov* and eleven brothers. His dream was that the sun, moon, and eleven other *kokavim* or star-clusters (or constellations) all bowed to his star. *Moshe* gave *Yaaqov's* interpretation of his son's dream, one of true and prophetic Star Worship. Father *Yaaqov* interpreted the celestial fire-ball called the sun to be analogous of him, he interpreted the lunar star orbiting the earth we call the moon that reflects the light of the sun to the earth, to be symbolic of Leah, his wife who was the matriarch of Israel, and *Yaaqov* interpreted the twelve stars or constellations of *Yoseph's* dream, analogous of his twelve sons (and their tribes), each one ruling the earth for approximately 30 days/one month, from the waxing to the waning of the moon. Daddy *Yaaqov* interpreted the night sky as analogous of his family when hearing *Yoseph's* dream (Genesis 37). Was *Yaaqov* correct?

In early Israelite history seven times it was told Israel *"you shall be as the stars"* (Genesis 15:5; Genesis 22:17; Genesis 26:4; Exodus 32:13; Deuteronomy 1:10; Deuteronomy 10:22; Deuteronomy 28:62). Then, Israel entered into battle and the Holy Scriptures say, *"the stars in their courses (or orbit) fought for Israel, the stars fought from heaven, from their courses they fought against Sisera [for Israel]"* (Judges 5:20). The patriarch *Yaaqov* knew as the patriarchs before him knew, that the heavens are like a scroll, they reveal God and His master plan.

C.S. Lewis wrote in his *Chronicles of Narnia, The Last Battle*, **"the stars never lie, but men and beasts do."** Paganism did not inaugurate stargazing, star study, or astronomy. Let's be clear by using the Bible as our main resource: the heavens declare the glory of God. Glory is not a trite word. Glory is *Elohim's* manifestation, His revelation, His authentication, and His presentation. *Elohim* is the tripartite essence of the triune Godhead, and His glory is His invisible Word. *Morning to morning and evening to evening the heavens speak, declaring His glory* (Psalm 19). If only we could read God's [first] revelation.

What the patriarchs read, paganism corrupted. Of course. That is what Satan and demons do; they counterfeit and/or corrupt. The stars in their courses were made for lights, signs, and seasons, says *Moshe* in Genesis 1. They shine, they reveal, they instruct, until the time God would decide to disclose His special revelation on canvas, His Holy Scriptures.

The study of the heavens to discover God's messianic plan, predates the study of God's messianic plan written on papyrus and vellum. The heavens heralded His Word, first. The written Word came later. I am not suggesting that astronomy is in anyway superior or a nexus or even comparable to the written *Davar* (Hebrew), *Logos* (Greek), or the Holy Scriptures. I am suggesting that before 1445 BC when *Moshe* began writing the Torah, God had already spoken by the witness of the stars. Man has NEVER been without the Word of God!

The Holy Scriptures describe God presenting to *Moshe* the schematic or design of the tabernacle. Yet, there was already a tabernacle. According to the Holy Scriptures, the heavens are the tabernacle, and the sun is described as a bridegroom leaving "his" chamber to run "his" course or his orbit (Psalm 19:5). Again, let's be clear. God never intended for His people to build *ziggurats* or pyramids in order to worship the heavens. That is idolatry. The cosmological bodies were purposed by God, however, to tell us about Himself and His Messiah, His Spirit, and His rule. When Messiah came, the stars witnessed of Him! Ask the *Magi!*

The magi from the east were Arab believers perhaps descendants of the Medes whom the prophet *Dani'el* referenced as *magoi* (Daniel 1:20; 2:2; 4:7; 5:7). These were Arabs on quest for truth. The *magi* of the NT era studied the biblical/Jewish prophecies and they studied the scrolls of heaven alongside them. The *magi* calculated the fulfillment of biblical prophecies in accordance with the stars and astrological equations. These men were not rogues or charlatans. They were not mystics, but disciples of the divine study. They having read of "Him" in the night sky, set out for the holy city, Jerusalem. They came with gifts of gold, for a king. They brought incense the scriptures tell us, for the king's death, and they brought myrrh for the king's resurrection. Because of the three gifts tradition has deduced there were three wisemen, and tradition has given them names. Yet, according to the prophecy of Isaiah, they came in great number. Isaiah prophesied, a multitude of camels will cover you (Isaiah 60:1-5). Read the text, it's a good messianic prophecy!

For nearly two millennia the world which God made was without a written word from Him. Yet, the patriarchs read God, knew God and walked with Him. The patriarchs read Him in His heavens. They sung His cantata. They knew some of what His glory was telling, not all, of course, but some! The corruption of God's first venue of the Gospel, the heavens, was by Satan and his powers of darkness.

God has rules, divine rules, that both He and the adversary must obey. The enemy was allowed to magnify himself, and he did. He was allowed to boast against God, and he did. He was allowed to corrupt God's creation, to corrupt God's man and woman, to corrupt God's garden, to corrupt God's divine scroll, the heavens, to corrupt God's prophets, priests, kings, and God's people. God allowed the adversary to counterfeit His messianic glory with occult astrology, and Satan has. However, God gets the final say which is given in Revelation 12, *the Star Gospel.*

Yochanon saw the virgin, clothed with the sun, under her feet the moon, and on her head a crown of twelve stars. She was pregnant and she cried out in labor and pain to give birth. Another wonder appeared in heaven. The dragon/serpent from the beginning was present to destroy her child THE MOMENT He was born. Yes, the dragon was in Bethlehem. Read the chapter to sense the rage and hate of the serpent for God. What *Yochanon* saw was a *last days* scenario of the beast, *antichrist*, the number 666, but he also saw the Lamb standing on Mount Zion.

The patriarchs were stargazers. *Adam, Set, Enos, Canaan, Mahallalel, Yared, Khanoch, Methuselah, Noach, Shem, Avraham, Yitzack, Yaaqov, Yoseph* and his brothers, all knew something of God's messianic plan since they studied the *Davar* (Hebrew), that is, the Word (English) in the heavens. What did they study? What do the heavens declare? The Holy Scriptures declare that the heavens, the sun and moon, the stars in their orbit all declare the glory of YHWH and His handiwork.

The patriarchs knew this! Day-to-day the Word is worded, and night to night, there is knowledge of the Word. There is no place where there is not a night sky, and no place where the Word is not 'voiced' or heard (Psalm 19:1-4). The heavens declare the dragon or serpent, the virgin, the Lion, and a single star that descends out from twelve stars who humble themselves and bow before Him!

The patriarchs studied and knew that the heavens with its stars are a tabernacle for *Yaaqov* and his dozen sons of whom the twelve stations called *mazzaroth* ("signs") in Hebrew, and *zodiakos* ("circle") in Greek commemorate, in the ecliptic circle or path for the sun (Psalm 147:1-4). The patriarchs studied and knew that the twelve major constellations in the heavens, each one 'ruling' the cosmos for approximately thirty days (a month), were pictures in the night sky of the messianic plan of *Elohim*. All twelve moons or months preach the glory of God.

The patriarch, Job knew of *Pleaides*, "the Seven Sisters" (38:31), *Orion* (38:31), *Arcturus the Bear* (9:9), and *Mazzaroth* (38:32) meaning, "twelve signs." *Yochanon* when writing the final scroll of Holy Writ, the Apocalypse wrote of a great sign in heaven, "a woman dressed with the sun, the moon under her feet, and a crown with twelve stars on her head." Another sign shown was "a dragon in the sky, with seven heads, ten horns (or, kings), and on his head a crown of seven diadems." What *Yochanon* saw in the heavens first, he then wrote on parchment (Revelation 12).

The Jewish historian, Flavious Josephus wrote of *Seth*, the son of Adam who Josephus said, *knew the zodiac and its language.* Josephus suggested that God gave the early patriarchs, the antediluvians, long lives so that they might perfect their astronomical inventions (Book 1; Chapter 2; Section 3).

"Now this Seth, when he was brought up and came to those years in which he could discern what was good, became a virtuous man; and as he was himself of an excellent character, so did he leave children behind him who imitate his virtues. All these proved to be of good dispositions. They also inhabited the same country without dissentions and in a happy condition, without any misfortunes falling upon them until they died. They also were the inventor of that peculiar sort of wisdom, which is concerned with the heavenly bodies and their order. And that their inventions might not be lost before they were sufficiently known, upon Adams prediction that the world was to be destroyed at one time by the force of fire, and at another time by the violence and quantity of water, they made two pillars, the one of brick, the other of stone. They inscribed their discoveries on them both, that in case the pillar of brick should be destroyed by the flood, the pillar of stone might remain and exhibit these discoveries to mankind. Now this remains in the land of Siriad to this day."

Persian and Arabian traditions ascribe the understanding of the zodiac (from the Hebrew *tsodi* meaning "the way" or "the path") to *Seth* and his great, great, great, great, grandson, *Enoch*.

Avraham was told by *Elohim* to count the stars and in doing so he counted his children. Neutron stars, protostars, pulsars, quasars, spiral galaxies, ring galaxies, Seyfert galaxies, white dwarfs, brown dwarfs, red giants, magnetars, X-ray busters, nebulae, globular clusters, globular clusters, circumstellar matter, dark matter, etc., all make up what is called "a cosmic zoo" (Stedman 202), and like the Hebrew language itself, the heavens display the world's first Picture Show of Messiah.

The star descending from *Yaaqov* was the star assigned to *Yeshua*, the star that the stargazing *Magi* saw in the east that led them to Jerusalem where the king was to sit. It was a star, in its course, not an apparition or ghost that led the *Magi* onward to *BeitLechem*. The *Magi* were perhaps *Zoroastrian* priests whose duties included the mapping and interpretation of the movement of stars. They lived close to a

Jewish seminary and were certainly familiar and studious of the messianic predictions. The *Magi* might also have been descendants of the Jewish captives in Babylon (609, 597, 586 BC) who remained behind from the 50,000 who returned to Jerusalem. The *Magi* were certainly esteemed students of prophecy and astronomy observing the seasons and the *kokavim* or stars, and interpreting their signs, since stars were created for this very the purpose (Genesis 1).

Are you a stargazer? The heavens are like musical notes, a grand cantata, and they are sign-posts of God to man. The heavens are eschatological banners of YHWH's soon coming. But, can we read His music? Not so good! We need the written Word, black ink on paper, since we are [more] fallen. Yet, the Word of God is living. He spoke to *Noach* in the fertile crescent, to *Avraham* in Ur, to *Moshe* in Egypt, and to Reggie in Lake Charles, Louisiana. The *Davar/Logos*/Word lives outside the confines of cosmology and outside the confines of paper. The Word of God is living!

The Word of God was initially written [first] in the heavens, then in creation, His Word was written in the sites of the holy land, then on papyrus, vellum, and pages of a book. His Word needs to be written on the hearts of man (John 1:9). We are without excuse!

Total solar eclipse in the United States, 2017; picture taken in Cleveland, TN, 1:30 PM in the afternoon.

Question 26

Who are the Two Witnesses that will come to Jerusalem?

Answer

The *Apocalypse* is the only scroll in the entire Bible that is said to be directly from *Yeshua* (Revelation 1:1), endorsed by *Yeshua* (Revelation 22:16), and that promises a blessing to those who read, hear, and obey the apocalyptic scroll (Revelation 1:3). In the *Apocalypse* are the words of *Yeshua* concerning two witnesses who are coming to Jerusalem.

"I will give power unto my two witnesses, and they shall prophesy a thousand two hundred and threescore days, clothed in sackcloth" (Revelation 11:1-14).

In context two men arrive as "witnesses" during the last days, and their arrival will be during a time when the Temple will be the epicenter of the Jewish (and Gentile) world. A Temple will be built in Jerusalem (Revelation 11:1,2) and that Temple will be desolated as prophesied by *Yeshua* (Matthew 24:15), just as the OT Temple was desolated by Antiochus Epiphanes IV. In concert with the desolation, the two men who are called "two witnesses" will prophesy for exactly 1,260 days, or 42 thirty-day months which is exactly three and one-half years (biblical months are thirty days from Genesis to Revelation).

Knowing the Word of God, we are to assume these *two witnesses* are *Moshe* and *Eliyah* since we know that *Eliyah* had power to shut heaven from rain (I Kings 17:1), and *Moshe* had power to turn waters to blood (Exodus 7:20). Also, these two men appeared with *Yeshua* on the

Mount of Transfiguration, and *Kefa*/Peter wanted to build a temple for all three (Matthew 17:3). *Yeshua*, the author of the *Apocalypse* wants the reader to have evidences and He gave us the information needed of recognizing the *antichrist*, by *the number of his [the antichrist] name*, so we may identify the *antichrist* (Revelation 13:17,18), and *Yeshua* wants the readers to identify the two witnesses as *Moshe* and *Eliyah* since He gave us the miracles performed by no one other, than these two.

For three and one-half years these two visitors from heaven are invincible. Dressed in sackcloth which was a sign of mourners in distress, they prophesy among Israelis. No one can touch them (Revelation 11:5) and their message is to the Jews! This is why their manifestation of powers are a nexus to OT events concerning Israel, the miracle of shutting the heavens from rain, and turning waters to blood (Revelation 11:6). Jews living in the coming last of the last days may recognize the two witnesses by their biblical powers, and they may also investigate the account of these two men with *Yeshua* on the Mount of Transfiguration. Many will believe and be saved due to the witness of *Moshe* and *Eliyah*, but the majority of Israel will not believe.

After three and one-half years, their assigned period of preaching, the *antichrist* will be permitted to kill the two witnesses (Revelation 11:7), and their bodies will lie in the street of the city of *Yerushalayim* without burial. Jerusalem will be so nasty that *Yeshua* in His apocalypse labels the city, "Sodom." Jerusalem will be so rebellious against God's manifestation of miracles, that *Yeshua* in His apocalypse labeled the city of Jerusalem, "Egypt" (Revelation 11:8).

Jerusalem and the entire world will be very happy that *Moshe* and *Eliyah* are murdered and their teaching silenced. The general reaction of the entire world when *antichrist*, the world Czar silences the preaching of God's Word by murdering these two men of God, is thanksgiving with a celebration of giving gifts (Revelation 11:10). The world will have become so bedeviled that the world will applaud God's two holy men being murdered while embracing the son of Satan, the antichrist, and his name, and the number of his name that they will wear on their forehead or hand.

After the 3½ days, *Moshe* and *Eliyah* who will have been lying in the street of Jerusalem, will resurrect and they will ascend out of this world back to heaven in accordance with an earthquake that will violently shake Jerusalem. The earthquake will be intense that one-tenth of Jerusalem will be killed (Revelation 11:13). In the year, 2020 as I write this book, that would be 95,000 Jerusalemites. The third woe is now unleashed! Oy Vey!

How is the coming of *Moshe* and *Eliyah* to Jerusalem relevant? A Jew cannot think of *Moshe* without remembering how he shepherded Israel to the promised land; he was the deliverer of the remnant. *Eliyah* is so famous that he is considered in any talk of messiah, the messianic age or era, and a messianic kingdom. Jews remember *Eliyah's* contesting the *Baals* in the land of Israel. He was a prophet of judgment and reform.

Dr. Hugh van Eaton, my former pastor once reminded me, when we preach, teach, write, sing, or give the Word, we are ALWAYS doing the work of God, for we are either giving someone the message of their salvation or we are giving them the message of salvation which they have rejected and will be their judgment. Everyone must hear the message! Messianic Ministry to Israel with whom I serve challenges modern Israel and the Jews of our world with a choice! The Gospel is the message of *Yeshua*, the Prophet like unto *Moshe,* and His new covenant (Deuteronomy 18:15). There is no other Gospel, so the alternative choice is believing anti-*Yeshua* "rabbis" with their oral traditions written in the Talmud, which is *Baal* worship. We have today in Israel, God's backyard, a contest [again] of *Baal* and *YHWH*!

Yeshua is YHWH's only way, truth, and life. All other faiths and religions are *Baal.* Modern Israel needs *Eliyah* to challenge their Judaism, a Judaism that is leading Jewish people away from *Yeshua.* *Moshe* and *Eliyah* are coming and will do just that!

On our Prayer Mission to Israel (May-June 2019) Crystal and I prayed in Haifa concerning the Baals in the land of Israel. The Bahai Shrine (above) on the slope of Mount Carmel is Baal in the land of Israel. Islam is also Baal in the land of Israel.

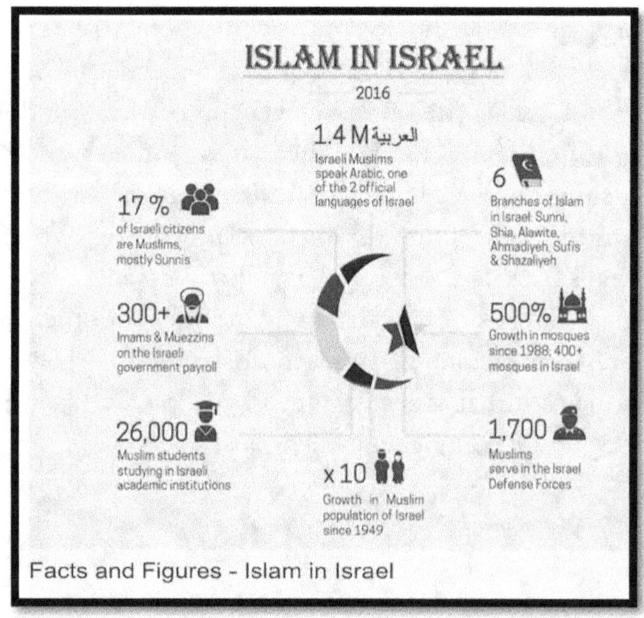

Question 27

Is Eschatological Babylon the Catholic Church?

Answer

Babylon is spoken of in Revelation chapters 17-19 as an ecclesiastical religious system which will corrupt the earth. This Babylon is reminiscent of ancient Babylon in Genesis 11. In fact, last-days Babylon is the same Babylon of Genesis, and Babylon in Revelation 17-19 is also the same Babylon of Nebuchadnezzar in the scroll of *Dani'el*. Eschatological Babylon is not the Catholic Church although the roots of Catholicism are Babylonian.[33]

The apocalyptic Babylon is not New York, America although many renown prophecy teachers interpret Babylon as the great commercial city. Someone has identified sixteen parallels between Babylon and modern New York, and Jack Van Impe, the former renown TV evangelist somewhat agreed, pointing to Jeremiah 50 and 51 to be in concert with Revelation 18 concerning Babylon and New York.

R.A. Coombes in his book, *America, the Babylon: America's Destiny Foretold in Biblical Prophecy* sites thirty-three markers of apocalyptic Babylon as America. I disagree with the analogous interpretation, but in lieu of the question, here are some of the parallels of Babylon and New York.

1. New York is the greatest commercial city of the world. Babylon is that city in Revelation 18:9-11.

---

[33] Adoration of a goddess (Maryolotry); prayers to and for the dead; purgatory; weeping for Tammuz; infant baptism; confession to a priest; system of sacraments; infallible Pope with a celibate hierarchy; worship of relics; bowing to idols; repetitious prayers are all remnants of the pagan Babylonian system.

2. New York was seen around the world as the World Trade Center burned. Babylon will burn in Revelation 18:9-11.

3. New York was destroyed in one hour, the merchants of the world mourning. Merchants of the earth mourn for Babylon in Revelation 18:9-11.

4. John the Apostle alludes in Revelation 18 of a rich land although laden with sins that glorified herself causing her to live deliciously. New York is promoted to be lavish in glory.

5. New York is the last of the superpowers. Babylon is such a superpower in Jeremiah 50:12.

6. New York is where the body of the world's leaders assemble and meet. Babylon is where the leaders of the world assembled, but will stream there no more, according to Jeremiah 51:44.

7. New York is extremely wealthy; Babylon has a treasury according to Jeremiah 51:13.

8. New York is a land of immigrants. Babylon was once sown and it harvested people (Jeremiah 50:16).

9. New York has no fear of invasion on its own soil. Babylon was the mistress of nations (Isaiah 47:5,8).

10. New York is known for its disrespect of the elderly. Babylon laid a heavy yoke on the elderly (Isaiah 47:6).

11. New York is guarded by a military air power and is a land of air travel. Babylon was noted for sending envoys by ship, swift messengers to nations far and near (Isaiah 18:1-2).

12. New York has stealth technology. Babylon had great wisdom and knowledge (Isaiah 47:10-13).

13. New York is the location of the only world-governing body, the United Nations. Babylon will be that body in Revelation 17:2,8.

14. New York is the world city of commerce, trading the following commodities daily: coffee, sugar, cocoa at the Coffee, Sugar, and Cocoa Exchange; cotton and orange juice at the New York Cotton Exchange; crude oil, gasoline, natural gas, heating oil, platinum, and palladium traded at the New York Mercantile

Exchange; gold, silver, and copper traded at the New York Mercantile Comex Division; diamonds, precious gems, iron, ivory, marble, spices, cosmetics, legal pharmaceutical drugs, and professional services related to advertising, media, and the arts; and fine foreign wines from the world. Babylon in the last days will be such a city of commerce (Revelation 18:11-13).

15. New York is home to the New York Stock Exchange, American Stock Exchange, NASDAQ, the largest banks in the world including the Federal Reserve Bank, the engine of wealth for the world economy. Babylon will be such a city (Revelation 18:11-19).

16. New York is the deep-water sea port, one of the greatest seaports in the world. Babylon is such a deep-water sea port (see Revelation 18:17-19).

17. New York is the key cultural city of the world. Babylon will be a key cultural city of the world in the last days (Revelation 18:22).

18. New York is the largest consumer of illicit drugs, especially heavy drugs like heroin and cocaine, and for merchandising occultism. Babylon will be noted for its sorcery (Revelation 18:23).

19. New York has the largest population of Jews in America, and the second largest population of Jews in the world. In the last days God will call His people out of Babylon (Revelation 18:4; Jeremiah 50:8, 28; 51:6, 45-46).

20. On Long Island overlooking the main harbor approach to New York City and within the view of the Statue of Liberty is the community of Babylon, New York. The city received its name due to the large influx of Jewish immigrants settling in the area.

All the above is interesting, so hence the list. However, eschatological Babylon is biblical Babylon and not New York, America. Babylon spoken of in the book of Revelation is the ancient biblical Babylon resuscitated, resurrected, and rebuilt. Babylon in the scroll of Revelation is presented as a wicked city and not a nation. It is presented as a city that persecutes God's people, especially the prophets and saints. New York City America has actually been a haven to Jewish and Christian immigrants from around the world (although it was years ago). Babylon the great city and capital of the *antichrist* is specifically called "Babylon" six times in Revelation (14:8; 16:19; 17:5; 18:2; 18:10; 18:21). Some suggest that the name "Babylon" is only a code name for New York City or Rome or Jerusalem or another. However, nothing in the biblical text indicates that Babylon is to be taken figuratively or symbolically.

Babylon is mentioned 290 times in the Holy Scriptures, more than any other city in the world except for *Yerushalayim*. At most every mention of the city in the Holy Scriptures Babylon is the epitome of evil and rebellion against God. Babylon is Satan's capital city on earth. For this reason, Babylon in Revelation is the Babylon of Genesis, the city of man's first organized rebellion, the capital city of the world's first ruler, *Nimrod* (Genesis 10:8-10; 11:9).

A literal rebuilt city of Babylon best fits the criteria laid out in Revelation 17-18. The renowned scholar, Dr. Robert Thomas notes, "Babylon on the Euphrates has a location that fits this description politically, geographically, and in all the qualities of accessibility, commercial facilities, remoteness of interferences of church and state, and yet centrality in regard to the trade of the whole world."

The vision of Zechariah (5:5-11) argues for a literal Babylon, as do the prophets of the Holy Scriptures who predicted that the city of Babylon will be destroyed. It is reasonable to read Babylon as literal and not figurative (Isaiah 13:19-22; 14:22,23; Jeremiah 50:9,10, 11-16, 21-27, 39-40, 41-42, 45,46; 51:7-9, 24-26, 29, 48-49, 54-58, 59-64). Jeremiah clearly describes the geographical city of Babylon on the Euphrates (51:13 cf. Revelation 17:1) in comparison with *Yochanon* describing the destruction of Babylon in Revelation 18:1-3.

Babylon was a city in the land of Shinar, the kingdom of Nimrod, east of the place of the beginnings, that is, east of Eden, away from

God. Eschatological Babylon will have a spiritual [religious] system. In prophetic language prostitution, fornication, harlotry, and adultery are equivalent to idolatry and religious apostasy (Isaiah 25:15-17; Jeremiah 2:20-31; Ezekiel 16:17-19; Hosea 2:5; Nahum 3:4). This spiritual system is reminiscent of the tower of Babylon in Genesis 10:9-10; 11:1-9. Ancient Babylon had such a spiritual system. Its name *Babylon* from *Babel* meaning "confusion," was the place where man rallied to build a tower to God rather than disperse across the earth. The intent of man was to organize a spiritual "gate" to God, not a literal stairway to the entrance of heaven from earth, but a cosmological system of worship or gate of inquiry.

Babylon became a communistic and socialistic kingdom associated with pantheistic religion. Gods were created representing every act of natural expression. Babylon was associated with pagan art, drama, music, and sexual and carnal satisfactions. Babylon's philosophical form of governmental was the control of the people.

Ur which was the capital of ancient Babylon, and God called *Avram* out of Babylon to another land, "the" land, the land of Israel. To *Avraham* God gave the gateway to heaven, which was His covenant (Genesis 12).

The heyday of Babylon was its golden age under the reign of Hammurabi (1792-1750) who codified the laws of Babylon and extended his empire. Babylon reached its glory in the days of Nebuchadnezzar, 604-562 BC. His empire stretched across the lands of Iraq, Saudi Arabia, Syria, Lebanon, Jordan, Israel and Kuwait. The historian Herodutus described the city of Babylon to be 15 miles square, surrounded by a brick wall 100 feet high and 87 feet thick where 6 chariots could drive abreast. There were 250 towers on the wall and outside the wall was a moat, and water from the Euphrates river ran inside the city. There were 25 magnificent streets 150 feet wide which ran from north of south, and an equal number ran east to west making 676 squares in the city. Babylon contained one of the ancient wonders of the world, the Hanging Gardens. This is the city that is coming to the world in the last days? Yes, it is!

In 541 BC Cyrus of the Medo-Persian Empire captured the city by draining the river that formed the moat and surmounted the banks and entered through the gates that had been unlocked because of a grand party. Darius took Babylon in 516 BC. Later, in 478 BC Xerxes captured Babylon.

In 331 BC Alexander the Great selected Babylon as his intended capital and he died there. Babylon came under the power of Seleucus in 293 BC and was later ruled by the Parthians who replaced the Greeks in about 140 BC. Jews from Babylon came to Jerusalem for the Feast of Pentecost mentioned in Acts 2 (Parthians, Medes, Elamites residents of Mesopotamia). In AD 60 Babylon still stood mentioned by *Kefa* (1 Peter 5:13), and by the 5th Century there were 3 Jewish universities.

Babylon is where the *Babylonian Talmud* was written by the academies of Babylon, actually the better Talmud of the two Talmuds, the Jerusalem Talmud and the Babylonian Talmud since the scholars in Babylon were able to live, work, study, and write, while those in the land of Israel were continually under aggression, facing wars, and were always moving and sometimes hiding.

Babylon slowly declined, yet in the last days the city will recover and resurrect to be the greatest commercial city on earth (Isaiah 13:19-22; 14:3-4, 22; Jeremiah 50:1-5, 8-10, 13-16, 41-46; Jeremiah 51:1-10, 24-32, 49-58; Micah 4:10; 5:6).

Below is an interesting comparison of the Woman on the Beast in Revelation 17 and the Woman of the Statue of Liberty. Yet, to answer the question, Babylon is not the Catholic Church, but Babylon is the revived ancient city of Babylon found throughout Holy Writ.

THE WOMAN ON THE BEAST	THE WOMAN OF THE STATUE OF LIBERTY
Robed in scarlet and purple (17:4)	Robed (originally in scarlet)
Golden cup in her hand (17:4)	Golden cup was originally in her hand; changed to a torch
Purpose denotes royalty; she may wear a crown	Wears a crown of seven spikes or horns
Cup contents are smelly pollutants connected to immigrants (17:15)	Cup/torch contents is natural gas flame for immigrants
She sits on seven heads or mountains/continents (17:3,7,9)	Her seven spikes or horns are seven continents
Represents Babylon the megacity	Overlooks Babylon on Long Island; a representation of the goddess of liberty, aka *Aphrodite, Venus, Isis, and Ishtar*
Reigns over the kings of the earth (17:2)	Overlooks the UN building; reigns over the largest commercial nation in the world
Mother of harlots (17:5)	Mother of exiles according to the poem on the base of the statue

Question 28

Couldn't the Rapture and the Second Coming of Christ be the same eschatological return of Christ?

Answer

Following the rapture of the saints, a great apostasy or defection from the Christian faith will occur. This will be natural, of course, since the Holy Spirit is the person and power of conviction, salvation, and regeneration, and unbelievers who have rejected *Yeshua* will be left behind to believe the deception. Coinciding with a great falling away or apostasy, the *Great Tribulation* or *Yaaqov's Trouble* occurs confirming what the Tanakh or Old Testament has prophesied to happen. The *Day of the Lord* has come. At the end of this horrendous seven years of the Great Tribulation, *Yeshua* returns to the earth to literally save the earth and to save humanity. The Second Coming of Christ is His literal return (Revelation 19:11; Matthew 24:27-30; Mark 13:24-26).

"And I saw heaven opened, and behold, a white horse, and He who sat on it {is} called Faithful and True, and in righteousness He judges and wages war."

"But immediately after the tribulation of those days THE SUN WILL BE DARKENED, AND THE MOON WILL NOT GIVE ITS LIGHT, AND THE STARS WILL FALL from the sky, and the powers of the heavens will be shaken. And then the sign of the Son of Man will appear in the sky, and then all the tribes of the earth will mourn, and

they will see the SON OF MAN COMING ON THE CLOUDS OF THE SKY with power and great glory."

"AND THE STARS WILL BE FALLING from heaven, and the powers that are in the heavens will be shaken. Then they will see THE SON OF MAN COMING IN CLOUDS with great power and glory."

Unlike the *Rapture* where *Yeshua* returns "in the air" as a bridegroom to seize His bride and to elope taking her into His wedding chamber for consummation, the Second Coming of *Yeshua* is to the earth, in wrath, to wage war. Holy War is a biblical precept that began with YHWH in Genesis 3:15.

"And I will put enmity between you (serpent) and the woman, and [enmity] between your (serpent) seed and her (woman) seed; He (of the woman) shall bruise you on the head, and you (serpent) shall bruise Him on the heel."

Holy War is biblical from Genesis to Revelation where *YHWH* is disclosed as the great warrior. God is love! However, He does not love everyone unconditionally. In fact, those without Messiah *Yeshua* are rebels, under God's wrath, and God abhors the wicked (Psalm 11:5; Psalm 5:5) It is true that God has a good will toward all, believers and the lost, and God blesses everyone to some degree (it rains upon them, just or unjust), but God's unconditional love is only for Messiah and those in Messiah, that is, the redeemed. God does not unconditionally love the lost. God's agape love is only for His own! God may show love or be loving toward the non-remnant, but only His children know Him as love. God has another face for the unbelieving and unrepentant, and that face is wrath (John 3:36; Romans 1:18; Romans 2:5)! The Holy Scriptures say that God hates the wicked (Psalm 11:5), and He has indignation, wrath for the wicked EVERYDAY (Psalm 7:11)! God unconditionally loved *Yaaqov* and God hated (not emotion of hate, but opposite of love) *Esav* (Malachi 1; Romans 9:13).

Elohim, the God of Israel often encouraged Israel to know and to remember that He was their warrior; He would fight their battles. He would rescue Israel. He would save Israel. He would deliver Israel. Yet, *Elohim* also promised Israel if they did not obey Him as Commander and Chief He would fight as a warrior against them (Deuteronomy 6:13-15; 28:15-68).

"But it shall come to pass, if thou wilt not hearken unto the voice of the LORD thy God, to observe to do all his commandments and his statutes which I command thee this day; that all these curses shall come upon thee, and overtake thee" (Deuteronomy 28:15).

"And it shall come to pass, that as the LORD rejoiced over you to do you good, and to multiply you; so the LORD will rejoice over you to destroy you, and to bring you to naught; and ye shall be plucked from off the land whither thou goest to possess it" (Deuteronomy 28:63).

The Son of God and Son of Man is all about justice and righteousness, setting good against evil, judging the wicked and blessing those who are His.

Following the *Great Tribulation* with its cosmological catastrophes that will affect the heavenly bodies, the sun, moon, planets, stars, and galaxies, the *"sign of the Son of Man"* in the heavens will occur (Matthew 24:27-30). The scriptures do not tell us what this sign is, but every family and tribe of the earth will see the sign, and they will mourn greatly.

When *Yeshua* comes for His bride at the *Rapture* He descends in the air to "catch away'" His beloved. But, at His Second Coming *Yeshua* comes to the earth in bodily form (Zechariah 14:4; Revelation 19:11; Acts 1:11). At the *Rapture Yeshua* will be clothed in His *kavod* or glory, but at His Second Coming *Yeshua* will be clothed in a robe dipped in blood (Revelation 19:13). His appearance is apocalyptic. When *Yeshua* comes in the *Rapture* He is coming for His saints (John 14:3; 1 Thessalonians 4:17; 2 Thessalonians 2:1), but at His Second Coming

Yeshua comes WITH His saints (1 Thessalonians 3:13; Jude 14; Revelation 19:6-14). At the *Rapture* only the *messianic* or Christian eyes will see Him (1 Thessalonians 4:13-18), but at His Second Coming every eye will see Him (Revelation 1:7).

At the *Rapture* the trumpet sounds to collect His bride (John 14; 1 Thessalonians 4:13-18; Revelation 4:1), but at His Second Coming He comes to wage war and judge (Revelation 19:11; Jude 15). At the *Rapture* when *Yeshua* comes for His beloved, a shout comes from His mouth (1 Thessalonians 4:16), but at His Second Coming from His mouth comes a sword to pierce the nations (Revelation 19:15). At His *Rapture* for His saints *Yeshua* comes with comfort (1 Thessalonians 4:18) and believers are saved from His wrath (1 Thessalonians 1:10, 5-9). At His Second Coming, *Yeshua* comes in wrath (Revelation 19:15; Jude 15) and the unsaved will experience terror of His indignation and wrath (Revelation 6:12-17). There will be no signs to precede His coming in the *Rapture* (1 Thessalonians 5:1-3), but many signs will precede His Second Coming (Luke 21:11,15).

Finally, the church who is His bride, His building/temple, His living epistle, and His body, is the focus and the intent of the *Rapture*. The focus of the Second Coming of *Yeshua* is judgment and then His reign for one-thousand-years in the kingdom He is coming to inaugurate (Matthew 24:14).

See Question 18: Why Would Jesus be Returning Twice....

Question 29

What precipitates the War of Armageddon?

Answer

Messiah *Yeshua* at His Second Coming is coming with His army to make war! The Holy Scriptures speak much of God as the warrior, a potent motif in the Holy Scriptures, and the ancient site of Megiddo will be the battlefield where "God murders the human race!" (Dr. Hugh Van Eaton). That may sound strong, but it is indeed the very intent of the *Armageddon* campaign. God will annihilate the human race of unbelievers.

Megiddo is situated in one of the most strategic points in the Middle East; it connects the east and west for those passing from Africa, Europe, and Asia whether for military, trade, and/or pilgrimage, and without having to cross mountains. The Bible (1 Kings 9) tells us that *Sh'lomo* in his greatness controlled Gezer, Megiddo in the central region of Israel, and Hazor north of Galilee. *Sh'lomo* in essence controlled the world, since the Jezreel Valley was the battlefield of the Bible. Today, the Jezreel valley is the "breadbasket" of Israel, but one of the final battles on earth will happen here.

In the Jezreel Valley tremendous sized armies can battle without mountains as obstacles. Devorah and Barak defeated Sisera and his armies in this valley (Judges 4:1-7, 10-13; 5:19,20). Judah's King Josiah was mortally wounded in battle in the Jezreel Valley by Egyptian Pharaoh Necho (609 BC) a crushing blow to Judah (2 Chronicles 35:20-24). Elijah ran some 20 miles down this valley from Mount Carmel ahead of King Ahab's chariot (1 Kings 18:46). Alexander the Great came through this valley as did Vespasian's armies. Napoleon led his army from Egypt through this valley to Acre where he was defeated; on his way Napoleon commented saying that this was the most ideal battlefield he had ever seen.

Prophecies about Megiddo are found in the Holy Scriptures (Zechariah 12:11; Revelation 16:16), and the valley of Megiddo is called the Valley of Jezreel (Hosea 1:5), the Valley of Decision (Joel 3:15), and the Plain of Estralon by the Greeks.

Jezreel means "God sows," *Har* in the Hebrew means "hill" or "mount," and *Megiddo* means "rendezvous" or "fighters." *Har Megiddo*, "mountain of rendezvous/fighters" in the valley of *Jezreel*, "God sows." The Greek *Armageddon* is derived from the Hebrew, *Har Megiddo*. The mount overlooks the plain of Megiddo the most fertile land in Israel. It was referred to as the most perfect, strategic, battlefield in the world by another great world leader, US President Eisenhower. Its measurement is 15 miles x 15 miles x 20 miles.

Megiddo was the classroom of *Yeshua*. He viewed the valley from atop the high places in Nazareth many times. In Bible prophecy, the greatest and most lopsided war ever to be fought will happen here. Revelation 16 says that in the latter days demons or unclean spirits will cause all nations to come to battle at this place; one army will lose every single soldier, while the other army will not have a single wound (Revelation 16:10-16; 19:11-21).

There are two words used for war in the Bible, *polemos* meaning "lengthy war," and *stratyoo'omahee* meaning short skirmish or battle. The word used in the Bible to describe this fight is *polemos*, a lengthy two-and-one-half-year war. All nations will gather here precipitated by Russia marching out of the north according to Ezekiel (38) to take prey of the unwalled villages of Israel. Russia will be destroyed by an act of God on the mountains of Israel. The great river Euphrates in Iraq will be dried up and a 200 million marching army will come out of China the kingdom of the rising sun marching over the Himalayas across to this part of the world. The battle will go back and forth on this plain, then down the valley past Jericho on down beyond the Dead Sea and almost to Egypt, then back again to the city of *Yerushalayim*. Outside *Yerushalayim* in the valley of Jehoshaphat the battle will end with the blood to the height of the bridle of the horse. *Yeshua* will Himself come and stand on the Mt. of Olives and end this war, which otherwise will have destroyed all flesh of the earth.

One of the last great battles of humanity will be fought on this one-hundred square-mile battlefield of the Bible. The war happens in a matter of sequences.

Phase 1. First, the Euphrates river in the east dries up to make way for the "kings of the rising sun" or "the kings of the east" (Revelation 16:12). Some bible commentaries suggest this invasion to be demonic rather than human. However, in context a human invasion is meant, and China may be the people of *the rising sun*. This invasion is prompted by earlier demonic invasions.

"And the sixth angel poured out his bowl upon the great river, the Euphrates; and its water was dried up, that the way might be prepared for the kings from the east."

Phase 2. The allies of the *antichrist* assemble and strategize how they may together annihilate world Jewry (Revelation 15; 16). Israel is the primary subject that incites the invasion.

Phase 3. All the nations of the earth who are allies of the *antichrist* will gather to attack *Yerushalayim* which is then captured, its myriad homes plundered, the women ravished, half of the city exiled, and the rest of the people murdered (Zechariah 14:1-3).

"Behold, a day of Jehovah cometh, when thy spoil shall be divided in the midst of thee. For I will gather all nations against Jerusalem to battle; and the city shall be taken, and the houses rifled, and the women ravished; and half of the city shall go forth into captivity, and the residue of the people shall not be cut off from the city. Then shall Jehovah go forth, and fight against those nations, as when he fought in the day of battle."

Phase 4. It is then, that *Yeshua "going forth to fight against those nations as when He fights on a day of battle"* (Zechariah 14:4) sets His feet on the Mount of Olives in front of *Yerushalayim*. There will be a colossal earthquake and the Mount of Olives will split from east to west forming a very large valley. Half of the Mount of Olives will move toward the north and the other half of the mountain will slide south just in front of the Temple Mount, directly in front of the Eastern Gate that once led to the Temple proper. A major earthquake is coming to *Yerushalayim*.

Phase 5. *Yeshua* and His armies will destroy all the armies of the nations which have gathered against *Yerushalayim* in the valley of *Yehoshaphat* (Joel 3:9-17; Zechariah 12:1-9; 14:3). It is here that the pruning hooks are made into spears and plowshares beaten into swords, as the Holy Scriptures prophesy. This great battle is likened by *Yoel* the prophet to a wine press at harvest, the Lord as a Lion roaring from Zion, speaking loudly from *Yerushalayim*. This combat is so great that heaven and earth tremble, yet all the Lord's army have *Yeshua* as a refuge and stronghold, and there is not one casualty to God's people. *ZecharYa* agreeing with *Yoel* says that *YHWH* will go forth to battle and fight against the nations as when He fights on a day of battle. It is also during this time that myriad of unbelieving Jews will come to believe in *Yeshua* mourning over Him whom they pierced as one mourns for an only son; these Jews will weep bitterly.

Phase 6. *Yeshua* descends upon Edom to destroy its inhabitants and deliver the Jewish remnant who have been in hiding at *Petra* where they had escaped earlier to be sustained by God (Isaiah 34:1-7; 63:1-5; Joel 3:19; Revelation 19:11-16).

Phase 7. At *Har-Megiddo* or "Mount of Megiddo" the *antichrist* will rally the armies that remain to fight against the Lord and His army (Revelation 16:16; 19:19-21). The *antichrist* and his armies will suffer total cataclysmic defeat under the mighty hand of the king (Psalm 2:9).

Phase 8. After *Armageddon* the birds will gather to feed upon the putrefying carnage that litters the land (Matthew 24:28; Luke 17:37; Revelation 19:17-21). The *abomination of desolation* is removed from the Temple (Daniel 12:11) and *Yeshua* will cast the *antichrist* and false prophet alive into *Gehenna,* the lake of fire (Revelation 19:20).

The Final War! The War of Armageddon occurs during and at the end of the Great Tribulation when Yeshua returns. The final war is spoken of in *Apocalypse* or Revelation 20:8 and Ezekiel 38, 39, the War of Gog and Magog following the Millennial Kingdom.

Rosalyn Small, one of our *From the Uttermost Back to Jerusalem* mission team members, at *HarMegiddo,* "Mount of Megiddo" overlooking the Valley of Megiddo also known as the Jezreel Valley.

From the Uttermost Back to Jerusalem Mission/Team getting a different view of the valley of Jezreel from Mount Precipice and Nazareth. As a young boy, Yeshua saw this view myriad times.

Question 30

Why is the Golan Heights so important to the people of Israel?

Answer

Dark Spirits Have Battled for the Golan From the Beginning

Today, people have no problem believing that old hotels, civil war hospitals, abandoned theme parks, or antique houses where people were once murdered, are haunted. We want to believe in the paranormal. But, speak of the biblical seraphim, cherubim, archangels, watchers, four living creatures, seven spirits, angels, demons, powers of darkness, spiritual wicked beings in the atmosphere all battling against God and for the souls of men, and people think it is novel and sensational. The sinister serpent has deceived the minds of man to consider the Bible as religious literature and its characters fictitious. The secular world who are children of the devil train their subjects with the same deception.

For the true believer, the Holy Scriptures are an everlasting treasure and the Divine Library. They speak of the truths of God, His sovereignty, His beginning, His creation, the mutiny of a cherub who became the devil, the creation of man, God placing man in the Garden in Eden, life and death, heaven and hell, eternity, and so much more. As Christians we don't believe with head knowledge, we believe and we do know with certainty the spiritual truths told us in God's Holy Scriptures. We believe and know that there are spiritual beings and that places are "haunted" although not by murdered victims or departed souls hanging about, but by deceptive spirits attempting to distract humans from biblical truth.

It is very probable that all wars fought on earth are haunted, that is, wars on earth are caused by phantom powers fighting in the heavenly atmosphere. One theatre of spiritual combat, is the battle for the *Golan*. There a supernatural link to the battle for the *Golan Heights* at the border of Israel, Syria, and Lebanon. The political and military struggle for the real estate bordered by the Sea of Galilee and the Hula Valley on the west, the Wadi Raqqad to the east, the Yarmouk River in the south, and Mount Hermon on the north is a satanically inspired and sinister struggle set in motion from the beginning from the dark spirits in the atmosphere.

Israel regained the Golan Heights during the Six-Day War in 1967 with modern Israel's victory and control of the *Golan*, the first time since one-thousand years before the days of *Yeshua*. That's over 3,000 years ago! That is quite amazing, even miraculous especially considering how Israel won the Six-Day War. If we use the term "miracle" for Israel's victory, we are interpreting the war to be biased toward Israel and because of supernatural inference and angelic help, the Jews won! God helped the Jews [Israel] -for some reason- win that "war" and capture the *Golan*. If we suggest that God helped the Jews and Israel to win the war and retake the Golan, then we are also saying that dark powers were helping Egypt, Syria, Jordan, and the other enemies of the Jews/Israel. Can that be true?

Israel in 1967 until today is not a regenerate community of believers. Less than 1% of the population of Israel are messianic believers. So, did God take sides with Israel among the unbelieving nations, since none of these nations, including Israel, are a redeemed people? Or, has God invested in real estate, and regardless of the national ethnicity, God is working His angle in regards to His holy land (Zechariah 2:12)? Israel is not a holy kingdom of saints, so why would God help Israel above the other nations? There is another reason beyond God's interest as a Landlord in His holy estate!

During the Six-Day War Israel tripled her land area, including the Sinai, all of southern Israel called the *Negev*, the West Bank, the Old City East Jerusalem, the Temple Mount, and the Golan Heights. The high place on the Golan is a 9,200-foot mountain called Mount Hermon, which some think is the mountain of the Transfiguration. Two-thousand years before *Yeshua*'s transfiguration on Mount Hermon (if, Mount Hermon was actually the place of His transfiguration), the mountain was considered by the Babylonians who held the Jews captive in the land of Babylon, as the mountain of the divine assembly, the chief God of the spiritual assembly being *EL*. One-thousand years before the Babylonians, about 1450 BC the Hebrews came to the Promised Land under the command of General *Yehoshua,* and they were to take that land from the immoral Amorites. Living among the Amorites were the nasty giant-worshippers of *Gezer* where I recently participated in an archaeological dig (see my pictures at the end of this chapter). Archaeology tells us more about these people and places than we get from the Bible, and archaeology agrees with the Holy Scriptures concerning hybrid-humans living at *Gezer*. The *Gezerites* were so dark and evil that neighboring peoples greatly feared these Amorites. Sumer in Mesopotamia (today, Iraq) built a border wall 170 miles in length to keep out one of the families of the Amorites, the *Tidanu* or *Tidnim*. The wall was called *bahd martu muriq tidnim*, meaning, "wall that keeps *Tidanu* away." The wall was breeched and the Amorites came to rule the peoples that today live in countries called Iraq, Kuwait, Syria, Lebanon, Jordan, Israel, and Egypt.

The Babylonians who took Israel captive in 609, 597 and 586 BC were the most renown and infamous of the Amorite dynasty. "Bad boys" is too genteel. The Amorites were cultic devil-worshipping humans devoted to pagan gods, their chief gods being *Yarikh* and *Marduk*, dwelling on *Hermon* (Lipinski, Edward. El's Abode: Mythological Traditions Related to Mount Hermon and to the Mountains of Armenia," Orientalia Lovanien sa Periodica 2, 1971: 19).

Yekhek'el (Ezekiel), *Dani'el, Shadrach, Mishach, Abednego*, and other Jews in Babylon certainly knew of the evil Chaldeans. Later, *Havvakuk* (Habakkuk) wrote of the fierce and impetuous Chaldeans. *Moshe* knew of the Amorite cultic practices for he wrote of *King Og of Bashan*, one of the *Rephaim*, or *Nephilim* whose bed of iron was nine cubits long and four cubits wide (Deuteronomy 3:11). The king's bed was a cultic one, where his cohorts engaged in ritual sexual copulation to bless the land, and his bed was the same dimensions as that of *Marduk* who resided in his temple in Babylon. *Moshe* was declaring *Og of Bashan* to be one of the giants (*Rephaim*) related to the god *Marduk*, although really a devil of Babylon. *Yehoshua* said the same.

"Og king of Bashan, one of the remnant of the Rephaim, who lived at Ashtarot and at Edrei and ruled over Mount Hermon and Salecah and all Bashan" (Joshua 12:4,5 ESV).

While at Gezer I did more than dig; I listened. When the profs and archaeologists spoke, I took notes and all of them without exception said that the tunnel we worked in, was cultic, and with my own eyes I saw the high ceiling cut meticulously by its long-ago inhabitants. For giants? Well, when I returned to *Neve Shalom* in the evenings where we lodged, I spent the remaining part of the day studying. I discovered *Gezer* was one of the places the Philistines was repelled by the fighting forces of Israel. Did the *Gezerites* dig the shaft down, down, down to pay homage to the netherworld? The Amorites did! They lived in the region of Bashan and Hermon the high place on the *Golan*, and they thought it to be the entrance to the netherworld. In fact, the Amorites believed they descended from the *Titans*, those gods of Greek mythology.

Let's fast-forward to *Yeshua*'s day, to the event when He brought His *talmidim* (disciples) to a place that they may discover for themselves exactly Who He was. *Yeshua* brought them to the foot of Mount Hermon, to a place in His day called *Caesarea Philippi*. Here *Pan* the goat-god was worshiped, along with myriad other gods. On the shelves carved in that mountain sat idols of myriad gods, and in the presence of these *Baals* in the Holy Land of God, Messiah *Yeshua* asked His followers a question. "Who do men say that I am?"

Here, at the strategic place to be heard, *Kefa*/Peter made his great confession concerning *Yeshua*, "YOU are the Son of the Living God!" Let's fast-forward now to the transfiguration of *Yeshua*. No one knows where the transfiguration took place, since the Scriptures do not say, but many think it was Mount *Hermon*. So, entertaining the possibility of *Mount Hermon* as the Mount of Transfiguration, *Yeshua* selected the mountain of *Hermon* on the *Golan* to be the place of His transfiguration into a being of Light, pronouncing Himself as God! The God of the mountain of gods.

In Psalm 68:15-18 is a reference to the spiritual war that has to do with God and gods, and the psalmist wrote of *Mount Hermon* as the mountain of *Bashan*, and of *Zion* as the Mountain of *YHWH* (much like *Shaul*/Paul did in Galatians of the two mountains, Sinai and Golgotha).

"O mountain of gods, mountain of Bashan; mountain of knolls, mountain of Bashan! To what you watched O mountain of knolls, [at] the Mount that Elohim desired for His abode, also YHWH will dwell forever? The chariots of God are myriads of thousands and myriad of thousands; my Lord is among them; Sinai is in the sanctuary. You ascended on high, leading a host of captives in your train and receiving gifts among men, even among the backsliders/rebellious, that YHWH Elohim may dwell there" (Psalm 68:15-18).

Hermon is the mountain of *Bashan*, not the mountain of God. *Tzion* (Zion) is the mountain of *YHWH*. Figuratively speaking, *Bashan* with many knolls or peaks is looking to *Zion* with jealousy. *Zion* is where God YHWH desired to dwell since the beginning of time (Ezekiel 28). It is possible that in early history the chariots of God led by YHWH came against the gods of that mountain. Psalm 68 may also be prophetic of the end times. It is reasonable if only by exclamation that *Yeshua* may have been transfigured here since He is YHWH to lead captives on high, even backsliders to Himself.

Another interesting reference to *Hermon* on the *Golan* is in the ancient Book of 1 Enoch.

"And it came to pass when the children of men had multiplied that in those days were born unto them beautiful and comely daughters. And the angels, the children of the heaven, saw and lusted after them and said to one another: Come, let us chose us wives from among the children of men and beget us children And Semjaza who was their leader, said unto them, I fear ye will not indeed agree to do this deed and I alone shall have to pay the penalty of a great sin. And they all answered him and said, "Let us all swear an oath, and all bind ourselves by mutual imprecations not to abandon this place, but to do this thing. Then sware they all together end abound themselves by mutual imprecation upon it. And they were in all two hundred; who descend in the day of Jared on the summit of Mount Hermon and they called it Mount Hermon because they had sown and bound themselves by mutual imprecation sup it."

It appears from the famous (although not canonical) book of *Khanoch* (Enoch) that the *titans* who may have been the "Watchers" began their rebellion on Mount Hermon before the flood of *Noach*. Mount Hermon throughout history was the gathering place of the gods or more accurately, the gathering place of the demons of the Sumerians, Amorites, Arameans, Assyrians, Babylonians, Phoenicians, Greeks and Romans. It is probable that these gods are the ones behind Buddhism, Hinduism, Catholicism, Islam, and all other religions to replace regenerative faith in *Yeshua*, and these gods have their eyes fixed on the land YHWH has decreed for spiritual Israel and their Messiah *Yeshua*, the Holy Land! Thus, all religions are about real estate (even churches) to replace or replicate *Yerushalayim*, the holy city of God. Even Christian preachers, teachers, and pastors call their spiritual location, the 'local church," and teach the people the local church is "your Jerusalem." The intent is to keep that particular community in focus for tribute, tithe, and attention. Biblically, Jerusalem was and one day will be the epicenter of the earth, and until that time, Jerusalem, Judea, and Samaria is the mandate for missions (Acts 1:8,9; Romans 1:16).

In the last days Israel will continue to reject *Yeshua*, but will desire and embrace a geopolitical messiah. They will welcome a god, one of the *Rephaim* from *Hermon*, the *antichrist*. Sensational?

In the beginning was a holy land, *Eden* where YHWH dwelt in a pristine environment until evil was found in Lucifer, a ruling cherub (Ezekiel 28:13-15). The fallen cherub was exiled from that land. YHWH made Adam, a man, in His image and placed His image in the Eden, in the garden in Eden. That man, Adam was beguiled by Lucifer to sin. Lucifer had become Satan meaning "adversary." Adam/man was exiled, although he was promised by YHWH a messianic savior, a champion (Genesis 3:15).

"And I will put enmity between thee and the woman, and between thy seed and her seed; it shall bruise they head, and thou shalt bruise his heel."

YHWH later found His man in the east and brought him back westward to His holy land and *Avraham* entered it. YHWH promised the land of milk and honey, His garden to *Avraham*, and a seed from *Avraham* was to inherit the Holy Land. *Avraham* begat *Yitzhak* and *Yitzhak* begat *Yaaqov* and *Yaaqov's* seed became a nation, a nation called Israel, the same name grandfather *Yaaqov* had inherited by the angel with Whom he wrestled (Genesis 32). Because of sin that nation was divided, and because of sin both Israel, the northern confederacy, and later, Judah the southern confederacy were exiled.

In God's perfect time, He arrived. The seed of *Avraham* was *Yeshua*. YHWH came to be a human using virgin *Miriam's* genome. YHWHshua had purposed limitations. He came to rule His kingdom but was murdered by mutiny. No worry. He came intending to die before inaugurating His kingdom. As the messiah, the champion of man, and the son of God, He has to die for the sins of the world, and

He did. Then, He resurrected and ascended back to heaven to await His time to receive His bride of the New Covenant, the Church. This will happen in the Rapture. Then, He will return to the Holy Land, and as the Second Adam will rule over all the earth as king sitting upon the throne of David, in the holy city of Jerusalem, upon the Temple Mount, the Mountain of Zion.

Until that day when He returns to inaugurate His kingdom, for God's mysterious purpose, the gods of Hermon will continue to fight in the heavenly realm for the *Golan* and its chief mountain, Mount *Hermon*, that high place Satan "willed" to be his seat!

"I will sit enthroned upon the utmost heights of the Mount of the Congregation in the north" (Isaiah 14:13).

MMI Office Manager, Lane Keith on Mount Bental at an abandoned army bunker on the Israel & Syrian border. Note Mount Hermon in the distant background, mentioned in the Book of Enoch as the place where the "Watchers" fell, the mountain in the north.

Gezer Archaeological Dig

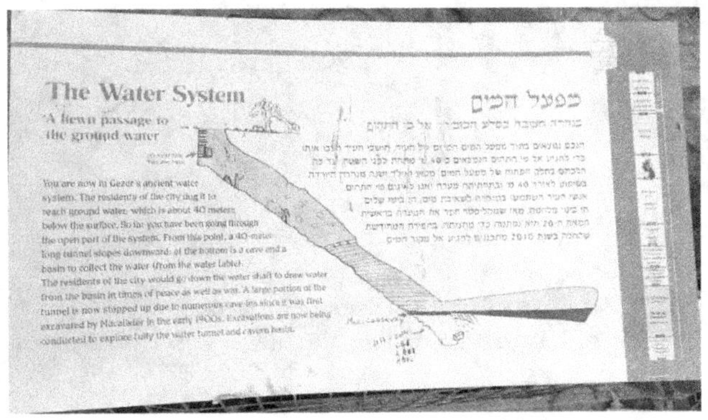

Pictures of Gezer by the author (left to right): Gezer tunnel 150 steps below earth. The author, Reggie Lisemby dug in the abyss for three weeks. Reggie cleaning pottery; standing stones from primitive times; archaeological team having lunch under tent; Gezer water system.

Gezer Calender, 925 BC is the oldest ancient Hebrew document ever discovered in the world. It is on display at the Istanbul Archaeological Museum. Believed to be a record of agricultural work.

Question 31

Does Christ begin His reign in Jerusalem immediately after the War of Armageddon?

Answer

Christ Autonomous Judgments

Following the War of Armageddon, one-third of last days Israel will be saved (Zechariah 13:9) in the valley of *Yehoshaphat* (Joel 3:1-3), also called the valley of decision, known as the valley of *Jezreel* which flows down to the *Kidron* valley in *Yerushalayim*.

Messiah *Yeshua* will judge the unbelieving Israeli survivors of the *Great Tribulation* (Ezekiel 20:30-39; Matthew 24:31; 25:1-30). Then, *Yeshua*, to whom all judgment has been given (John 5:21-23, 27; Revelation 1:14; 2:18), judges the unbelieving Gentile survivors of the Great Tribulation (Joel 3:1,2; Matthew 25:1-46). *Yeshua* also judges all the nations of the earth based on their relationship with Him, and their mistreatment of the regenerate remnant, Israel. Finally, *Yeshua* judges and awards the Tribulation saints (Revelation 20:4).

Perhaps it is here, now, that *Yeshua* judges the OT saints (Daniel 12:1-3; Isaiah 26:19; 20:4; Matthew 16:27; Revelation 20:4-6).

Christ's Binding of Satan (Revelation 20:1-8)

Revelation 20:1 reads, *"an angel coming down from heaven...."* The angel coming down from heaven in Revelation 20:1 (as in 10:1 and 18:1) seems to be a special angel commissioned for the task assigned him. The angel descends just as Satan in antiquity descended and was confined to the earth (Revelation 12:9,12). This angel comes *"having the key of the abyss."* Perhaps this is the same key that locks or unlocks the mouth of the shaft that leads downward to the *abyss* as in Revelation 9:1 (cf. Luke 8:31; Romans 10:7). The *abyss* mentioned in this passage is also mentioned in Revelation 11:7 and 17:8. This *abyss* is not *Gehenna fire* of Revelation 19:20 and 20:10 which comes later and is the eternal state for the devil, the *antichrist*, and the wicked. In context the *abyss* is a special compartment under the earth.

The angel comes with *"a great chain in his hand."* There is a spiritual binding that occurs. *Shaul* (Paul) once wore a chain while in Rome (2 Timothy 1:16). *Kefa* (Peter) wore a chain in Jerusalem (Acts 12:6,7). The chain spoken of in Revelation 20:1-8 shackles a spiritual being, the devil (cf. Jude 6). The chain is a spiritual binding and not for physical restraint only. The chain is one stronger than that which bound *Shamshon* (Samson, Judges 6:6), and stronger than that which bound *Legion* (Mark 5:3,4).

An angel, perhaps Michael spoken of in Jude 9, who has authoritative power, lays hold of the *dragon*.

"And he laid hold of the dragon, the serpent of old, who is the devil and Satan" (Revelation 20:2).

The words *laid hold* means "to seize without moderation." The term *dragon* is frequently used in Revelation (12:3,4,7,13,16,17; 13:2,4,11; 16:13) reminiscent of the serpent at the beginning of the Holy Scriptures (Genesis 3:1). The *dragon* is the *devil* the divine opponent from [before] the beginning as *Yochanon* suggests (Revelation 2:10; 12:9, 12; 20:10) who is *Satan,* the title meaning "adversary" (Revelation 2:9, 13, 24; 3:9; 12:9).

Satan, the devil and our divine opponent, will be bound (Revelation 9:14) and confined (Isaiah 24:22-23) according to *Yochanon* *"for a thousand years."* The thousand years are the years of the millennial kingdom. This binding or incarceration is literal! The *amillennialist* interprets this binding as symbolic just as the *amillennialist* interprets the thousand years as symbolic and the present age in which we live. *Oy Vey! Yochanon* writes "a thousand years" in his scroll, six times (Revelation 2:2,3,4,5,6,7); how could it be mistaken? His repetition solidifies a literal interpretation! Also, no number in the scroll of Revelation is symbolic. Clearly there is symbolism within the *Apocalypse* itself, for example, the scroll, seals, trumpets, bowls, etc., are symbolic, and *Yochanon* gives the interpretation of what these means. Yet, the number of the churches, seals, trumpets, and bowls, which is seven (7) is literal. Anyone reading the Holy Scriptures from the beginning to the end should know this. To have read through Holy Writ and read of three days and nights, four cherubs, six creation days, seven feasts of Israel, twelve sons, forty days in the wilderness, etc. then come to the Apocalyptic scroll of *Yeshua* and interpret seven years to be symbolic displays a appalling blunder in biblical interpretation. This is how false faiths and beliefs, denominations and religions are formed.

The *thousand years* is literal just as every other number in the scroll of Revelation is literal. The two witnesses are two in number. The three unclean spirits are three in number. The three angels are three in number. The three woes are three in number. The 1,260 days are the 1,260 days. The seven churches are seven churches. The seven angels are seven in number. The seven spirits, seven seals, seven trumpets, seven bowls are seven in number. The twelve apostles are twelve in number. The twelve tribes of Israel are twelve in number. The 144,000 are twelve thousand from each of the twelve tribes of Israel multiplied which equal 144,000. What the seals, bowls, and trumpets are may be figurative, but the numbers are literal to those who read the Holy Scriptures earnestly. Beware of interpreters who teach otherwise. *Oy Vey!*

The biblical text says that the strong angel throws, or casts Satan, the adversary, the devil into the pit, *"and threw him into the abyss, shut it, and sealed it over him."* Satan presently prowls the earth to devour, so the devil has not yet been confined to this pit of incarceration. Satan will be handled without mercy. This *abyss* is the prison of the demonic horde (Revelation 9:1) and the beast (Revelation 11:7; 17:8). The terms "laid hold," "chained," "thrown," "shut," and "sealed over" guarantees incarceration and confinement. The reason is given, *"so that he should not deceive the nations any longer, until the thousand years were completed.* The purpose of his incarceration is not necessarily punitive; that comes later. The purpose of Satan's incarceration is strategic so that he should not deceive man for one-thousand years.

Man will not be hindered by the enemy of souls for one-thousand years, and the celestial and terrestrial beings will discover the kingdom God that was intended for *Adam* and *Havva* and mankind in the beginning. The kingdom of *Yeshua*'s reign will be without Satan's deceit, unlike the initial kingdom *Adam* and *Havva* experienced. Yet, we must note that this is not the eternal state, this is not heaven, not yet!

Question 32

What is the purpose of a millennium? Couldn't the one-thousand years be analogous of a long duration of time, such as the church age?

Answer

The Millennium Fulfills the Biblical Covenants

The Millennium will be the fulfillment of the *Abrahamic* covenant, and the land promised *Avraham* and his descendants (Isaiah 10:21,22; 19:25; 43:1; 65:8,9; Jeremiah 30:22; 32:38; Ezekiel 34:24, 30-31; Micah 7:19, 20; Zechariah 13:9; Malachi 3:16-18). Just before the millennial age, the holy, promised land of Israel will have been ravaged by the *Great Tribulation*. Following earth's final Holocaust, the holy land will be reconstructed for the reign of the Second Adam, *Yeshua* (Isaiah 32:16-18; 49:19; 61:4,5; Ezekiel 36:33-38; 39:9; Amos 9:14,15).

The land of Israel will be renewed with fertility and productivity (Isaiah 29:17; 32:15; 35:1-7; 51:3; 55:13; 62:8,9; Jeremiah 31:27,28; Ezekiel 34:27; 36:29-35; Joel 3:18), and the holy land will receive an abundance of rainfall (Isaiah 30:23-25; 35:6,7; 41:17-18; 49:10; Ezekiel 34:26; Zechariah 10:1; Joel 2:23,24).

The Millennium also fulfills the Davidic covenant, the covenant God made with David concerning his seed who is to reign as king, both in the land of Israel and over the entire world. The reign of David and the reign of Sh'lomo did not fulfill the covenant promises God made with David. During the Millennium there will be a new model for the Garden in Eden. That model will be the Temple!

The Millennial Temple (Ezekiel 40:5-43:27)

The Millennial Temple will be the largest of all Temples in biblical and Jewish history. *Shlomo's* Temple was 40 acres which was very impressive. However, the millennial temple will cover approximately one-mile square. The present Temple mount, Mount Moriah in modern Jerusalem is miniscule for such a house of *Yeshua*.

The millennial Temple will be sanctioned by God, and the Lord Himself will come to the Temple. He will come from the direction He departed two-thousand years ago, from the east.[34]

YHWHshua will sit upon the messianic throne of David, promising never again to depart (Ezekiel 43:1-9). This is perhaps the purpose of the closing of the eastern gate. The Millennial Temple as all former Temples will be entered from the east (Ezekiel 43:17), and it will be *kadosh YHWH* or *Holy* to *YHWH*.

The Millennial Temple will be unique in that it will be different from the former Temples. Here is a list of those things occupied *Shlomo's* Temple and *Zerubbabel's* Temple, but that will NOT appear in the millennial Temple.

- no Wall of Partition
- no Court of Women
- no Laver
- no Golden Lampstand
- no Table of Showbread

---

[34] Adam was exiled from *Gan Eden* out the eastern gate. God found *Avraham* in the east and called him back to "the land" which God gave him. *Yehoshua* and Israel left Egypt and entered Yericho and the Promised Land from the east, after circling through the Sinai in the south, and having looked down upon the land from Mount Nebo. The Temple built in Jerusalem faced east, and the High Priest, the holiest man of humanity and the new Adam, entered God's presence from the east, from the direction Adam had been sent away. *Yeshua* the Messiah of Israel will enter the millennial Jerusalem from the east as the last and final Adam, and will rule in the Holy Land upon the throne of David over all the earth. At His eastern gate will be the tribe of Judah, the Lion guarding the entrance.

- no Alter of Incense
- no Veil
- no Holy of Holies
- no Ark of the Covenant
- no Pot of Manna
- no Tablets of Stone
- no Budding Rod
- no Mercy Seat
- no High Priest
- no Levitical Priest (rather, the sons of Zadok)
- no evening sacrifice
- no Day of Atonement
- no Feasts except Passover and Tabernacles

The duration of the millennial kingdom is given in Revelation 20:2-7. Six times "one-thousand years" is given. The *amillennialist* doubts the literal meaning of one-thousand years due to the scriptural inference of Christ to reign over an endless kingdom (2 Samuel 7:16; Psalm 89:3,4; 45:6; Isaiah 9:6,7; 51:6; 55:3; 56:5; 60:19, 20; Jeremiah 32:40; 33:14-17; 37:24-28; Daniel 7:13,14; Hosea 2:19; Joel 3:20; Amos 9:15; Revelation 11:15). However, any doubt can be greatly helped by one simple passage.

"Then cometh the end, when he shall deliver up the kingdom to God, even the Father; when he shall have abolished all rule and all authority and power. For he must reign, till he hath put all his enemies under his feet. The last enemy that shall be abolished is death. For, He put all things in subjection under his feet. But when he saith, All things are put in subjection, it is evident that he is excepted who did subject all things unto him. And when all things have been subjected unto him, then shall the Son also himself be subjected to him that did subject all things unto him, that God may be all in all" (1 Corinthians 15:24-28).

Yochanon records, *"one-thousand years…one-thousand years…one-thousand years…one-thousand years….one-thousand years…one-thousand years"* in the scroll of the *Apocalypse* (Revelation 20:2-7). Repetition was always used for emphasis. One cannot suggest that the number *one-thousand* is symbolic, and believe the binding of Satan and the rule of Christ are literal. Amillennials do. One may not hold that the *one-thousand years* to be symbolic, but interpret the first resurrection and the second death as literal. Amillennials do.

Yochanon used symbols in Revelation and the symbols are usually explained either in the book or elsewhere in the Scriptures. *Yochanon* frequently used numbers in Revelation as did every Jewish author in the Holy Scriptures, and they all used numbers for a literal meaning and the numbers are to be interpreted as literal. There is no number in Revelation that may be interpreted as symbolic though certainly the direct objects of which numbers speak may be symbolic and are said to be so by the author, *Yochanon.*

Question 33

During the millennium, will the land of Israel be different than it is today?

Answer

At Messiah's Second Coming the land of Israel will undergo tremendous geographical and topographical changes. The highest mountain in the world today is said to be Mount Everest which is 8,850 meters or 29,035 feet above sea level. The mountain of *YHWH* in Israel will become the tallest, and will be the epicenter of the earth, since atop this mountain will set the millennial city of Jerusalem with the millennial Temple of God (Isaiah 2:2-4; 27:13; 56:6-8; 66:20; Micah 4:1-2). This mountain will become the center of both Jewish and Gentile attention and worship. The prophet *Yekhek'el* speaks most of the mountain of *YHWH's* house (Ezekiel 17:22-24; 20:40-41; 40:1-4; 45:1-8; 48:8-22). The highest mountain in the world will have a 50 square-mile plateau; this plateau will be subdivided into three units, each part to have a special segment that will play a role in the messianic Kingdom:

The <u>Northern section</u> will be twenty by fifty (20 X 50) miles, and at the center of the northern section will set the Millennial Temple. The rest of this section is reserved for the descendants of *Zadok* who will live there as a reward for their faithfulness.

The <u>Central section</u> will be twenty by fifty (20 X 50) miles, and will be reserved for the Levites from the tribe of Levi who do not belong to the line of *Zadok*. Their responsibility will be to serve as caretakers of the Temple.

<u>The Southern section</u> will be ten by fifty (10 X 50) miles and *Yerushalayim* will be the very center of this southern section, measuring ten by ten (10 X 10) miles. The two remaining parts of the southern section, east and west of *Yerushalayim* will each measure ten miles by twenty miles (10 X 20) and will be for the purpose of growing food for the inhabitants of the holy city. *Yerushalayim* will not belong to any particular tribe, but will be inhabited by members of all twelve tribes of Israel. The *holy mountain* is referred to as the holy oblation because the Temple is to sit somewhere on the holy mountain in the city of *Yerushalayim*.

<u>The River Flowing out of Israel</u> according to Joel 3:18 will originate in the Temple area. *Yekhek'el* (Ezekiel 47:1,2) wrote that a river will begin in the Temple area at the front part of the Temple, by the threshold of the door and the right side of the altar in front of the Temple. The river will gush out, first heading east until it passes the eastern gate and then eventually making its way south to the Dead Sea. Zechariah 14:8 states that the river will flow southward from the city of *Yerushalayim* where it will divide into two channels. The western branch will flow down the mountain and empty into the Mediterranean Sea. The eastern branch will flow down to the Dead Sea, healing or changing the Dead Sea into a lake that will swarm with life. There will be fisherman who will stand on its shores fishing, and nearby in *Engedi* a fishing resort will exist. To envision such a thing today is unbelievable, if the holy scriptures did not say so.

> *"Then said he unto me, These waters issue forth toward the eastern region, and shall go down into the Arabah; and they shall go toward the sea; into the sea shall the waters go which were made to issue forth; and the waters shall be healed. And it shall come to pass, that every living creature which swarmeth, in every place whither the rivers come, shall live; and there shall be a very great*

multitude of fish; for these waters are come thither, and the waters of the sea shall be healed, and everything shall live whithersoever the river cometh. And it shall come to pass, that fishers shall stand by it: from En-gedi even unto En-eglaim shall be a place for the spreading of nets; their fish shall be after their kinds, as the fish of the great sea, exceeding many" (Ezekiel 47:8-10).

<u>The Promised Land of Israel</u> (Ezekiel 47:13–48:29). The northern boundary of the promised holy land will extend from the Mediterranean Sea incorporating much of modern-day Lebanon and parts of modern Syria, over to the Euphrates River (Ezekiel 47:15-17). The eastern boundary will move south from the Euphrates River, incorporating the Golan Heights and portions of Syria up almost to Damascus, and continues south to the Jordan River where it exits from the Sea of Galilee. The border will then run along the river all the way down to the southern end of the Dead Sea (vs.18). The southern border will move from the southern end of the Dead Sea incorporating the *Negev* and parts of Sinai all the way along the Brook of Egypt, the modern *Wadi-el-Arish* to the point where it reaches the Mediterranean Sea (vs. 19). The western border will be the Mediterranean Sea (vs. 20).

Sailing the Galilee, the lowest lake in the world
(photo taken using a Nikon fish-eye lens)

The Golden Menorah in the Jewish Quarter of Old Jerusalem was built by the Temple Institute, plated with 45kg (95lb) of 24 caret gold, worth two million dollars. The Menorah is said to be a declaration to God by Rabbinic Judaism that "we are home, as you said we would be, and we are ready to build the Temple."

Question 34

Christ was God's Lamb, crucified two-thousand years ago for the sins of the world. So, why are there sacrifices during the Millennium?

Answer

Under the Mosaic code or the covenant God made with Israel at Sinai, sacrifices were prescribed by God. These sacrifices did not forgive sin because they could not forgive sin, and the sacrifices also did not remove the guilt of the sinner (Hebrews 10:4,11).

"For it is not possible that the blood of bulls and of goats should take away sins."

"And every priest standth daily ministering and offering oftentimes the same sacrifices, which can never take away sins...."

Why would God prescribe rituals of slaughter if the sacrifices slaughtered did not atone? What about *Yom Kippur*, the Day of Atonement, the most holy day for Jewish people throughout their history. Did the sacrifices not atone for sins? They did not! The sacrifices served as types of Him Who was coming. *Yeshua!* According to Ezekiel 43:18-46:24; Zechariah 14:16; Isaiah 56:6-8; 66:21; Jeremiah 33:15-18; Ezekiel 20:40,41 there will be sacrifices and worship during the millennium. We can assume that the sacrifices during the millennial kingdom will serve the same purpose as sacrifices before *Yeshua* came. Sacrifices during the millennial kingdom will be for remembrance, a major *motif* in Holy Writ, just as ancient sacrifices before the coming of *Yeshua* were for anticipation, looking ahead? The sacrifices during the millennium will be a worship response to our Lord and King, *Yeshua* for His life, brutal torture and death, burial, resurrection, ascension, atonement, and priesthood.

The Millennial Kingdom includes the sacrifice of animals. After all, that was the purpose of many creatures, some to give milk, some to give meat, others to give wool or clothing, and myriad more for visuals of the Almighty God, so that by their life and death, they could preach *Yeshua.* Animals today are showcased and preserved in parks and zoos, and they are beautiful, yet much more beautiful when they foreshadow God's Son in their slaughter, death, and burning.

Salvation came to man by faith in the ritual sacrifices of clean animals. Salvation has always been by faith; it was the offeror's faith that saved him, even in the era of the Tanakh or OT. Never did sacrifices atone for man, since all sacrifices fall short of *Yeshua*, the true and only sacrifice. Any sacrifice other than *Yeshua*, is limited, unworthy, and falls short, terribly short. The one-and-only final sacrifice that saves, has always been and now is, *Yeshua,* the Lamb of God. The purpose of OT sacrifices and offerings were to serve as visual pictures, types, and foreshadows of the coming Messiah (Isaiah 53:10-12).

The New Covenant Church has been commanded by our Lord to keep His Passover, our Lord's Last Supper, which we perform monthly, quarterly, or yearly. The Lord's Supper is a remembrance of the ritual of His sacrifice. If for the sake of a better and more dramatic presentation of *Yeshua* dying for our sins, what if we were to add to the Lord's "supper" along with the itty-bitty cracker and thimble of juice, the death of a lamb? What if we also added the butchering, burning, and eating of that same lamb? That's Passover!

We actually do this once a year. Each spring *Messianic Ministry to Israel* hosts our anniversary Passover Seder Supper. It is a beautiful two-hour dinner-theatre. Part of our meal is lamb. We don't slaughter and divide the meat ourselves, but we purchase the meat and prepare it. A lamb did die -somewhere, and he is there on our tables having come from the oven!

The Passover is a remembrance of His body and His blood and His sacrificial offering. We remember His body as we break the bread, we remember His blood as we drink the wine, and as we eat the lamb, we remember He was the Lamb of God Who took upon Himself the sins of the world. We don't suggest *Yeshua* is dying again at every Passover Seder. We do the drama of Passover and eat the meal of theology to remember and remind ourselves of what Messiah did (past tense) one time for all time, on the cross, for those of us who have and will receive Him.

God intends to carry this drama into the kingdom age, a physical and visual picture of what the Messiah accomplished on the cross. The Passover or Lord's Supper is a drama of remembrance, and it is also anticipatory, that is, a dinner rehearsal! During the millennial kingdom sacrifices will be offered, *"in remembrance of me"* just as *Yeshua* told us to do, and the meat will be eaten with bread and wine, just like we do today.

The sacrifices during the millennial kingdom will not be for expiation, to take away sins (Hebrews 10:4). The sacrifices will be a memorial, a reminder, and will provide the opportunity for worship and praise of God. Consider the impact upon people's minds if their church decided once a year to have a worship service, with a live lamb brought before the congregation, its throat slit, its blood drained, and its blood sprinkled on every attendee in the service as the pastor walks down every isle sowing the shed blood upon sinners saved by grace. That may sound primitive and gory, and animal rights activist would have us arrested, maybe imprisoned. Yet, this is, in fact, part of the worship during the millennium, and how impressionable such a ritual will have on those observing and realizing their savior was that lamb.

The Prophet *Yekhek'el* peeked into the future of the kingdom age and he saw the realization of blood offerings, sin offerings, and trespass offerings (Ezekiel 40:39). Blood will be sprinkled on the altar (Ezekiel 43:18), meal offerings will be observed (Ezekiel 42:13), there is to be a cleansing for the altar (Ezekiel 43:20-27), there will be an observance of the New Moon and the Sabbath (Ezekiel 46:1), morning sacrifices will be offered daily (Ezekiel 46:13), and perpetual inheritance will be recognized (Ezekiel 46:16-18). The *Passover* will be observed (Ezekiel 45:21-25) and also the *Feast of Tabernacles* (Ezekiel 45:25) and the *Year of Jubilee* (Ezekiel 46:17) will be kept. Dr. John C. Whitcomb says the following.

> *"The Millennial sacrifices will not simply memorialize Christ's redemption, but will primarily function in restoring theocratic harmony. The future animal sacrifices will not have to do with salvation, nor be primarily memorial (like the eucharist in church communion). They will be efficacious in terms of provision for the ceremonial theocracy."*

The Priesthood of *Zadok* will be present and the Levites will be the caretakers although according to *Yekhkek'el* they will be excluded from the priestly ministry (Ezekiel 44:10-14). The *beni-Zadok* or "sons of *Zadok*" will be in charge of the sacrifices (Ezekiel 40:46; 44:15,16; 48:11).

Adam and *Havva* were exiled from *Gan Eden* out the eastern gate. The Lord stationed *Cherubs* to guard reentry. Later, the entrance to Israel's Temple where God dwelt behind the veil, upon the Ark of the Covenant, guarded by two cherubs, was from the east. Only "the Adam" of Israel, the holiest man of the nation, the Cohen Gadol or the Great High Priest could enter. *Yeshua's* millennial Temple will have the eastern gate.

Question 35

Who are the people that will live in the millennial kingdom; how do they arrive to the kingdom, and will there be Jews and Gentiles during the Millennium?

Answer

All who initially enter the millennium will be the born-again regenerate survivors of the Great Tribulation. Myriad children will be born during the millennial kingdom to redeemed parents who will raise their children as believers. All participants in the kingdom will have a new heart (Jeremiah 31:33), and they will not need to be taught "know the Lord," but will know Him from birth (Jeremiah 31:34) having the fullness of Spirit (John 2:28,29). *Yochanon the Immerser* had such a birth, leaping in his mother's womb being filled with the Holy Spirit in the womb. After all, Messiah *Yeshua* had come, in the womb of a virgin girl from Bethlehem, and the messianic age of *Yeshua's* reign was about to be realized. Babies born during the millennial kingdom era will have such a birth as *Yochanon the Immerser* and *Yeshua*, regenerate from birth, or at least a potent inclination toward a virtuous moral character. Complete perfection does not happen until the eternal state, yet all who are saved during the millennium will be under the New Covenant (Jeremiah 31:31), curses will be removed, and sin is almost completely eradicated (Zechariah 14:11).

During the millennium the Jews will possess and settle all of the Promised Land for the first time in Israel's history. The Real Estate will again be divided into twelve tribal divisions. The tribal divisions will be different than those in the biblical book of *Joshua*, and the divisions will be God's final covenant promises fulfilled. The land of Israel which is the Holy Land will be the Garden of Eden (Amos 9:11-15; Psalm 102:16; Ezekiel 36:8-12, 33-38; Isaiah 35:1; 41:19,20; 44:26; 51:3), and the Jewish people in Israel will be *Adams* and *Havvahs* (Ezekiel 36:10-12, 19-24; 37; Isaiah 43:5,6; 11:11,12; Zechariah 8:4-6).

Seven of the twelve tribes will settle in the northern section. North to south the tribes will be Dan, Asher, Naphtali, Manasseh, Ephraim, Reuben, and Judah (Ezekiel 48:1-7). Situated south of Judah's border and north of Benjamin's border serving as a dividing line between the northern seven tribes and the southern five tribes will be the location of the mountain of YHWH's house, the *holy oblation* (Ezekiel 48:8-22). Settling the remaining part of the land are the five remaining tribes, Benjamin, Simeon, Issachar, Zebulun, and Gad (Ezekiel 48:23-29).

The Jews for the first time ever will possess ALL the land of Israel and will experience a series of prophetic occurrences that brings about Jewish revival.

1. The revival begins by the **re-gathering** of world Jewry into all the land of Israel; this will actually precipitate during the latter end of the *Great Tribulation* and carry over in to the millennial kingdom era (Isaiah 11:11, 16; 27:12,13; 43:5-7; Zechariah 8:6-7; 10:10; Jeremiah 12:15; 16:14,15; 23:3,4; 24:6; Amos 9:14,15).

2. Second, regathered Israel will experience **regeneration** (Micah 4:7; 7:18-20; Joel 2:28-32; Zechariah 13:9; Isaiah 45:17; Romans 11:26,27; Jeremiah 23:6; 24:7; 50:19,20; Ezekiel 11:19; 36:25-27; Zephaniah 3:9-13). "All Israel will be saved" (Romans 11).

3. Third, Israel will be **reunited** (Jeremiah 3:18; 33:14; Ezekiel 20:40; 37:15-23; 39:25); the two sticks or confederacies, Israel and Judah will have assembled back as one stick or one people. They will be a witness to the nations (Micah 5:7-8; Zephaniah 3:20; Zechariah 4:1-7; 4:11-14; Isaiah 44:8, 21; 61:6), and the nations will be interested to visit this people who now possess

all the Promised Holy Land (Zephaniah 2:7, 9; Zechariah 8:12; Ezekiel 20:42).

4. Finally, Israel will be **reminiscent** of living with God in Eden. Israel will live securely and sinless (Zephaniah 3:13) and the Jews will be the tour guides to the Holy Land (Zechariah 8:20-23; Isaiah 49:6).

Messiah *Yeshua* will be the hallmark, the zenith, the locus, the celebrity of the millennial age and kingdom. He will be the light and the salvation of the nations (Isaiah 11:10; 42:1; 49:5-7; 56:1-8; 60:3-5; Zechariah 8:22,23). The nations will have a place among the millennial Temple worship service (Isaiah 66:18-24), and a delegation from the nations will go up each year at the Feast of Tabernacles (Zechariah 14:16-19).

According to Isaiah and Zechariah the *goyim* or nations will be servants to Israel (Isaiah 14:1-2, 49:22-23; 60:14; 61:5; Zechariah 8:22-23). With *Yeshua* on the throne the world will finally be like what would have been had *Adam* and *Havvah* not sinned. In hindsight, perhaps the nations of the world would have been going up to Eden thrice yearly to serve our first parents. The millennium is reminiscent of such a world. *Yeshua* is *Adam,* the last Adam!

All of modern Lebanon will be encompassed by Israel (Ezekiel 47:13-48:29). Moab in Jordan will be destroyed, but a remnant will return to Moab (Jeremiah 48:1-47). Ammon will also be destroyed and become a possession of Israel (Jeremiah 49:1,2) though a remnant will return (Jeremiah 49:6). Edom/Mt. Seir will be a perpetual desolation (Isaiah 34:8-15; Jeremiah 49:7-13, 19-20; Obadiah 5-917-21; Ezekiel 25:12-14; 35:6-9). Egypt will experience destruction and conversion (Isaiah 19:1-22; Joel 3:19; Ezekiel 29:1-16). Syria will have peace with Israel (Isaiah 19:23-25), and Saudi Arabia (Hazor) will be a total devastation forever (Jeremiah 49:33). Iran (Persia or Elam) will be partially destroyed (Jeremiah 49:34-39), while Babylon will never again be inhabited (Isaiah 13:20-22; Jeremiah 50:39,40; 51:41-43; Revelation 19:3; 18:1-2).

Yerushalayim will be the center of the millennial earth (Isaiah 2:2-4; Jeremiah 31:6; Micah 4:1; Zechariah 2:10,11). There will be twelve gates named after the twelve sons of *Yaaqov*. In the North, Reuben, Judah and Levi; in the East, Joseph, Benjamin, and Dan; in the South, Simeon, Issachar, and Zebulun; in the West, Gad, Asher, and Naphtali. The measurements of *Yerushalayim* will be ten (10) miles square. The holy city will be called *YeHoVeh Shammah* ("YHWH is there"), *Jehovah Tsidquenu* ("YHWH is our Righteousness"), and *Yerushalayim* ("Yah Provides Shalom"), and the city will be characterized by holiness, justice, and righteousness (Isaiah 4:3-6; 52:1,2; 60:14-21; Jeremiah 30:18; Joel 3:17; Zechariah 2:1-13).

The golden age of Jerusalem is yet to come. Jerusalem will be accessible to all (Isaiah 35:8,9), and Jerusalem will endure forever (Isaiah 9:7; 33:20-21; 60:15; Joel 3:19-21; Zechariah 8:4; Ezekiel 48:30-35).

The "holy ones" or saints of the millennial era will be (1) the resurrected New Testament saints, those of the earlier rapture (1 Corinthians 6:2,3; 2 Timothy 2:12), (2) the resurrected tribulation saints will also comprise the "holy ones" (Revelation 20:4,6), (3) the redeemed survivors of the Great Tribulation (Zechariah 12:10-13:1; Matthew 25:1-30; 31-46), and (4) the resurrected OT saints (Daniel 12:2,13).

Near the end of the millennial era Satan who has been locked in prison for one-thousand years will then be released for one last "Eden reenactment."

PROPHECIES CONCERNING THE NATIONS

NATION ↓	Amos	Ezekiel	Isaiah	Jeremiah	Other Books
Ammon	1:13-15 judgment by fire to consume; exile	25:1-7 spoil to the nations; to perish from the land		49:1-6 desolate heap; terrorism; possessed by Israel; to be restored	
Babylon			13:1-14:23 destruction; extermination; waste; none to survive	50, 51 captivity; great destruction; ruin habitation for unclean spirits	Habakkuk 2:6-17 disgrace & devastation
Damascus	1:3-5 judgment by fire to consume; cutoff; exile		17:1-3 ruin; remnant left for glory; conversion (19:23-25)	49:23-27 helpless; distress; destruction	
Edom	1:11-12 judgment by fire that will consume	25:12-14 become a waste	21:11-12 devastation possible survival	49:7-33 total desolation; object of horror; a wasteland	Obadiah total destruction with no one surviving
Egypt		29-32 overcome by Babylon; waste and desolation	19 civil war; famine; economic decline; to know YHWH	46:1-26 conquered by Babylon; no healing; to be inhabited as at the beginning	
Moab	2:1-3 judgment by fire to consume; death	25:8-11 captivity	15-16 distress; ruin; mourning; impotent remnant left	48 captivity; exile; cursed; calamity; remnant restored	
Ninevah					Nahum: besieged; destroyed
Philistia	1:6-8 fire to consume; destruction	25:15-17 great vengeance; destruction	14:29-32 famine; extermination	47 wailing; destruction; mourning	
Tyre	1:9-10 judgment of fire to consume	26-28 desolation	23 destruction; ruin; restoration		

Question 36

Will the kingship and reign of Yeshua during the Millennium be political?

Answer

The Kingdom of the Millennium will be a *Theocracy*, the rule of God. The millennium will be reminiscent to the Kingdom that would have been in *Gan Eden* (Garden in Eden) in the beginning had the federal head of the human race, *Adam* and *Havvah* not sinned. During the millennial kingdom the provoker of deception is removed since Satan will be bound (Revelation 20:1-3). Divine righteousness is displayed (Isaiah 1:26; 11:5; 26:2; 32:1; 46:13; 51:5; Jeremiah 23:6; Daniel 9:24; Malachi 4:2) and a divine Kingdom of holiness is installed (Psalm 60:6; Zechariah 2:12; 14:20,21; Psalm 48:1; Jeremiah 31:23; Ezekiel 39:7; Isaiah 4:3,4; 35:8-10; Joel 3:17; Zechariah 14:20,21).

The millennial kingdom will be the Davidic Kingdom with David as Prince (Isaiah 55:3,4; Jeremiah 30:9; 33:15,17,20-21; Ezekiel 34:23-24; 37:24-25; Hosea 3:5; Amos 9:11; Psalm 89). Some theorize that *David* in the texts is only a type of Messiah, that is, the kingdom is not ruled literally by David, but the seed of David, that is, the Messiah/Christ (Matthew 1:1; Luke 1:32-33). Their interpretation is that *David* means a biological seed of David to rule (Jeremiah 33:15, 17, 20-21). *Yeshua* was often called the "son of David," in fact, fifteen times in Holy Writ, *Yeshua* is called the "seed of David" (John 7:42; Rom.1:3; 2Timothy 2:8), and the "root of David" (Romans 5:5). Yet, Messiah is never called David. The prophecy of *Yekhek'el* (Ezekiel 46:2) declares that the prince is engaged in acts of worshipping God, so the prince cannot be *Yeshua* for He is Messiah and God Who will be worshipped.

David in the texts means literally David. This is consistent with a literal interpretation. David alone could sit on the Davidic throne promised him without violating the prophecies. For example, resurrected saints will have positions on thrones as kings, without violating the kingship of *Yeshua*. So, David may be Prince, King, and Lord along with many other subordinate rulers (Matthew 19:28; Luke 19:12-27) under *Yeshua*, the Prince of Peace, the King of Kings, and the Lord of Lords. In Ezekiel 46:16, the Prince has sons and divides an inheritance with them. In Ezekiel 45:22, the Prince is said to offer a sin offering for himself. *Yeshua* will not be offering a sin offering for Himself; He has no sin. "David" in the texts must be David.

The Kingdom is characterized by the dominion of Messiah in the following ways.

- the fullness of Spirit (Joel 2:28,29; Ezekiel 36:27; 37:14; cf. Jeremiah 31:33; Isaiah 32:13-15; Isaiah 41:1; 44:3; 59:19,20; 61:1).
- the dominion of the "Son of God," "Son of Man," the "Lord of Hosts" (Isaiah 24:33; 44:6).
- the dominion of the Lord our righteousness (Jeremiah 23:6; 33:16).
- the dominion of the Ancient of Days (Daniel 7:13).
- the dominion of the LORD (Micah 4:7; Zechariah 14:9).
- the dominion of the Son of God (Isaiah 9:6; Hosea 11:1).
- the dominion of YHWH (Isaiah 2:2-4; 7:14; 9:6; 12:6; 25:7-10; 33:20-22; 40:9-11; Jeremiah 3:17; 23:5,6; Ezekiel 43:5-7; 44:1,2; Joel 3:21; Micah 4:1-3, 7; Zechariah 14:9).
- the dominion of the Son of Man, the rod of Jesse (I Samuel 11:1,11).
- the dominion of the Son of Man (Daniel 7:13), the servant (I Samuel 42:1-6; 49:1-7; 53:11).
- the dominion of the branch of David (Isaiah 11:1; Jeremiah 23:5; 33:15).

- the dominion of the King (Isaiah 33:17,22; 44:6; 24:21-26; 31:4-32:2; Daniel 2:44; 7:15-28; Obadiah 17-21; Micah 4:1-8; 5:2-5, 15; Zephaniah 3:9,10; Zechariah 9:10-15; 14:16,17).
- the dominion of the Judge (Isaiah 11:3,4; 16:5; 33:22; 51:4,5; Ezekiel 34:17,20; Joel 3:1,2; Micah 4:2,3).
- the dominion of the Lawgiver (Isaiah 33:22).
- the dominion of the Shepherd (Isaiah 40:10-11; Jeremiah 23:1,3; Ezekiel 34:11-31; Ezekiel 37:24; Micah 4:5; 7:14).

As *Yeshua* promised, He and His twelve *talmidim* or disciples will govern the kingdom age.

"Then answered Peter and said unto him, Lo, we have left all, and followed thee; what then shall we have? And Jesus said unto them, Verily I say unto you, that ye who have followed me, in the regeneration when the Son of man shall sit on the throne of his glory, ye also shall sit upon twelve thrones, judging the twelve tribes of Israel" (Matthew 19:28).

Believers also will reign with them.

"Thus saith Jehovah of hosts: If thou wilt walk in my ways, and if thou wilt keep my charge, then thou also shalt judge my house, and shalt also keep my courts, and I will give thee a place of access among these that stand by" (Zechariah 3:7).

The millennial government may be structured as Modern Israel's government is structured, derived from the *Knesset Hagedolah* or "Great Assembly" that convened in *Yerushalayim* under Ezra and Nehemiah in the 5th century BC. The "Great Synagogue" founded near 400 BC was composed of 120 men who finalized the *canon* of Holy Scripture. Later, this group was reshaped and came to be called *"The Great Sanhedrin"* composed of 70 men. Modern Israel's government is structured similar to the *Great Sanhedrin*.

POSSIBLE THEOCRATIC GOVERNMENT
STRUCTURE OF THE MILLENNIUM

Head of State
YHWHSHUA, THE KING/MONARCH
Psalm 2:6-8; 24:7-10
Isaiah 9:3-7; 11:1-10
Jer.23:5,6; 33:20-26
Ezek.34:23-25; 37:23,24
Zec.14:9
Luke 1:30-33

Reigning with a *Rod of Iron* (Ps.2:9; Rev. 2:27; 12:5; 19:15; Isa.11:4) due to some wickedness eventually displayed (Ps.72; Isa.11:1-5; 29:17-21; 65:20; Zec.14:16-21)

LEGISLATIVE	**EXECUTIVE**	**JUDICIAL**
The Knesset/Parliament	Government of Prime Minister and Cabinet	Court System

PRINCES, JUDGES, COUNSELORS	**DAVID, PRINCE/ REGENT**	**CHURCH & TRIBULATION SAINTS**
Isaiah 32:1; Ezekiel 45:8,9 Isaiah 1:26	Isaiah16:5; 55:3,4 Jeremiah 30:9; 33:15-21 Ezekiel 34:23,24; 37:24,25 Hosea 3:5 Amos 9:11,12	1 Corinthians 6:2 2 Timothy 2:12 Revelation 20:4-6 Psalm 89

DISCIPLES
Matthew 19:29
Luke 22:28-30

SUBJECTS

The saved of all the earth
The saved of Israel who survive the Great Tribulation
The saved Gentiles who survive the Great Tribulation
(Daniel 2:35; 7:14,18,22, 27; Micah 4:1,2; Zechariah 9:10)

Question 37

What will life be like during the Millennium?

Answer

The Millennium will be characterized by the following:

1. **Longevity of Life** (Isaiah 65:20). During the one-thousand-year reign of the Second Adam, *Yeshua* and His bride, the Church, there will be no infant mortality. There should be no death until the age of one hundred, in fact, anyone dying at the age of 100 or younger will be thought to be cursed, and those of the age of one hundred will be considered youth. Note: there is no resurrection mentioned of millennial saints who perish. The resurrection prior to the millennium is the "first resurrection." Perhaps, death is for unbelievers.

2. **Complete Israeli Salvation** (Jeremiah 31:31-34). There will be no Jewish unbelievers during the millennial kingdom. Jewish people will be related to *YHWH* like unto marriage (Isaiah 54:1-17; 62:2-5; Hosea 2:14-23). The two confederacies of Israel, Israel and Judah will be reunited as one stick (Jeremiah 3:18; 33:14; Ezekiel 20:40; 37:15-22; 39:25), and Israel will be exalted for God's own purpose above the Gentiles (Isaiah 14:1,2; 49:22,23; 60:14-17; 61:6,7), the Gentiles being servants to Israel (Isaiah 14:1,2; 49:22,23; 60:14; 61:5; Zechariah 8:22,23). Israel will be revered as the true Jehovah's Witnesses (Isaiah 44:8,21; 61:6; 66:21; Jeremiah 16:19-21; Micah 5:7; Zephaniah 3:20).

3. **The Curse from the Beginning Will be Removed [somewhat]** (Genesis 3:17-19; Isaiah 11:6-10; 35:9; 65:25). There will

be unbelieving Gentiles during this period, so it is not completely eradicated.

4.   **Peace/Cessation of War** (Isaiah 2:4; 9:4-7; 11:6-9; 32:17-18; 33:5-6; 54:13; 55:12; 60:18; 65:17-25; 66:12; Ezek.28:26; 34:25; Hosea 2:18; Micah 4:2,3; Zechariah 9:10). One of the main characteristics of this era is that the kingdom of *Yeshua* will be a kingdom of peace, similar to the kingdom of *Sh'lomo*. There will be no war, no threats of war, no rumors of wars, but prosperity and shalom.

5.   **Glory** (Isaiah 24:23; 4:2; 35:2; 40:5; 60:1-9). The kingdom will be a glorious kingdom somewhat like Adam enjoyed in the Garden in Eden although brief. The Glory of *Yeshua* will overshadow those living in the millennium. There is no biblical reference that man returns to his nakedness as at the beginning. There is no reference that *Yeshua*'s physical frame nor man's will be hidden in God's *shekinah*.

6.   **Justice** (Isaiah 9:7; 11:5; 32:16; 42:1-4; 65:21-23; Jeremiah 23:5; 31:23, 29-30). God is a God of judgment, because God is a God of justice. During this era *Yeshua* will rule over the globe in His justice.

7.   **Great Knowledge** (Isaiah 11:1,2; 41:19-20; 54:13; Habakkuk 2:14). Knowledge in this present generation has increased unbelievably but will greatly magnify during the age of the millennium. Think of what that will mean in comparison to the information and technology we have today (year 2020). Man has created the model T Ford to guided missiles, unmanned drones, and space craft to Mars. Our world has increased from cranked party-line phones to the I-phones that are a radio, walkie-talkie, GPS, camera, video camera, recording studio, maps, clock, alarm timer, guitar tuner, games, compass, notepad, calculator, bible of any/every version and of any/every language, and more all in one small box that fits in our pocket. Imagine the increase of knowledge during the millennial kingdom.

8.   **Healing from all Deformity** (Isaiah 29:17-19; 35:3-6; 61:1,2; Jeremiah 31:8; Micah 4:6-7; Zephaniah 3:19; 33:24; Jeremiah 30:17; Ezekiel 34:16), and sickness is removed (Isaiah 33:24; Jeremiah 30:17; Ezekiel 34:16). This age is not only reminiscent of the beginning and *Adam* and *Havva* ruling the world, but is the fulfillment of that design. Sickness will be uncommon.

9.   **Freedom from Oppression** (Isaiah 14:3-6; 31:29; 42:6-7; 49:8,9; Zechariah 9:11,12). All demonic spirits, powers of darkness, and spiritual wicked ones in hierarchal places are removed. The presence of heaven on earth heals the atmosphere, environment, and the physiology of man.

10. **Voluminous Reproduction** (Jeremiah 30:20; 31:29; Ezekiel 47:22; Zechariah 10:8). *Adam* and *Havvah* (Eve) had myriad children though we only know of three, Cain, Abel, and Seth. The millennial kingdom will be like the beginning, married couples having myriad (25/50) children.

11. **Unified Language** (Zephaniah 3:9). The prophet says the nations will speak with purified lips. Hebrew scholars suggest a purified language, meaning the original pure language of Hebrew. Certainly, man's mouth will be clean, righteous, helpful, and wholesome.

12. **Unified Worship** (Isaiah 45:23; 52:1; 66:17-23; Zechariah 13:2; 14:16; 8:23; Zephaniah 3:9; Malachi 1:11; Revelation 5:9-14). As *Yeshua* prayed in John 17 (the authentic Lord's Prayer) we will be in harmony and "as one" with He and the Father. Central to our worship will be a harmonious fellowship of everyone kissing toward Him.

13. **Presence of God** (Ezekiel 37:27,28; Zechariah 2:2; 2:10-13; Revelation 21:3). *Yeshua* will literally reign on the Davidic throne and the world will have the very presence of God in human form. This is

the reason that Gentiles will grasp the garment of a Jew and say, *"let us go-up with you for we have heard YHWH is with you."*

14. **Economic Prosperity** (Isaiah 4:1; 35:1,2, 7; 30:23-25; 62:8,9; Jeremiah 31:5; Ezekiel 34:26; Micah 4:1; Zechariah 8:11,12; Joel 2:21-27; Amos 9:13,14). The earth will be at rest, the people will be at rest, and there will be no want. The peoples of the earth will be as David said to his shepherd, "I have no want!" The prosperity Gospel belongs here.

Christ will manifest His kingdom in world history. The millennium will provide a demonstration of the truthfulness of the divine person and witness of Messiah and His followers. Although Satan will be locked away during the millennial rule, the test must come, again. Adam's sin gave Satan his authority (Luke 4:6) who has since operated as the "god of this world" (John 12:31; 14:30; 16:11; 2 Corinthians 4:4; 1 John 5:19). The Millennium will reveal that man's rebellion against God lies deep in man's own heart, and with Satan 'bound and gagged' for one-thousand years, there will be some who will still rebel against God and His righteousness.

The final release of Satan will demonstrate the hidden evil of the devil as the originator of sin. The release of Satan after the Millennium will show the invulnerability of the city of God, and the extent of the authority of Christ, since the devil is immediately defeated and cast into the lake of fire forever. The Millennium is required to do some general "housecleaning," needed after all the preceding generations and ages of sin.

All of this has a purpose, perhaps to teach the righteous who will live in the coming eternal state, the consequences of rebellion, pride, and disobedience.

Question 38

What "last days" event follows the millennium?

Answer

Immediately following the kingdom age of the one-thousand years reign of *Yeshua*, Satan is released from the abyss for his final revolt.

"Then I saw an angel coming down from heaven, holding the key of the abyss and a great chain in his hand. And he laid hold of the dragon, the serpent of old, who is the devil and Satan, and bound him for a thousand years; and he threw him into the abyss, and shut {it} and sealed {it} over him, so that he would not deceive the nations any longer, until the thousand years were completed; after these things he must be released for a short time."

"When the thousand years are completed, Satan will be released from his prison, and will come out to deceive the nations which are in the four corners of the earth, Gog and Magog, to gather them together for the war; the number of them is like the sand of the seashore. And they came up on the broad plain of the earth and surrounded the camp of the saints and the beloved city, and fire came down from heaven and devoured them. And the devil who deceived them was thrown into the lake of fire and brimstone, where the beast and the false prophet are also; and they will be tormented day and night forever and ever."

During the millennial kingdom Satan has been incarcerated in the *abyss* (shut and sealed) and in chains by a great angel from heaven for one-thousand years. Satan is now released for one last campaign. He will go forth to deceive the nations and will gather the nations with *Gog and Magog*. Then, Satan will be destroyed.

First, are the Judgments

Earlier, at *Yeshua*'s rapture of His church, *Yeshua* judged believers at the *Bema Seat* Judgment. That judgment is about rewards, and not about sin (the believer has no sin on record).

Later, at *Yeshua*'s Second Coming to the earth, *Yeshua* will judge the unbelieving Israeli survivors of Great Tribulation (Ezekiel 20:30-39; Matthew 25:1-30). *Yeshua* will also judge the unbelieving Gentile survivors of the Great Tribulation (Matthew 25:1-46), then, God judged Satan and the fallen angels and they were bound for 1,000 years (Revelation 20:1-3). God has judged the Tribulation saints, and God has judged the OT saints (Daniel 12:1-3; Isaiah 26:19; 20:4). Then, following those judgments, the Lord reigned for 1000 years, the millennium, as we just studied (above).

During the millennium, Satan has been bound for one thousand years (Revelation 20:3). At the end of the millennium Satan is released (Revelation 20:3,7), and amazingly Satan finds myriad people, even after the thousand-year reign of *Yeshua*, who defy the Lordship of *Yeshua*. The final battle of eternity is the battle of *Gog and Magog* (Revelation 20; Ezekiel 48). After that battle Satan is judged and cast into *Gehenna* fire where the *Antichrist* and False Prophet were cast earlier after the war of *Armageddon*.

> *"And the beast was taken, and with him the false prophet that wrought the signs in his sight, wherewith he deceived them that had received the mark of the beast and them that worshipped his image: they two were cast alive into the lake of fire that burneth with brimstone"* (Revelation 19:20).

Gehenna is the final and eternal state of Satan, the Anti-Christ, and the False Prophet.

The judgment of unbelievers before the Great White Throne Judgment now occurs (Revelation 20:11-15).

"And I saw a great white throne, and him that sat upon it, from whose face the earth and the heaven fled away; and there was found no place for them. And I saw the dead, the great and the small, standing before the throne; and books were opened: and another book was opened, which is the book of life: and the dead were judged out of the things which were written in the books, according to their works. And the sea gave up the dead that were in it; and death and Hades gave up the dead that were in them: and they were judged every man according to their works. And death and Hades were cast into the lake of fire. This is the second death, even the lake of fire. And if any was not found written in the book of life, he was cast into the lake of fire."

This judgment, the Great White Throne Judgment, is for unbelievers and their works (Revelation 20:11-15). Here is a visual that may help in understanding the judgment.

The Courtroom

The **Judge** is *Yeshua* (John 5:22; Acts 17:31; 2Timothy 4:1) and the Defendants are the dead, small and great (Revelation 20:12) standing before the throne; the dead from the sea, the dead from *hell/hades/sheol* have been summoned by the Judge.

The **Evidence** is from the books. Exhibit A is the Lamb's Book of Life, written before creation (Revelation 13:8; 17:8). This is a book of names (Revelation 21:27), an enrollment (Hebrews 12:23), a divine register of loyal believers (Isaiah 4:3; Psalm 69:28), an enrollment of redeemed Gentiles (Philippians 4:3), an enrollment of redeemed Jews (Daniel 12:1) who are in heaven (Luke 10:20). It appears this book originally contained the names for all whom Christ died, that is, the whole world, every person ever born. Yet, at the judgment of the Great White Throne (Revelation 20:12) many blank spaces will signal the removal of many names (Psalm 69:28); these are those who rejected the Gospel of *Yeshua* and chose not to believe and be saved (3:5).

Exhibit B are the "other books" (Revelation 20:12). These are a register of human actions (Deuteronomy 32:34; Psalm 56:8; Isaiah 65:6; Daniel 7:10; Malachi 3:16; Matthew 12:37); a certain record of evil deeds in comparison to holy standard or commands (Revelation 20:12,13).

The **Verdict** is all are guilty. There will be no appeal. The Word of God is a serious matter. It pays for us to know the Word, now, and let it save us, rather than judge us later to be damned.

The **Sentence** will be eternal damnation in *Gehenna*-fire, and without parole.

Gehenna

The word *Sheol* occurs 65 times in the Hebraic OT, translated "hell" thirty-one times, "grave" thirty-one times, and "pit" three times. It is a place of conscious existence (Deuteronomy 18:11; 1 Samuel 28:11-15; Isaiah 14:9). The NT equivalent of the Hebrew *Sheol* is the Greek word *Hades. Hades* is translated "hell" in every instance except one (1 Corinthians 15:55), and *hades*/hell is described three times as a place of punishment (Matthew 11:23; Luke 10:15; 16:23), a place where souls enter at death (Matthew 16:18; Acts 2:27, 31; Revelation 1: 18; 6:8; 20:13, 14). Believers entered the section or compartment called *paradise* (Luke 23:43) or *Avraham's bosom,* and *hades* was a place of fire and torment for unbelievers (Luke 16:19-31).

The word *Tartarus* (Greek) was the residence especially built for the fallen angelic *watchers* referred to in Revelation 9 and also in 2 Peter 2:4, Jude 6, and the *Book of Enoch*. This is the lowest strata of *Sheol* or *Hades.* The word *Abussos* (Greek) describes a "bottomless pit" where demons are imprisoned (Revelation 9:1,2,11). Satan will be imprisoned here for 1000 years (Revelation 20:1-3). There are other references given in Revelation 11:7; 17:8.

The term *Gehenna* (Greek) is from *Gehinnom*, the valley of *Hinnom* on the south and east of Jerusalem, that was once the garbage dump of the city, the "place of burning." The term is used in every instance by *Yeshua* with one exception where James speaks of it (Matthew 5:22, 19-30; 10:28; 18:9; 23:15, 33; Mark 9:43, 45, 47; Luke 12:5; James 3:6). Under *Ahaz* and *Manasseh* (1 Kings 16:3; 2Kings 21:6; 2Chronicles 28:3; 33:6) *Hinnom* was a notorious place of human sacrifice and idolatry. This is the final state, the lake of fire! There will be different levels or degrees of punishment, more tolerable for some (Matthew 11:20-24) who have fewer sins (John 19:11).

<u>The Judgment of the Earth</u> (2Peter 3:7-13; Revelation 6:12-14; 20:11; 21:1; Matthew 24:35).

The present earth is not renovated, but according to the Holy Scriptures it is cremated, and a preexisting one descends from heaven. This is the picture *Yochanon* gives in Revelation 21. The present earth will be consumed (Isaiah 34:4; 51:6; Psalm 102:25-26; Matthew 24:35; 2 Peter 3:10,12; 1 John 2:17) and a new earth will fall and suspend in space just as our present earth has been hung (Isaiah 65:17; 66:22; 2 Peter 3:13; Revelation 21:1-8). The city of God, the New Jerusalem in the center of the new earth, follows as does the eternal state (Revelation 21:9-22:5).

Reginald. K. Lisemby

Question 39

If God dwells in heaven and He is perfect, and Jesus will reign on earth in His kingdom, why is there a need for a "new heaven and earth" spoken of in Revelation 21 and 22?

Answer

There are two interpretations of Revelation 21 and Revelation 22. The first interpretation is that these chapters are simply a recapitulation of the millennial kingdom mentioned in chapter 20 due to the mention of Jerusalem, "*He who sits on the throne,*" the high mountain and holy city, Jerusalem, the walls with 12 gates named after the 12 tribes of Israel in both places. The second view is that Revelation 21, 22 disclose a chronological description of the next and final event, the eternal state. The second view is supported by the Holy Scriptures.

The eternal state consists of a literal "new heaven and new earth," a new garden in Eden, which is the New Jerusalem, and a new world order. *Yochanon* is continuing the chronological order of things. Revelation 20 concerns the millennial city, Jerusalem described in Ezekiel 40-48, yet the holy land of the millennial kingdom of chapter 20 of Revelation though grand, could not contain such a city as described in Revelation 21 and 22. The eternal city is 1500 miles long, 1500 miles wide, and 1500 miles high. Clearly, Revelation 21 and Revelation 22 both describe the eternal state and not the millennial kingdom.

The present *heavens and earth* that were created and have existed since Genesis 1:1 will be destroyed (Revelation 21:1). *Heaven and earth* is a *merism* or a figure of speech for all that is above and beneath, from "top to bottom." The present *heavens and earth* will be destroyed because they are the abodes of Satan. (1) The first abode of Satan was heaven (Isaiah 14:12-14), that is, the heaven where God dwells. (2) The second abode of Satan was the primeval earth, the holy mountain of God, the mineral Garden in Eden mentioned by the prophet Ezekiel (28:11-15) which he ruled before his mutiny. (3) The third abode of Satan is the atmospheric heavens that *Shaul* (Paul) describes in his letter to the Ephesians (Ephesians 2:2; 6:12). Satan still has access to heaven as in the presentation of Job (1:6; 2:1), and he remains the accuser of the saints "*before God night and day*" (Revelation 12:10). (4) The fourth abode of Satan is the present earth (Job 2:2; John 12:31; 1 Peter 5:8; 2 Corinthians 4:4). Satan is not yet confined or chained to the *abyss* which happens, as you remember, after the Second Coming of *Yeshua* and during the millennial reign of *Yeshua* (Revelation 22:7-12). (5) The fifth abode of Satan is to be the *abyss* (Revelation 20:1-3), and (6) the sixth and final abode of Satan is to be *Gehenna*, the lake of fire (Revelation 20:7-10). He knows it!

According to Holy Writ the present *heaven and earth* is destined for judgment because of sin (Isaiah 34:4; 2 Peter 3:7) and is wearing out like a garment (Psalm 102:25,26), like our flesh, due to the entrance of sin and death. Most of the present earth is water, the seas which are the result of the former sin of Lucifer and the *Luciferian* fall and flood before the beginning (2Peter 3:5,6; Genesis 1:1,2,6,7,9,10), and also the result of sin and the *Noahic* flood upon the earth (Genesis 7:19-8:2). The sea was and perhaps still is the home for *Leviathan*, the [symbolic] monster of the deep, the twisted serpent, the dragon (Isaiah 27:1). The sea is the domain of the beast who arises from the 'sea' (Revelation 13:1). "Sea" is metaphoric and figurative speech in the Holy Scriptures for death, hell, judgment, disorder, violence, and unrest (Revelation 20:13; Isaiah 57:20; Psalm 107:25-28; Ezekiel 28:8), perhaps because the real watery sea is home to dark spirits or the entrance to the *abyss*.

Interestingly, the eternal state has an absence of seven evils. These are given in *Yeshua*'s Apocalypse, Revelation 21:1,4; 22:3; 21:25; 22:5.

(1) there is no sea;

(2) there is no death;

(3) there is no mourning;

(4) there is no weeping;

(5) there is no pain;

(6) there is no curse; and

(7) there is no night.

The present creation is in slavery to corruption (Romans 8:19-22), so it must be remade, recreated, reformed, and renewed. The present *heavens and earth* are cursed and must be utterly destroyed (2Peter 3:7,10,12). They will be.

The schematic for the eternal state, in particular the *new heavens and the new earth* is a fulfillment of biblical prophecy (Isaiah 65:17; 66:22; Psalm 102:25-26; 2 Peter 3:13; Revelation 3:12). One interpretation suggests that the "new heavens and new earth" is simply a renovation of this present heavens and earth (Genesis 48:4; Psalm 119:90; Ecclesiastes 1:4; Acts 3:21; Matthew 19:28). Another interpretation is that the "new heavens and new earth" is a replacement (Revelation 21:5; Psalm 102:25-26; Isaiah 34:4; 51:6; Matthew 24:35; 2 Peter 3:7, 10-13).

The language of Revelation 20:11 depicts a complete dissolving of the old, a vanishing into nothingness followed by a new creation with the absence of the former creation and its condition. The millennial kingdom has seas (Psalm 72:8; Isaiah 11:9, 11; Ezekiel 47:10, 15, 17-18, 20; 48:28; Zechariah 9:10; 14:8) though the eternal state will have no sea (Revelation 21:1).

Jerusalem in the distance, across the Kidron Valley from the Jewish cemetery on the Mount of Olives. The cemetery is the most ancient and most important Jewish cemetery in Jerusalem containing 80,000 to 150,000 tombs.

Question 40

Is the "New Jerusalem" a real city coming down from heaven? Couldn't the city be allegorical?

Answer

There is symbolism in Revelation and the new city, the New Jerusalem is symbolic in *Yeshua*'s Apocalypse of a bride, although it is quite clear in the same context that the new Jerusalem is a literal city. *Avraham* reached a city in Israel that he had looked for, yet the scroll of Hebrews tells us *Avraham* continued to look for that eternal city, and that heavenly city is the New Jerusalem (Hebrews 11:10-16 cf. 12:22-24).

The New Jerusalem is a bride-city (Revelation 21:2, 9) and is reflective of purity and devotedness. The old Jerusalem was called the "holy city" and also a "bride" (Isaiah 52:1; 61:10; Matthew 4:5; 27:53), although it has fallen greatly since the crucifixion of God two-thousand years ago and will be so fallen in the last days that the Holy Scriptures name last-days Jerusalem, *Sodom* (Revelation 11:8) due to despicable sins. The meaning of the word *Sodomy* will be applicable to Jerusalem in the end times. Perhaps modern Jerusalem will come to be a seat of the reprobate homosexual community in the last days where sodomites will dwell in their demonically inspired lusts. This will happen during the time prior to the Rapture and more especially during the period of the Great Tribulation.

During the millennium, Jerusalem will be purified and prepared to become the seat of *Yeshua* for His millennial kingdom. *Yeshua* will reign for one-thousand years from Jerusalem, yet even that city will come to an end and give way to the *New Jerusalem* mentioned in Revelation 21 (Galatians 4:25-31; Hebrews 11:10; 12:22; 13:14).

In likeness of the earthly Jerusalem which represented the covenant community of God, the New Jerusalem will be the new community of God where all saints will reign with *Yeshua* for eternity. The historical Jerusalem, the present Jerusalem, and the millennial Jerusalem are all copies of the heavenly New Jerusalem which is presently being built and is the prototype, just as the heavenly Temple is the prototype for the historical Temple.

Yeshua will rule over the earthly millennial Jerusalem to fulfill its earthly purpose, and then transition into the eternal state to rule from the New Jerusalem forever as King.

The New Jerusalem has many names. It is called the *Holy City* (Revelation 21:2), the *New Jerusalem* (Revelation 21:2) which presupposes a recognition of the old Jerusalem (Isaiah 52:1), the *Tabernacle of God* (Revelation 21:3), *My Father's House* (John 14:2), *Mount Zion* (Hebrews 12:22), the *City of the Living God* (Hebrews 12:22), *heavenly Jerusalem,* and *YHWH Shammah* (Ezekiel 48:35). This city is presently under construction (John 14:2-4) though we assume the schematic has been known since eternity past.

The Walls

The wall around the New Jerusalem is "great and high" measured at 144 cubits or 226 feet which equals 72 yards. The measurement is incompatibly small compared to a city 1500 miles square. Perhaps this is the width of the wall though not even this width would support a wall 1500 miles high. Some suggests that the model is a pyramid figure which would constitute the "holy mountain" spoken of here in Revelation and elsewhere in the Holy Scriptures. Rabbinic Judaism believes in a "new Jerusalem" that is said to rise 1500 miles to the throne of God.

The wall is made of jasper and it has twelve gates. The twelve gates each face a direction, three face north, three face south, three face east, and three face west which parallel the former creation where Satan desired to sit (Ezekiel 28). The twelve gates actually correspond to the moving Tabernacle and the northern, southern, eastern, and western gates where tribes were assigned as guardians.

The Gates

Each of the twelve gates are a single pearl. Pearls were the ultimate treasure in the ancient world (Matthew 13:46; 7:6; 1 Timothy 2:9); this is interesting since a pearl comes from an unclean fish, but under the new covenant of *Yeshua*, all men, all things are made clean as told *Kefa* (Peter) in the vision given him on the housetop in Joppa.

The gates are inscribed with the twelve names of the twelve tribes of Israel. Note that the tribe of Judah is now in the north and not in the east. The twelve angels stationed at the twelve gates need not suggest the possibility of attack. The angelic stations function as seats for the *Seraphim* who cry, *kadosh, kadosh, kadosh*, or "holy, holy, holy" before the throne which they guard. These twelve gates are never closed.

The Foundation Stones

The twelve foundation stones of the New Jerusalem have twelve names who are the names of the twelve apostles. These foundation stones are precious stones: jasper; sapphire; chalcedony; emerald; sardonyx; sardius; chrysolite; beryl; topaz; chrysoprase; jacinth; amethyst. Eight of these stones correspond to the stones in the breastplate of the high priest. Nine of these stones correspond to those found in Eden (Ezekiel 28:13). Twelve of these stones correspond to the sign of the zodiac and the tribal standards each tribe bore of the zodiac (according to Josephus and Philo).

The holy city, the New Jerusalem will rest upon the new earth. It is not suspended as a satellite city, nor is it a cosmological satellite city. The New Jerusalem will be as earthly as the modern city of Jerusalem today, only the New Jerusalem will be on the new pristine earth.

The City & Streets

The city streets of the New Jerusalem are pure gold, like transparent glass (Revelation 21:18,21). There is no night, no sun, no moon, no created light source or artificial light source. The *Menorah* in the Temple referenced the light in Eden before the fall, and it referenced the light in the New Jerusalem after the curse is removed. The Tree of Life in the new city, the New Jerusalem references the twelve loafs of bread in the Temple, which referenced the Tree of Life in *Gan Eden*. The Altar of Incense in the ancient Jewish Temple referenced the walk with God in Eden, and also prophetically, in the New Jerusalem.

Nothing unclean and no one unclean enters the holy city through the twelve gates. There are millions of mansions presently being constructed by the carpenter from Nazareth (John 14:2, *"I go away to prepare a place for you"*). Perhaps *Yoseph* His father and other great biblical carpenters are -right now as you read this- helping *Yeshua* build this gated community.

The Citizens

The citizens of the holy city are those whose names are written in the *Lambs Book of Life* that was written before creation (Revelation 13:8; 17:8). This *Book of Life* is a book of names (Revelation 21:27), an enrollment (Hebrew 12:23), a divine register of loyal believers (Isaiah

4:3; Psalm 69:28), an enrollment of redeemed Gentiles (Philippians 4:3), and redeemed Jews (Daniel 12:1). This Book of Life is presently in heaven (Luke 10:20), and contrasted from the "books" (Revelation 20:12) which are the register of human actions (Deuteronomy32:34 ; Psalm 56:8; Isaiah 65:6; Daniel 7:10; Malachi 3:16; Matthew 12:37). The dead will be judged out of those things written in "the books," a certain record of evil deeds, in comparison to the holy standard or commands from God that were to be embraced and obeyed. The judgment will have been according to their works (Revelation 20:12,13).

Also, in the city with its citizens, are myriad of angels (Hebrews 12:22).

The Nations

There are nations outside the walls of the beautiful New Jerusalem, which are spread over the surface of the new earth. These nations will have kings or political leaders who will occasionally *aliya* or "come up" to the holy city. We are not told how often they come, although Israel was commissioned to "come up" to Israel thrice yearly. Such an edict will be issued to the nations, and they will come up to the city of God.

The New Jerusalem in the midst of the new earth is reminiscent of the garden in the midst of Eden. The New Jerusalem will be the epicenter of the universe, and it will be home to Adams and Eves, the glorious ones, the holy ones, the saints, the body of Messiah, believers in *Yeshua*, the Church.

The nations outside the eternal city, New Jerusalem are those people carried over into the eternal state from the former Millennium, those who did not join Satan's final revolt (Revelation 20:7-11). As the sons of *Noach* repopulated the earth after the flood, these saints or holy ones in the image of God will repopulate the new earth in the eternal state. There will be a new race of man living on the new earth, nations created for the new earth just as Adam and Eve and their seed should have propagated. These offspring will be in the likeness of God and organized under kings.

The nations outside the 1500-mile city are the seed of reproductive man. There will be marriage and families and holy sons of God living in the eternal state forever! These nations outside the holy city, Jerusalem are those over whom the saints will reign for eternity (Revelation 22:5). The nations of eternity will be descendants from the millennials who *"shall inherit the earth for a thousand generations."*

These people will eat of the Tree of Life for life and for healing, that is for longevity as *Adam* and *Havva* should have enjoyed. The Greek word here is *therapeaun* from which comes the word, *therapeutic*. What is in view is not healing from sickness, but eating for flavor, enjoyment, and sustenance (Revelation 22). Again, this is reflective of how it would have been in Eden had *Adam* and *Havva* not sinned.

We are going back to the beginning! The eternal state will consist of life, consummation, pregnancy, and offspring on the new earth, and the new heavens will be a new vast solar system and a new lodging for God for eternity, future.

Once the earth is repopulated to its fullness, perhaps the human race in the image of God or sons of God may colonize other spheres in the myriad of galaxies. We are not told, so we may only ponder the possibilities. Space really is the final frontier!

Question 41

Will the eternal state mentioned in Revelation 21 and 22, be like the eternal state before Genesis 1:1?

Answer

The Eternal State is Reminiscent of Eden (Revelation 21:3)

The Tabernacle of God in the Old Testament was somewhat a revelation of eternity. *"Behold the tabernacle of God is among man and He shall dwell among them"* (Revelation 21:3). The "tabernacle" (Greek, Strongs #4633, *skay-nay*) is a noun meaning "tent for habitation." This is, in fact, the purpose of the ancient Tabernacle to Israel, that God might dwell among them. To "dwell" (Greek, Strongs # 4637, *skay-no'o*) is the Hebrew verb form of *skay-nay* meaning "to tent" or "to tabernacle." This is the same word used in John 1:14 and Revelation 7:15, 12:12, and 13:6. The tabernacle of God was "to occupy," and in the eternal state, the Tabernacle of God is reminiscent of Eden.

The *apocalypse* or revelation that God gave *Yeshua*, that He gave the angel, and that he gave *Yochanon* (the book of Revelation is the scroll of *Yeshua*) presents the eternal state as a *nexus* with paradise-like qualities. That is, the eternal state is the fulfillment of Eden (Revelation 2:7). The New Jerusalem in eternity future will be a city of unity, no longer two variants of believers, Hebrew Christians and Gentiles Christians, but one people, likened to "one new man" (Ephesians 2:11-22). The New Jerusalem will be a city of saints; it will be pristine and divine, and the city will reflect Israel, Jerusalem, the messianic lamb, the twelve sons of Israel, the twelve Apostles, the temple, and the throne of God.

The New Jerusalem will be the forever "Eden." The city is a cube city (Revelation 21:16) like unto the inner sanctuary or *Kodesh Kodeshim* or Holy of Holies (1 Kings 6:19,20). The New Jerusalem is also like the garden in the "midst" of Eden (Genesis 3:3; 3:24). The New Jerusalem is 1500 miles long, wide, and high, a perfect square which equals the combined areas of the western United States between the Pacific coast and the Mississippi River and the distance from New York to Houston squared; or from London, England to Athens, Greece squared.

The New Jerusalem is a city of pure gold like transparent glass (Revelation 21:18, 21) as was Eden (Genesis 2:12; Ezekiel 28:13,14). The New Jerusalem is a city with twelve gates, three on each side, named of the twelve tribes of Israel, made of single pearls and never closed (Revelation 21:21-25), with [12] angels stationed (Revelation 21:12). The city has walls like Eden as its perimeters; the walls are 72 yards high and made of jasper. The city also has foundations, twelve foundation stones named for the Apostles and with precious stones (Revelation 21:19,20). The city has no darkness so there is no need for sun or moon. Thus, there is a new reckoning of time. The city is illumined by the glory or *kavod* of God. The Lamb *Yeshua* is the lamp. The Tree of Life and the water of life are the main distinguishing marks of the city.

The new city has *"come down,"* and is *"a great and high mountain, and the holy city, Jerusalem."* The city is indeed reminiscent of Eden (Ezekiel 28:14, cf.28:13; Ezekiel 20:40; Micah 4:1-3; Genesis 22:14; Psalm 132:13; and more: Isaiah 2:2,3; 8:18- 18:7; 24:23; 62:1-7; Hebrews 12:22; Psalm 2:6, 9:11; 50:2; 87:1,2).

The account of Revelation finalizes the ongoing motif that began in Genesis, with man's banishment from Paradise until his restoration to a *Garden in Eden* state! A Tabernacle for God to dwell is the new city (Revelation 21) with a river, throne, the Tree of Life, its leaves medicinal (Revelation 22:1) are all reminiscent of God's original throne, the Garden in Eden, its river, the Tree of Life, and everlasting life (Genesis 2:8-10, 3:22).

The river of the New Jerusalem (Revelation 22:1) is like the one that flowed in Eden (Genesis 2:10), and the river is in context to the city (Psalm 46:4; Ezekiel 47:1, 9), and is a water of life (Jeremiah 2:13; 17:13; Psalm 36:9; Proverb 10:11; 13:14; 14:27; 16:22). The New Jerusalem is truly new and it is holy (Revelation 21:1), and the New Jerusalem is only for those who are clean (Revelation 21:27; 22:14, 15; 21:8), just like the Garden in Eden.

The New Jerusalem parallels the Garden in Eden continuing the *land motif* in Holy Scripture. This city is reserved only for the clean (Genesis 3:17, 23,24; 15:16; Leviticus 18:24-28; Ezekiel 36:17-19), a city for man to dwell with God (Revelation 21:3,4), and it parallels the Garden in Eden where God dwelled with man (Genesis 2:8).

The new garden, the New Jerusalem will have no death, no tears, no mourning, no crying, and no pain (Revelation 21:4). The new holy Jerusalem presently exists and is the glory of God (Revelation 21:10) with costly and precious metals (Revelation 21:19,20), which parallels the historical Garden in Eden which had costly and precious gold (Genesis 2:11), and bdellium and onyx (Genesis 2:12).

The New Jerusalem will be without a Temple because it is itself the Temple, again, paralleling Eden which was itself the house of God (Revelation 21:22). The New Jerusalem will have gates that never close (Revelation 21:25) reminiscent of the gate in Eden that was closed and never opened following Adam's expulsion (Genesis 3:24). The city with angels stationed at its twelve gates is certainly reminiscent of the *Cherubim* stationed at the entrance to Eden to guard its way.

In this new city, the New Jerusalem, the angels have an eternal function. They are even now crying out (perhaps practicing) *"Kadosh! Kadosh! Kadosh!"* or, *"Holy! Holy! Holy!"* The walls of the city are not for defense for no sin enters there and no enemy exists. The walls of the New Jerusalem are reminiscent of the boundaries of Eden before sin and before the fall, and is reminiscent of eternal security. Amen!

The Tree of Life (Revelation 22:2) at the center of the city (Revelation 22:1; 21:21) is reminiscent of the Tree of Life in the midst of the Garden in Eden (Genesis 2:9; 3:3). The Tree of Life in the Garden lost to man because of his fall, is now accessed (Revelation 22:2,14). This Tree of Life is good for food (Revelation 22:2) as was the Tree of Life in Eden (Genesis 2:9). The Tree of Life is medicinal (Revelation 22:2) as was the Tree of Eternal Life in the Garden (Genesis 3:22).

Eating from the Tree of Life in the New Jerusalem does not suggest disease will exist in eternity. The eternal state is one of immortality as at the beginning in Eden (Genesis 3:22). Eating from the Tree of Life implies the exclusion of the curse that has been lifted (Revelation 22:3,14), medicinal eating, and healthy sustenance. Amen!

Question 42

What are the main views of eschatology today?

Answer

There are three main eschatological views of the last days. (1) the Premillennial view, (2) the Amillennial view, and (3) the Postmillennial view. These three views revolve around three key issues. (1) When *Yeshua* is returning, that is, the timing. (2) How *Yeshua* will return, that is, returning in physical form, or by His spirit. (3) Where *Yeshua* will return, that is, from heaven to the hearts of His people (at Pentecost), or His literal return to the city, Jerusalem.

THE PREMILLENNIAL VIEW

The Premillennial view was the dominant view of the disciples of *Yochanon* (John), the early church, and the early church fathers, Papias, Tertullian, Clement of Rome, Barnabus, Ignatius, Polycarp, and Justin. Modern premillennialists are Charles Ryrie, John Walvoord, J. Dwight Pentecost, Hal Lindsey, John MacArthur, Charles Swindoll and myriad others, myself, the author, Reginald K. Lisemby included.

<u>When does *Yeshua* Return?</u> The Premillennial view of eschatology is that *Yeshua* will return at the end of the seven-year Great Tribulation and then He will inaugurate His millennial kingdom.

<u>How does *Yeshua* Return?</u> *Yeshua* presently reigns in heaven and He also reigns in the heart of His saints, but He will reign in a literal,

physical, earthly kingdom for one thousand years. The curse of the fall from the beginning will be reversed as Satan is bound and the Jewish people are restored to the Holy Land.

<u>Where will *Yeshua* Reign?</u> *Yeshua* will reign on the [literal] Jewish and Davidic throne in Israel, in Jerusalem, on the Temple Mount in the New Jerusalem.

THE AMILLENNIAL VIEW

The Amillennial view is presently the dominant view in the modern Catholic, Greek Orthodox and a large number of Protestant Churches. The view is said to have begun with Augustine in AD 354 and was also the view of Calvin and Luther. In fact, Calvin wrote a commentary of every book of the Bible except Revelation which he did not understand. Actually, these may not have wished to hear that another kingdom was coming, Messiah's Millennial Kingdom which is to be greater than the "Christian" church which was then being made greater thanks to Constantine and his 1st Reich and his Edict of Toleration (AD 311) which made the State Church the Kingdom Church.

<u>When does Jesus return?</u> This view regards Jesus as already reigning. His reign exists from the ascension until His Second Coming. Thus, there is no rapture, no seven-year tribulation, and no literal millennium.

<u>How does Jesus return?</u> Jesus is presently reigning in a spiritual kingdom which is analogous to the millennium.

<u>Where does Jesus return?</u> Jesus is reigning in heaven over the souls of the redeemed, and Jesus is reigning on earth in the hearts of His people, the Church.

THE POSTMILLENNIAL VIEW

The postmillennial view was the major view of the 18th and 19th Centuries due to the advances of technology, science, the industrial revolution, etc. man was being enabled to advance and also spiritually in order to bring in the Kingdom of God. However, the World Wars dealt this view a hard blow.

<u>When will Jesus reign?</u> Jesus will return after (post) the millennium which is a symbolic time frame from His first coming to His second coming; the thousand years is not taken literally.

<u>How does Jesus reign?</u> Jesus will reign spiritually and politically within the Church as it ushers in the golden age. This golden age will come about as believers in Christ exercise more and more influence over the affairs of this earth. Ultimately, the gospel will prevail, and the earth will be a better world. The world will be Christianized then Jesus will come to resurrect and judge before eternity.

<u>Where does Jesus reign?</u> Jesus is already reigning from heaven, but in particular, in the hearts of His people over all the earth from the first coming to the second coming.

**There are four major approaches to eschatology
with regards to the timing of eschatology.**

(1) The *Preterist* (*preter* meaning "past") which developed fully in the 17th Century believed that the destruction of Jerusalem in AD 70 and the spread of the gospel across the Roman Empire in the earthly church fulfilled the prophecies of the New Testament. *Preterism* is a form of *amillennialism,* while mild *preterism* still sees a future return of Christ although the millennial kingdom has already been established on earth. The rise of the allegorical school of interpretation and the

"Christianizing" of the Roman Empire (the Catholic Church) brought change in the church's interpretation of prophecy. Church historian, Eusebius (263-339) saw the *Olivet Discourse* of Christ already fulfilled in the destruction of Jerusalem by Rome and the change of Rome itself. David Chilton who is a *preterist* says of the book of Revelation, "the book of Revelation is not about the Second Coming of Christ. It is about the destruction of Israel and Christ's victory over His enemies in the establishment of the New Covenant Temple." *Preterism* sees no future for national Israel and no literal earthly tribulation or millennium. Contemporary preterists view the book of Revelation as already fulfilled and Christ now in the covenant Temple which is in the heavenly Jerusalem.

(2) The *Historicist* view developed after *Preterism* and grew in popularity through the Middle Ages. It was, in fact, the Franciscans who promoted this view (perhaps birthed it). The Reformers adopted and popularized *historicism* and Augustine (354-430) abandoned his early premillennialist view in favor of *historicism* and the amillennial view seeing Satan already bound, the church as the kingdom, and the present age ending in tribulation. The *historicist* sees prophecy fulfilled throughout church history in contrast to the *preterist* who sees the prophecies fulfilled in the first century.

> The *preterist* – prophecies fulfilled in the first century
> The *historicist* – prophecies fulfill throughout church history

Generally, the *historicist* sees the Tribulation (Revelation 6-19) as being fulfilled in the current church age. The *historicist* like the *preterist* uses the allegorical method of interpretation and he spiritualizes both the Tribulation and the Millennium. The churches of Revelation 2 and 3 were equated with developments in church history and prophecy was being fulfilled in the church in the present age. The pope is viewed as the *antichrist*, Rome is viewed as Babylon, and the church is viewed as the godly remnant persecuted by Rome. *Historicism* declined due to date setting and false predictions of the Lord's return, as in 1843 and then revised to 1844.

(3) The *Idealist* sees the prophetic elements of scripture as neither literal or important. These react to whichever view is dominant in their day and whichever view is favored. To this group, prophecy is a vehicle for expressing spiritual truth and does not require a framework or literal fulfillment. Thus, the book of Revelation does not predict any specific historical event. On the contrary, it sets forth timeless truths concerning the battle between good and evil that continues. The *idealist* view is more recent and more difficult to distinguish from the earlier allegorizing approaches. In general, the *idealist* refuses to identify any of the images with specific events historic, present, or future.

(4) The *Futurist* was the view of the early church though not developed and articulated as pretribulationism and premillennialism. The early church held to a future tribulation and millennium separated by the return of Messiah. The early church interpreted prophecy quite literally and anticipated a climatic return of Messiah to the earth. The *futurist* sees the prophecies of the Old Testament, the Olivet Discourse of *Yeshua*, and the book of Revelation (*Yeshua*'s disclosure, Revelation 1:1) as awaiting a time of fulfillment, and though *futurists* differ on the timing of the rapture, we agree on a literal, future tribulation, and millennium. *Futurism* was the dominant view in the first three centuries and is the view today of the majority of conservative, fundamental institutions and churches. The rise of the allegorical figurative and spiritual method of interpretation along with the Christianizing of Rome (the Catholic Church) led to a decline of *futurism*, though some *futurists* remained in the church throughout the Middle Ages.

Reginald. K. Lisemby

Question 43

With different views of eschatology, why do you think the pretribulation, premillennial view of eschatology is correct?

Answer

Different views of eschatology are not the result of the Holy Scriptures being confusing or conflicting forcing the reader to choose an eschatological view he or she likes the best. Different views of eschatology are the result of interpretation of the Holy Scriptures. Interpretation is everything!

The difference in the premillennial and amillennial view of scripture is a question of literal versus figurative interpretation.[35] An example is how one interprets *Israel* in the New Testament. The premillennial interprets *Israel* to be the same throughout the entirety of the Holy Scriptures, from *Yaaqov* given that name, his sons, his posterity, his twelve tribes, and the nation those tribes formed, even to Real Estate, the Promised Land. Sounds reasonable, doesn't it? *Israel* was the name given to *Yaaqov* and *Yaaqov's* posterity, so *Israel* is always *Israel.* When the New Testament opens, the nation and the land were both called *Israel.* However, the amillennial (beginning with Augustine) chooses to allegorize the name *Israel* and interprets *Israel* to be the "people of God," and in the New Testament Israel is said to be the church.

Allegorizing the scriptures always perverts the true meaning of the Holy Scriptures as one attempts to get to some deeper, secret meaning

---

35 Oswald T. Allis, Prophecy and the Church, p. 17

of the Word.[36] Allegorizing disregards the meaning of the biblical author who was inspired (the reader is not inspired), and allegorizing disregards the interpretation the Holy Spirit intends for the reader to have, but twists the meaning and often to a point toward cultic orientation. This is gravely dangerous.

One might argue that the Apostle *Shaul* used allegory, and that is correct. However, the Apostle *Shaul* was inspired by the Holy Spirit of God to do so. We can trust *Shaul's* use of allegory. I do not trust man's allegorizing, and especially not Augustinian allegory.

The Holy Scriptures are messianic (Luke 24:27-44), yet, when *Yeshua* came as prophesied in the Holy Scriptures, those who were supposed to know the Holy Scriptures did not recognize Him? Some recognized Him, but only a few. The intelligentsia of Israel, the religious leaders missed Him His entire life. There were those like *Sh'meon* and *Anna* who recognized their Messiah when He was an eight-day old baby come for His *brit-melah*. *Lukas* records for us that *Sh'meon* took baby God and held Him in his arms and exclaimed that his eyes were seeing His messiah, his hope, and his salvation.

Yochanon the immerser recognized his cousin as the Lamb of God to take away the sins of the world. *Andreas* recognized *Yeshua* and ran to tell *Kefa*, his brother. Those who recognized *Yeshua* had studied the Word and had a literal hermeneutic or interpretation.

Someone has said that a study of hermeneutics (the science of interpretation) is foundational for knowing prophecy and should be studied first. Here are some helps for a correct and dependable approach to the interpretation of the Holy Scriptures.

1. Recognize that the Holy Scriptures were written using the laws of human language, and thus should be interpreted according to the laws of written communication. Take the Bible at its word!

---

36 Dwight Pentecost. Things to Come, p.5.

2. Recognize that the authors of the Holy Scriptures were inspired, but we the recipients are not inspired. Read and interpret the Bible through the lens of the author since he wrote the scroll and he anticipated his audience would understand him.

3. Recognize that above the human author was the Holy Spirit Who superintended the human author. He, the Holy Spirit remains with us though the human author does not, and He is able to make the interpretation known to us, not secretly just for you, but to anyone and everyone who possesses Him, the Spirit of God. To truly know the Word, one must be born again or regenerated by the Holy Spirit.

4. Recognize that the Holy Spirit often hides the true meaning from those who are prideful, and reveals to those who are humble and approach Him as children (Matthew 11:25,26).

    "Thou has hidden these things from the wise and prudent, and has revealed them unto babes."

    The Holy Spirit also hides the true meaning from those who reject His Word, as Herod for example. *Yeshua* did not answer him.

5. Recognize it is absolutely essential to have some knowledge or resources to help you grasp the original languages. All translations are translations and not the original tongue God Almighty chose to reveal His Word. The original languages are veils between the biblical author and the interpreter. Get help to get beyond the veil.

6. Recognize that the Word itself is inspired! The Bible is not a record of inspired events. The Word itself is inspired. You and I have the privileged perspective on any/every subject, for the

Word speaks to all. A Southern Baptist Church where we were members was going to ordain a young man whom the church loved. Everyone loved Danny, and the mission field representative wanted Danny to plant a church in a particular state, but to do so, Danny had to be ordained. Problem. Danny had two wives, with a child by his first wife. Actually, the mission field representative didn't see this as a problem, nor the previous pastor of our church, and neither did the present pastor. The issue was so big for others of us, that the pastor called a meeting of the deacons, and for the first time in my life (and, I have been a Southern Baptist all my life) I was blackballed. My email was removed from the church's list of ordained men (until this present day), I was not asked to attend, and two deacons called me to argue that leaders in the church with PhD degrees interpreted the scriptures other than my interpretation, what made me think I was correct? That is a very good question. How would you answer it? Sad to say, they ordained Danny, and this disobedience of the church remains a blight to them until this day.

The answer to the qualifications of an elder is not difficult, since the Word of God is inspired and gives us the inspired perspective (and not the perspective we may want). The authors of the Holy Scriptures were simple men and sensible men of God, and they did not write to confuse their audience or mislead us. The leaders of the church I mentioned above were trying to find that secret, hidden meaning of "husband of one wife" while the Holy Scriptures and especially the New Testament scriptures are explicit about the seriousness of marriage, the one condition for divorce, the impact of divorce, the command to remain hopeful of reconciliation, the consequences of remarrying while the other spouse remains alive, the consequence of marrying a divorced person, and the qualifications of the elders and deacons of the church.

7. Recognize that there is a literal interpretation to every passage of Holy Writ, but to acquire it means that you are willing to embrace the grammatical, historical, and cultural context using the ordinary and original sense of the author according to the normal, customary, usage of words. An example of this would be the passage in Psalm 122:6, "Pray for the Peace of Jerusalem." The context of that entire Psalm, which is an *aliya* psalm or a hymn Israel sang "going up" to Jerusalem three times each year, is messianic with Messiah on the throne of David. Read it! This is not a passage that you can claim for present day Jerusalem to have peace, since present day Jerusalem continues to ignore *Yeshua*/Jesus, the Messiah! Thus, Israel is not going to have peace, and God will see that Israel does not until they repent! Nor is this passage a word you can apply in your prayers to the Christian Church. Your church is not your Jerusalem (Replacement Theology). Jerusalem is Jerusalem!

8. Recognize that there is the context, an inner-text, and an inter-textual meaning to correctly interpret a text. The context is the meaning of a text where it lies in location of the scroll. The inner-textual meaning is the meaning within the book the text occurs. There is also the intertextual meaning which is the meaning found within the whole of the Bible. Here is an example. In the book of Revelation, *Yochanon* writes *"and to the woman were given two wings of a great eagle, that she might fly into the wilderness, into her place, where she is ..." (Revelation 12:14).* The *two wings* is often interpreted to be a jet airliner carrying Jews. However, *Yochanon* borrowed that phrase from Exodus 19:4, *"you have seen what I did unto the Egyptians, and how I bare you on eagles' wings and brought you unto myself."* This is an example of the intertextual interpretation, where the meaning is found beyond its location (Revelation 12) even beyond the book

(Revelation), but within the entirety of the Holy Scriptures (Exodus).

9. Recognize that only using a literal interpretation will your biblical devotions and/or your study be anchored on solid scriptural assurance.

10. Recognize that a literal interpretation means to take the texts as they were meant by the inspired author. Figurative and metaphoric speech is to be interpreted as figurative and metaphoric, as the author intended. Types are types, symbols are symbols, and if symbols have a meaning the author may say so, even sometimes he has given the meaning explicitly. An example of this is *Dani'el* 8 where *Dani'el* is given the prophecy of a ram with two horns, a goat with one horn, and the goat with four horns and an antler. *Dani'el* gives us the interpretation: Medio-Persia, Greece, Alexander the Great (Greece's first king), his four Generals (Cassander, Ptolemy, Lysimachus, and Seleucus), and Antiochus Epiphanes IV.

11. Recognize that 'spiritualizing' a text could mean 'demonizing' a text. Be very careful! Certainly, the Holy Word of God is spiritual, in its origin, in its content, and in its application. Yet, what is spiritual is the truth that is revealed, and the power of truth changes lives. There is a truth war and the enemy will use every tactic to deceive us from the spiritual truth within, even by 'spiritualizing' the truth texts. It is evident that the most powerful cults use the Bible and its holy scriptures though they spiritualize and twist them: Mormonism; Jehovah's Witnesses; Christian Science; Holiness; Kabbalah; Gematria, etc. During the Middle Ages many were taught to first learn what you believe, and then go to the Scriptures to find it.

W.A. Criswell, pastor of the First Baptist Church of Dallas Texas once said, "if we preach the Bible literally, it is like telling the truth. You do not have to remember what you said. But if you spiritualize…what you said about a passage yesterday may be diametrically opposed to what you make it mean today…a man will find himself contradicting himself over and over again as he preaches though the years."[37] Also, if you spiritualize a text there is no way to test the validity of the conclusions.

12. Recognize that the Word of God (and Prophecy) was meant to be understood (Matthew 24:15), and if God is indeed the author of the Holy Scriptures, we should enter the Word to find a wealth of meaning.[38] After all, God invented language and chose it as His medium of communication, and He will use it for the final judgment.

---

[37] W.A. Criswell. Why I Preach that the Bible is Literally True. Nashville, TN: Broadman Press, 1969. Page 145.

[38] Cited by Anton Berkeley Mickelsen, Interpreting the Bible (Grand Rapids, Mich. Eerdmans, 1963, page 37).

Reginald. K. Lisemby

Question 44

What is your chronology of eschatology; how do you arrange the last days events in their chronological order of prophetic fulfillment?

Answer

PRIOR TO THE RAPTURE

- The remnant of Jews and the fullness of Gentiles are coming into the Church.
- The resurrection of the Dry Bones to Israel; the resurrection of the land of Israel.
- Violence, sexual immorality, sodomy, natural disasters, fabricated Christs and prophets, earthquakes, etc. continue worldwide and will grow worse.
- The church becomes divided as God gathers His people, and the non-remnant tares are separated.
- Apostasy increases; moral implosion in every country.
- The antichrist is being groomed for political arena.
- The spirit of antichrist (lawlessness) with growing apostasy or defection from Christianity.

THE RAPTURE

- The Church is raptured; the *Bema* or Judgment Seat of Messiah; Marriage of the Lamb; rewards/crowns distributed; Song of the lamb; Lamb receives the Seven-Sealed Scroll.

- Global hysteria; continued pandemics, plagues, false peace and security. Stampede of Jews to Israel (perhaps ethnic groups to their origin).
- Holy remnant and hindrance of evil is removed.

THE GREAT TRIBULATION

- World in colossal chaos.
- Antichrist appears and signs covenant/accord with Israel (the Great Tribulation now begins).
- The Day of the Lord has begun.
- Ark of Covenant discovered or rebuilt and revealed
- The Red Heifer is proclaimed; the Third Temple promoted; the Mosaic Covenant reinstituted.
- Reunited Roman Empire emerges as a league of ten nations.
- 144,000 Jewish believers in *Yeshua* are sealed; they begin their evangelistic campaign.
- Two witnesses, *Moshe* and *Eliyah* appear and begin preaching to Israel and the Gentiles; worldwide revival.
- Seal Judgments unleashed.
- Trumpet Judgments unleashed.
- Religious Babylon controls the world.
- Antichrist breaks covenant with Israel; commits *abomination of desolation* (or, perhaps later).
- Antichrist violently murdered; Satan cast down from heaven and begins his rage toward the end.
- Antichrist is miraculously healed and resurrected.
- Israel is forced to flee the land of Israel (perhaps to Petra).
- Antichrist seizes control of 10-nation empire. Antichrist becomes world czar.
- *Moshe* and *Eliyah* are murdered; bodies not permitted burial, but lie in street of *Yerushalayim*; the two messengers suddenly resuscitated, resurrected, and ascend to heaven.

- Antichrist breaks covenant with Israel; commits *abomination of desolation* (or, perhaps earlier).
- Judgment upon Babylon.
- Three world kings murdered by antichrist; false prophet rises with Mark of the Beast.
- Mark of the Beast/666 introduced as personal identity prefix and credit card.
- Worldwide persecution/martyrdom of saints.
- Bowl judgments poured out.
- Armageddon campaign begins.

THE SECOND COMING OF YESHUA

- Second Coming of *Yeshua*; judgments of Israel and Gentiles; birds gather to clean carnage; Satan bound for one-thousand years.

THE MILLENNIUM

- Millennial rule of *Yeshua* with David, *Yeshua*'s disciples, the Church.
- Land of Israel restored like the Garden in Eden.
- Millennial Kingdom is built

POST MILLENNIUM

- Satan is loosed; Satan leads final revolt/*Gog and Magog* War.
- Great White Throne Judgment; death and hades cast/hurled into Gehenna fire.
- Cremation of the present heavens and earth by fire.

THE ETERNAL STATE

- A new heaven and the new earth descends.

Reginald. K. Lisemby

Question 45

Is there a correlation between the book of Revelation and the book of Genesis?

Answer

Yes! The relationship of *Yeshua's* Apocalypse and *Moshe's* Torah is striking. *Yeshua* truly is the prophet like unto *Moshe. Yeshua* is actually the new *Moshe.* He is better than *Moshe*, and the covenant of *Moshe* having become obsolete (Hebrews 8:13), the covenant of *Yeshua* is eternal.

MOSHE OF THE BEGINNING (Genesis) *YOCHANON* OF THE END (Revelation)

The Eternal State before Genesis (John 17:5,24)
The Eternal State after Revelation (Revelation 22:5)

The beginning: the Heavens and Earth (Genesis 1:1)
The end: the New Heavens and New Earth (Revelation 21:1-22:5)

The original Holy Mountain of the Lord on first earth (Ezekiel 28:14)
The first earth passed away; the Holy City coming down (Revelation 21:1,2)

The Garden in Eden, God dwelling with man (Genesis 2)
The New Jerusalem, God tabernacling with man (Revelation 21:3,4)

The fall of Satan, he deceiving mankind (Genesis 3)
The binding of the serpent, he deceiving the nations (Revelation 20:1-8)

The angelic amalgamation, the ungodly judged by flood (Genesis 5,6)
The devil, ungodly serpent judged at Great White Throne (Revelation 20:7-15)

The woman and her seed versus Satan's seed (Genesis 3:15)
The two women (Revelation 12 & 17)

Avraham out of Babylon into the wilderness
The Apostle *Yochanon* carried into the wilderness as *Avraham*

Babylon, world center (Genesis 11), Nimrod ruled, unity of nations
Babylon, world center of religion, politics, economy of all nations
(Revelation 17-19)

The plaques of Egypt (Exodus 7-12)
The bowls of judgment (Revelation 16)

The Exodus (Exodus 12:51)
The victorious from the beast with harps of God (Revelation 15:1,2)

The Song of Moshe (Exodus 15)
The Song of Moshe (Revelation 15:3,4)

The Tabernacle and priestly garments (Exodus 25 +)
The Tabernacle and angelic garments (Revelation 15:5,6)

The *Shekinah* of God fills the Sanctuary (Exodus 40:34)
The *Shekinah* of God fills (Revelation 15:8)

The expectation of God's holy people (Leviticus)
The 144,000 from the 12 tribes marked (Revelation 14)

KEY TERMS IN ESCHATOLOGY

Abrahamic Covenant - God made an unconditional covenant with *Avraham* promising personal blessings, universal blessings, and a national blessing to *Avraham*. The personal blessings are a name, a land, and a seed. The national blessings is a nation among the nations, and the universal blessings are that all the families of the earth will be blessed in him and by him. Unlike the Mosaic covenant, the Abrahamic covenant is eternal not temporary, it is unconditional in the sense that God is going to fulfill the promise Himself although it is conditional in the sense that every individual who wishes to participate in the covenant must be obedient in faith.

Advent – The term refers to *Yeshua*'s first coming or "arrival" as Messiah. His second advent will be *Yeshua*'s second "arrival" as Judge.

Amillennialism – The "A" prefix is a negation in the Greek and means "no." Amillennial means, "no millennium." Amillennialists deny a literal one-thousand-year reign of *Yeshua* in bodily form on earth, in Israel, in Jerusalem, on a Davidic throne. Amillennialists believe that *Yeshua* rules spiritually. He rules earth from heaven. Amillennialists do not believe in a literal return of *Yeshua* to earth that will usher in the eternal state, and they also see no need for a return of national Israel to the land of Israel.

Annihilationism – The term annihilate means "to cause to cease to exist." Annihilationists believe the unregenerate will cease to exist after death rather than experience eternal conscious punishment. Annihilationism is also known as, "condition immortality."

Antichrist – "anti" means against, in place of, or instead of. Christ is the Greek equivalent for the Hebrew term Messiah. The *antichrist* will be a single person who is opposed to Messiah or Christ and for the nation of Israel and the world will be against Messiah or Christs. The term is also used in the plural form, *antichrist*s, for all who oppose Messiah or Christ. (see 1 John 2:18,22; 4:3; 2 Thessalonians 2:3-12).

Apocalypse – The term is from the Greek apocalypses meaning "to unveil," "disclose," or "reveal." In the common usage it means to take the cover off something or to reveal. Old Testament Apocalyptic scrolls include *Yekhek'el*, *Zecharyah*, and *Dani'el*.

Apostasy – The term is from the Greek *apostasia* found twice in the New Testament (Acts 21:21; 2 Thessalonians 2:3). The meaning is to intentionally defect or fall away, or to forsake one's faith. The concept of a spiritual revolt or departure from God is predicted in the Holy Scriptures to happen near "the end" of the age (2 Corinthians 4:10; 1 Timothy 1:20; 4:1). The general state of religion in the last days will be apostate (Revelation 13:11-17).

Armageddon – The term comes from two Hebrew words, *Har* meaning mountain and Megiddo, a place in northern central Israel, also called the Jezreel valley and valley of decision. Armageddon is mentioned only in Revelation 16:16, and it is not a battle, but a series of military campaigns, *polemos* in the Greek.

Bema Seat – A *bema* in Jewish society is an elevated platform on which a judge was seated above his subjects (Acts 18:12, 16). The *Bema Seat* or *Judgment Seat of Messiah* is for the believer, and has nothing to do with sin or sins, but rather the believer's works for which he will be rewarded.

Bodily Resurrection – In reference to the body of *Yeshua*, the same physical body that was crucified and buried, with nail holes and a spear gash in His side, was raised with scars (which *Yeshua* showed Thomas) and yet glorified. In reference to believers, the same physical body will be resurrected and glorified.

Chiliasm – The term is a Greek one describing those who believer in a one-thousand-year reign of Messiah as described in Revelation 20, one-thousand years occurring six times.

Davidic Covenant – God made an unconditional covenant with David ben Jesse involving a posterity that is, his seed, a kingdom which is David's dynasty, and a throne which is David's kingdom rule (2

Samuel 7:11-17; 23:5; 1 Chronicles 17:10-15; Psalm 89; Isaiah 9:6-7; Jeremiah 23:5-6; Luke 1:3-35; Acts 15:14-18).

Day of the Lord – The term day of YHWH occurs twenty-one times in the Holy Scriptures and relates to the seven years of tribulation culminating in the Second Coming of Messiah in judgment. Premillennialists include the tribulation, the Second Coming of *Yeshua*, and the Millennium all together in the Day of YHWH based on 2 Peter 3:10 and OT promises of blessing.

Dispensationalism – The term dispensational is a transliteration of the Latin dispensation which is a translation of the Greek word, *oikonomia i*dentifying a system of theology that categorize the program of God and how He deals with man in three essential characteristics. 1. Israel and the Church are distinct entities and have distinct purposes in the plan of God. 2. Prophecy is to be interpreted in a literal, normal sense. 3. God's purpose in the world is to manifest His glory. The word in its variations appear twenty times in the New Testament and means "to manage, regulate, administer, and plan (1 Corinthians 4:1-2; Ephesians 3:2-11; Colossians 1:25).

Epiphaino – The term *epiphaino* means to visibly "appear" and is found in Titus 2:13, "the glorious appearing of our great God and Savior, Jesus Christ." His appearance will not be an apparition but a literal and visible appearance although certainly in His divine glory.

Eternal State – The eternal state involves the new heavens and new earth and new Jerusalem (Revelation 21; 22). The eternal state of the Old Testament saint follows the millennium (Revelation 20:4-6); the eternal state of the Christians follows the Rapture and glorification (1 Corinthian 15:50-54; 1 Thessalonians 4:13-18). The eternal state of the unbeliever follows the Great White Throne Judgment where he is hurled into Gehenna Fire.

Futurism – The term futurism references a future fulfillment of prophecy. Premillennialist are futurists distinguished from *preterism* which sees prophecy as fulfilled in the first century. *Historicism* interprets prophecy as fulfilled in church history. Both *historicism* and *preterism* are views of *Amillennialists*.

Great Tribulation – The term Great Tribulation was used by *Yeshua* in Matthew 24 to describe the latter half of *Dani'el*'s seventieth week. This time is also known as Jacob's Trouble (Matthew 24:21-25; Revelation 4-19). Many maintain a distinction between the Great Tribulation and Jacob's Trouble. Amillennialists see the tribulation as current, not a literal seven-year time yet to occur.

Great White Throne Judgment – The final judgment for unbelievers in contrast to the Bema Seat or Judgment Seat of Messiah is the Great White Throne Judgment where all unregenerate souls will appear before Messiah for judgment of their sins, being in a sinful state, and thus hurled into everlasting Gehenna Fire.

Heaven – The Hebrew term is *shemayim* which is plural and refers to more than one. The atmospheric space surrounding the earth is heaven, the space of the planets and stars is heaven, and higher to the third heaven where *Shaul*/Paul was "caught up," and perhaps all the way to the fifth heaven. Heaven typically denotes the dwelling place of God (Matthew 18:10; Luke 11:13). Heaven is the believer's final and eternal home (John 14:2; 2 Corinthians 5:1-2; Revelation 21).

Hermeneutics – The science of interpretation is hermeneutics. *Yeshua*'s *hermeneutic* is found in Luke 24:27-44; He saw Himself walking through the pages of the Holy Scriptures.

Hell – Sheol or Hades is the current holding place or "hell" of the unrepentant and unregenerate souls. It is a place of conscious memory and punishment for Satan, the fallen angels, and one day to be emptied into Gehenna Fire or the Lake of Fire.

Historicism – This is a view that prophetic events of the Bible have been continuously fulfilled throughout church history. See "Futurism" above.

Imminency – This is the belief that Messiah *Yeshua* may return at any moment, a belief strongly maintained by Premillennialist and characteristic of the Apostles and the early church fathers.

Intermediate State – The status of the redeemed saints between physical death and resurrection of the body is the "intermediate state." The soul of the believer does into the presence of *Yeshua* at death (2 Corinthians 5:6) and on the body experiences death. The unregenerate are conscious in *hades/hell* at death, but not consigned Gehenna fire until after the Great White Throne Judgment (Revelation 20:11-15).

Idealism – Idealists see no specific fulfillment of prophecy in either the past or the future. Rather, the coming of Messiah occurs within the individual believer's experience at the present.

Jacob's Trouble – The term describes the latter half of *Dani'el* seventieth week, also known as the Great Tribulation. Many maintain a distinction between the Great Tribulation and Jacob's Trouble. Amillennialists see the tribulation as current, not a literal seven-year time in prophecy. See Matthew 24:21-25; Revelation 4-19).

Judgment Seat of Christ – Following the rapture of believers, the Church or Body of *Yeshua*, we will give an account to Messiah for our works and will be rewarded accordingly (2 Corinthians 5:10; Romans 14:10).

Kingdom – The Holy Scriptures refer to (1) an earthly kingdom, like Assyria, Babylon, etc. (2) the universal and eternal kingdom where God rules over all including creation, man, angels, etc. (Psalm 103:19; 145:10-13). The kingdom of God refers to God's rule over all elect creatures, angels and regenerate man (John 3:3; Hebrews 1:4-14). Everyone saved and born again is born into the kingdom of God. Everyone is elect. Everyone is an heir of the kingdom. There are no redeemed saints outside the King or His reign over His Kingdom.

Midtribulationism – This is an eschatological view that interprets the church sharing the first half of the Great Tribulation with Israel, but then raptured and spared the second half of the seven-year Great Tribulation.

Mystery – *Shaul*/Paul defines "mystery" in his epistles to the Roman believers, Ephesian believers and Colossian believers (Romans 16:25-

26; Ephesians 3:2-11; Colossians 1:24-27) as a truth previously hidden but now revealed, specifically, that the church is a work of God not revealed in the Old Testament, but now made known.

New Covenant – The "new" covenant was made by YHWH with Israel (Jeremiah 31:31-34) and guarantees a future regeneration for Israel which Gentiles will also participate (Isaiah 61:8,9; Ezekiel 37:21-28).

Normative Dispensationalism – Also known as classical, traditional, and historic dispensationalism that believes the church was a mystery unrevealed in the Old Testament and was formed by the baptizing work of the Holy Spirit at Pentecost. It also maintains that Messiah is now seated at the right hand of the Father in heaven, but not now on the Davidic throne (see Progressive Dispensationalism).

Olivet Discourse – This is Messiah's most significant teaching about the tribulation and his return as recorded in Matthew 24 and 25.

Palestinian Covenant – This is an eternal, unconditional covenant guaranteeing Israel possession of the land in Deuteronomy 30:1-10 which relates to the land portion of the Abrahamic covenant. Though obedience was required for blessing in the land, the right to the land and Israel's ultimate restoration to it are guaranteed (Ezekiel 16:53-63; Amos 9:11-15; Zechariah 8:6-8; 14:5-21).

Parousia – The term meaning "alongside of" occurs frequently and describes the return of Messiah.

Partial Rapture – Some believe that only "spiritual" Christians will be raptured before the Great Tribulation and unspiritual Christians will remain behind to experience the tribulation in order to "clean" them up for heaven.

Postmillennialism – This eschatological view sees the church as part of a currently existing redemptive and spiritual kingdom which will progressively transform the world in preparation for Messiah's return. Theonomic postmillennialism sees the kingdom advancing through imposition of kingdom law. Pietistic postmillennialism sees the kingdom as a spiritual kingdom advancing in the hearts of believers. Both maintain that we are presently advancing toward a golden age that will be climaxed by Christ's return.

Posttribulationism – This eschatological view sees the rapture of the church as occurring at the end of the tribulation. It is the prevailing view in covenant (historic) premillennialism. This view holds the rapture and the Second Coming of Messiah as a single event.

Premillennialism – This eschatological view holds that Messiah will return prior to establishing a literal one-thousand-year reign on earth. Covenant Premillennialists hold that the rapture will occur at the same time (or simultaneous with) the Second Coming and that the millennium will not involve Israel as a nation distinct from the church. Dispensational Premillennialism holds that the church will be raptured before or during the tribulation. Messiah will then return to the earth with the church to judge the nations and establish the earthly kingdom promised to Davie (Revelation 19:20; Zechariah 14:3-11).

Preterism – This views the Old Testament and New Testament prophetic scriptures as fulfilled with the destruction of the Jewish State in AD 70. Bible prophecy has already been fulfilled and is not now being fulfilled and does not have a future fulfillment.

Pretribulationism – This eschatological view maintains a distinction of the Church and Israel and sees the church as raptured prior to the Great Tribulation of the 70th Week of *Dani'el*. It distinguishes between the coming of Messiah in the air FOR the saints (John 14:1-3; 1 Thessalonians 4:13-18) and the return of Messiah to the earth WITH the saints (Zechariah 14:4,5; Matthew 24:27-31; 1 Thessalonians 5:1-10).

Pre-Wrath Rapture – This view suggests that the rapture occurs three-quarters way through the seven years of the Great Tribulation coinciding with the seventh seal and trumpet judgments. The first half of the Great Tribulation is the wrath of man, the second half of the Great Tribulation is the wrath of God.

Progressive Dispensationalism – Also known as reconstructed, modified, new, revised, kingdom and changed dispensationalism, it is distinct from classical dispensationalism in several significant ways. (1) it advocates complementary hermeneutics; (2) it has a more or less unified sense of the kingdom of God in both testaments; (3) it holds that the church was revealed in the Old Testament, but not realized until the New Testament; (4) it argues that the Davidic kingdom was inaugurated at the ascension of Messiah so that Messiah is now ruling on the Davidic throne in heaven; (5) the church is the present revelation of the future messianic kingdom; (6) the New Covenant has already been inaugurated with the church, but will also have a future enactment with Israel.

Reconstructionism – a recent development with reformed theology is the belief that the Christian is obligated to keep the whole law of God and that civil government should enforce the law of God. It is essentially postmillennialism. The goal is world dominion under Messiah's lordship, a "world takeover." The first steps are reformation, then reconstruction of the church, then social and political reconstruction, a flowering of Christian civilization.

Replacement Theology – This is the view that promises made to Israel are now fulfilled in the church. The church is the "new" Israel.

Resurrection – Ultimately all souls will be raised from the grave, the regenerate to eternal blessing and the unregenerate to eternal condemnation and damnation. The dead in Messiah will be resurrected at the Rapture (1 Thessalonians 4:16), Tribulation and Old Testament Saints will be resurrected at the Second Coming of *Yeshua* prior to His millennial reign (Revelation 20:3-5; Daniel 12:2). The unregenerate will be resurrected for the Great White Throne Judgment (Revelation 20:5, 11-14).

Revelation – This refers to God's disclosure to man. There is general revelation, that is God's disclosure through creation, and there is special revelation which is God's disclosure through His Holy Scriptures and the incarnation of Messiah.

Rapture - The seizing or "catching up" of the church resulting in her eternal union with Messiah. There are five different views of the rapture among evangelicals: partial rapture; pre-rapture; mid-rapture; post-rapture; and pre-wrath rapture views.

Soul Sleep – The belief that the soul remains in a "suspended animation" at death without being united to Messiah or destroyed.

Tribulation – The commonly used term for the seventieth week of *Dani'el* during which the events of Revelation 4-19 will occur. See Great Tribulation.

Theonomy – A combination of the Greek words for "God" and "law." This stresses the need to being the secular world under the jurisdiction of the Mosaic law (see Reconstructionism).

Theocratic Kingdom – This refers to the sovereign rule of God on earth through the various epochs of biblical history. It finds its ultimate consummation in the future eschatological or millennial kingdom on the earth when God's sovereignty will be universally recognized.

BIBLIOGRAPHY

Anderson, Robert. *The Coming Prince*. London: Hodder & Stoughton, 1894.

Blasing, Craig and Darrell Bock. *Dispensationalism, Israel, and the Church*. Grand Rapids: Zondervan, 1992.

Bradley, Mark. *IRAN*. Colorado Springs, CO: Authentic Media, 2007.

Bullinger, E.W. *The Witness of the Stars*. Grand Rapids: Kregel, 1983.

Dyer, Charles H. *The Rise of Babylon*. Chicago: Moody Press, 2003.

Dobson, Ed. *The End*. Grand Rapids: Zondervan, 1997.

Fruchtenbaum, Arnold. *Footsteps of Messiah*. Tustin, CA: Ariel Press, 1979.

Fruchtenbaum, Arnold. *Israelology*. Tustin, CA: Ariel Press, 1989.

Grenz, Stanley. *The Millennial Maze*. Downers Grove, IL: Brentwood, 1992.

Hanna, Dr. Ken. *Eschatology*. Dallas Theological Seminary. Class notes, 2001.

Hindson, Ed. *Is the Antichrist Alive and Well?* Eugene, OR: Harvest House, 1998.

Hindson, Ed. and Mark Hitchcock. *Can We Still Believe in the Rapture?* Eugene, OR: Harvest House, 2017.

Hitchcock, Mark. *Bible Prophecy*. Wheaton, IL: Tyndale Publishers, 1996.

Hitchcock, Mark. *The Second Coming of Babylon*. Sisters, Oregon: Multnomah, 2003.

Jeffrey, Grant. *Prince of Darkness*. Toronto: Frontier Research Publications, 1994.

Jeremiah, David. *Agents of the Apocalypse*. Carol Stream, IL: Tyndale Publishers, 2014.

Kennedy, James D. *The Real Meaning of the Zodiac*. Ft. Lauderdale: TCRM Publishing, 1993.

Lipinski, Edward. *El's Abode: Mythological Traditions Related to Mount Hermon and to the Mountains of Armenia,*" Orientalia Lovanien sa Periodica 2, 1971: 19).

Payne, J. Barton. *Encyclopedia of Biblical Prophecy*. New York: Harper and Row, 1973.

Pentecost, J. Dwight. *Things to Come*. Grand Rapids: Zondervan, 1965.

Pink, Arthur W. *The Coming Antichrist*. Chicago: Moody Press, 1974.

Rhodes, Ron. *Unmasking the Antichrist*. Eugene, OR: Harvest House, 2012.

Ryrie, Charles. *Dispensationalism*. Chicago: Moody Press, 1995.

Walvoord, John F. *Major Bible Prophecies*. Grand Rapids: Zondervan, 1991.

ABOUT THE AUTHOR

Reginald Kent Lisemby came to faith in *Yeshua* the Messiah in his early teen years and immediately began to share his love for his Lord with friends, baseball team mates, peers, even running five miles each day to the Lake Charles beach to share the Gospel of Jesus. Evangelism is his spiritual gift.

Reginald is the son of James Travis and Dorothy Sue Grice Lisemby, the second born of their four sons, James Ricky, Reginald Kent, Joel Keith, and Darren Burl. The Lisemby Family became renown in Baptist churches in the deep south for their music, revivals, and annual music schools and camps. The Lisembys sang Christian music and played a variety of string, percussion, woodwind, and keyboard instruments. The family initially recorded 14 LP albums and appeared with major recording artists, like the Oak Ridge Boys, Blackwood Singers, Happy Goodman Family, Amigos, Florida Boys, and Johnny Cash and June Carter Cash.

Reginald and his older brother, Ricky attended the Stamps-Baxter School of Music in the 1970s, and Reginald became a registered songwriter with BMI (Broadcast Music Incorporated) in Nashville, TN. He has written a number of Christian songs that have been recorded.

The Lisemby Family moved from Lake Charles, Louisiana to Kingsland Arkansas in 1984 to build *Psalms Bible and Music Camp* on the 40 acres his mother, Dorothy Sue Grice Lisemby inherited from her family and where she and her family once farmed cotton. Psalms encampment contains log dormitories, a log chapel, a log cafetoria, and a 7-acre lake, most of which Reginald and his father and brothers built.

In 1988 Reginald married Crystal Faith McNeely from Lismore, Louisiana. Their final concert with the Lisemby Family before leaving the family ministry and Psalms Camp to attend Moody Bible Institute in Chicago, was a homecoming concert in Kingsland, Arkansas that featured Johnny Cash and June Carter Cash. Reggie played his twelve-string Legend Ovation guitar in the shadow of his long-distance cousin, Johnny Cash who was born and farmed cotton in Kingsland, Arkansas with Reggie's father, James Lisemby. James and Johnny's grandmothers were sisters.

The most colossal experience for Reginald Lisemby and the one that changed his life, was his first trip to the Holy Land in 1979. This experience was the impetus that propelled Reginald toward Jewish ministry.

While at the Moody Bible Institute in Chicago, Reggie received many accomplishments: the Rachmiel Frydland Scholarship for his accomplishments in Jewish Studies; an honor graduate; Dean's List; Who's Who Among Students in American Universities & Colleges; and he graduated with a BA in 1998 having completed the *Jewish and Modern Israel Studies* program on campus and his intern in Nazareth Illit, Israel.

Mr. Lisemby is a Cum Laude Honor Graduate from Temple Baptist Seminary in Chattanooga, TN receiving his Master of Arts degree, and he later received an Honorary Doctorate of Divinity for studies and work in his field from a seminary in Georgia.

In 1998 *Messianic Ministry to Israel* in Chattanooga, TN called Reginald for an interview and Rev. Lisemby become the Executive Director of the one of the oldest Jewish Mission Boards in the South. *Messianic Ministry to Israel* is a mission board in Chattanooga, TN that was formed in 1944 for the purpose of sharing the Gospel with Jewish people.

Reginald has led mission/study/tours to Israel on twenty different occasions at the time of this writing. In 2017 Reginald participated on an archaeological dig at Tel Gezer Israel with the New Orleans Theological Seminary. Reginald has also studied and ministered in

Egypt, Jordan, Uganda, Kenya, Ukraine, Albania, and England, and has performed ministry with the Native-American and Korean people.

Reginald served as adjunct professor at Covington Bible College in Rossville, GA teaching Missions, the Tabernacle, the Holy Spirit, Eschatology I and II, and Nehemiah. He also taught History of Israel, Hebrew, Jewish Studies, and the Pentateuch at the Chattanooga Bible Institute. Rev. Lisemby also taught at Redemption Point School of Ministry in Chattanooga, TN, and he currently teaches a READ HEBREW class every Wednesday evening.

Reginald Lisemby is the first Three-Dimensional Artist with the Regional Art Alliance in Chattanooga, TN for his hand-thrown clay pottery. Rev. Lisemby has served as Interim Pastor on two occasions. He was the Youth & College Pastor at Midwest Korean Presbyterian Church in Park Ridge, IL for four years while attending Moody Bible Institute, and he served as Interim Pastor at Calvary Bible Church in Chattanooga, TN.

Dr. Reginald K. Lisemby has authored seven books:
The Land of Israel The Lord of Israel: Do the Ancient Holy Scriptures Validate the Modern Jewish and Palestinian Claim to the Land of Israel;
HOLY LAND from the Garden in Eden to the New Jerusalem;
He Throws Me Down to Make Me a Prince;
Crumbs from the Jewish Table;
Messiah Yeshua in the Hebrew AlephBeit;
He Came Upon a Midnight;
The Watchlist: The Most Chaotic Chapters of Human History are Ahead

Reginald K. Lisemby theological persuasion is the following: *"If there is a liberal bone in my body, I would seek the service of the Great Physician to have it removed. Rocked ribbed conservative; inerrancy of the Holy Scriptures without question!"*

Reginald's hobbies include reading, writing, Hebrew language study, pottery, carpentry, camping, gardening, hunting, photography, and travel.

Reginald. K. Lisemby

BOOKS BY DR. REGINALD K. LISEMBY

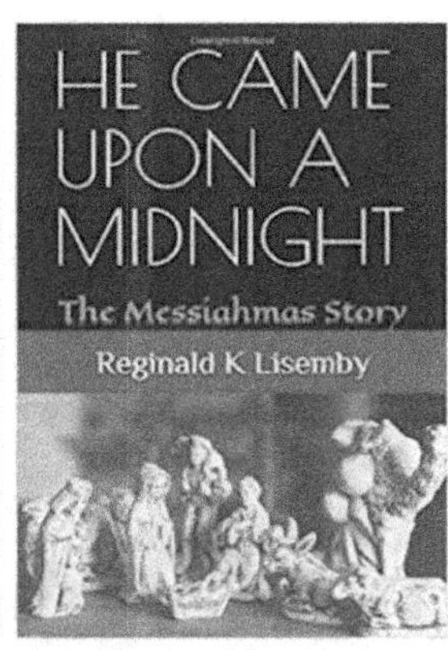

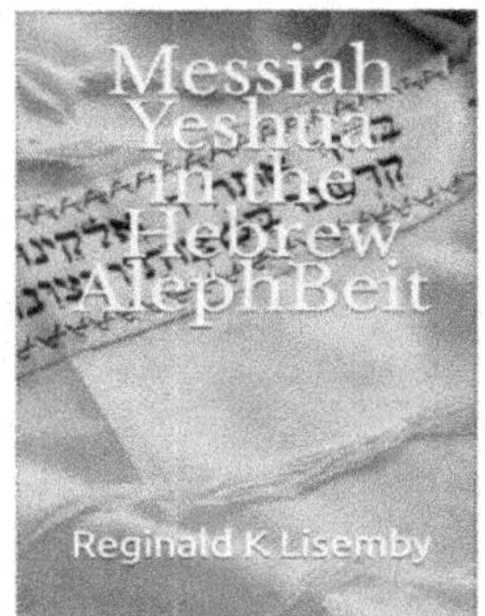

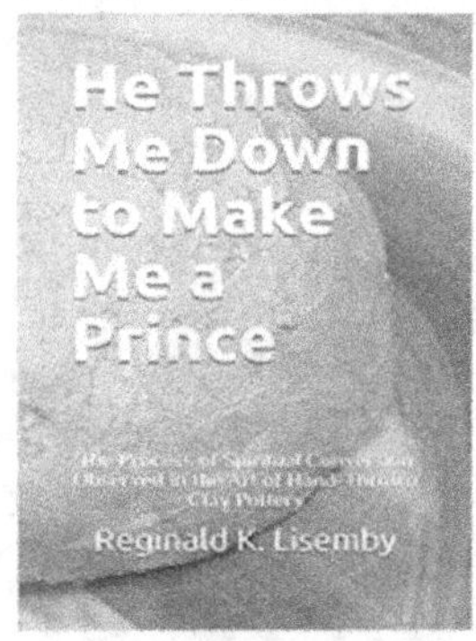

LEVITES AND MUSICIANS
Sue Grace Lisemby
SONGS IN THE NIGHT

THE FEAST OF FIRST-FRUITS
He Arose a Victor from the Dark Domain
Reginald Lisemby

THE LIFE OF YESHUA
a chronological, messianic, and hebraic record of the life of Yeshua from birth to ascension
Reginald Lisemby

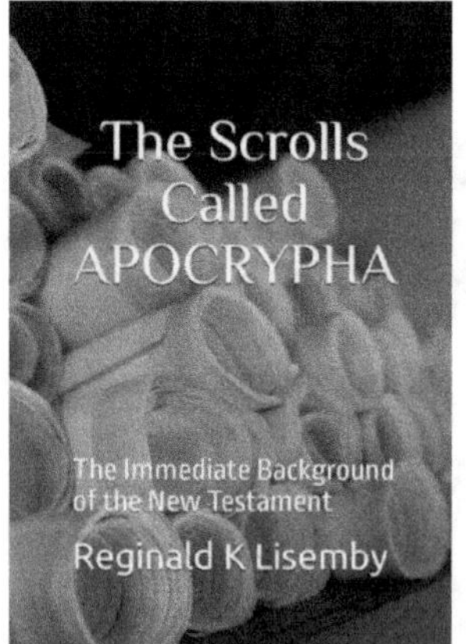
The Scrolls Called APOCRYPHA
The Immediate Background of the New Testament
Reginald K Lisemby

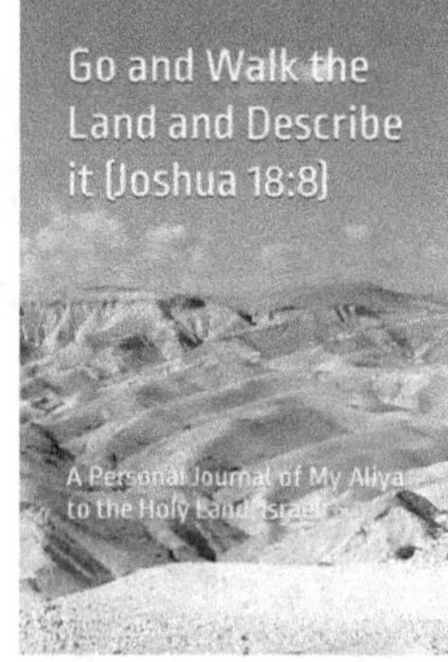
Go and Walk the Land and Describe it (Joshua 18:8)
A Personal Journal of My Aliya to the Holy Land, Israel

A BOOK CALLED ENOCH
A Man Walked with God, Angels Fell with Satan, Stars Proclaimed the Gospel, Dreams Revealed the Messiah, Prophecies Foretold the Times
Reginald K.Lisemby